THE POETICS OF TRANSLATION

THE POETICS OF TRANSLATION

A Thinking Structure

GENEVIÈVE ROBICHAUD

McGill-Queen's University Press
Montreal & Kingston • London • Chicago

© Geneviève Robichaud 2024

ISBN 978-0-2280-2194-0 (cloth)
ISBN 978-0-2280-2195-7 (paper)
ISBN 978-0-2280-2196-4 (ePDF)
ISBN 978-0-2280-2197-1 (ePUB)

Legal deposit third quarter 2024
Bibliothèque nationale du Québec

Printed in Canada on acid-free paper that is 100% ancient forest free (100% post-consumer recycled), processed chlorine free

This book has been published with the help of a grant from the Canadian Federation for the Humanities and Social Sciences, through the Awards to Scholarly Publications Program, using funds provided by the Social Sciences and Humanities Research Council of Canada.

Funded by the Government of Canada | Financé par le gouvernement du Canada | Canada | Canada Council for the Arts | Conseil des arts du Canada

We acknowledge the support of the Canada Council for the Arts.
Nous remercions le Conseil des arts du Canada de son soutien.

McGill-Queen's University Press in Montreal is on land which long served as a site of meeting and exchange amongst Indigenous Peoples, including the Haudenosaunee and Anishinabeg nations. In Kingston it is situated on the territory of the Haudenosaunee and Anishinaabek. We acknowledge and thank the diverse Indigenous Peoples whose footsteps have marked these territories on which peoples of the world now gather.

Library and Archives Canada Cataloguing in Publication

Title: The poetics of translation : a thinking structure / Geneviève Robichaud.
Names: Robichaud, Geneviève, 1983– author.
Description: Includes bibliographical references and index.
Identifiers: Canadiana (print) 20240293851 | Canadiana (ebook) 20240294068 | ISBN 9780228021940 (cloth) | ISBN 9780228021957 (paper) | ISBN 9780228021964 (ePDF) | ISBN 9780228021971 (ePUB)
Subjects: LCSH: Translating and interpreting—Philosophy.
Classification: LCC P306 .R58 2024 | DDC 418/.0201—dc23

This book was typeset by True to Type in 10.5/13 Sabon

Contents

Acknowledgments   vii

Introduction: The Poetry of Translation   3

1 Friendship and Translation in Erín Moure and Chus Pato's *Secession/Insecession*: Writing on an Incline   25

2 Rewriting Fernando Pessoa's *The Book of Disquiet*: PME-ART and the Afterlife of Translation   61

3 Standing in Translation's Wake: Gail Scott's *The Obituary*   89

4 The Snag of Translation and the Before Unapprehended Relation of Things   125

Notes   149

Bibliography   177

Index   187

Acknowledgments

Heartfelt thank you to Lianne Moyes, Jane Malcolm, Anne Quéma (thought-companion and generous mentor), the International Research Training Group (IRTG) on Diversity in both Montreal and Germany, Jessi MacEachern and Julia Charlotte Kersting, Gail Scott, and Erín Moure (thank you for your ardent reading and comments). I am grateful for the financial support that carried me through my studies: SSHRC (Social Sciences and Humanities Research Council), IRTG (International Research Training Group) on Diversity, and l'Université de Montréal's FESP (Faculté des études supérieures et postdoctorales). I am thankful to McGill-Queen's University Press for the opportunity to publish and circulate this work. I am also beholden to Richard Ratzlaff, my editor, for his invitation and accompaniment, and to Matthew Kudelka for his brilliant edit. Deep, heartfelt thank you to my peer reviewers for their enthusiasm and insight. And to you, dear reader, may some curious line follow you throughout, the line beneath the lines.

THE POETICS OF TRANSLATION

INTRODUCTION

The Poetry of Translation

The language of poetry is a language of inquiry, not the language of a genre.
Lyn Hejinian, *The Language of Inquiry*

The buried speech that creates a soundless gap between languages is at the heart of translation.
Gail Scott, on translating France Théoret's *Laurence* (*How2*)

INTRODUCTION:
POETRY AND TRANSLATION'S IN-BETWEEN(S)

Translation's relationship to a conceptual in-between hardly seems to demand a learned or scholarly explanation. In many respects, it seems self-evident: there are differences among languages; there are challenges to finding the meaning of a word in one language and then in another; there are ways of exploring, with translation, the (un)common networks to which words belong; there are misunderstandings and losses that can occur; but there is also a widened understanding of linguistic and cultural differences, the addition of new meanings, and the emergence and discovery of a new relationship to language(s).

All these readings of in-betweenness are fascinating and thought provoking in their own right, but they are not exclusively the kind of betweenness I have in mind throughout this book. In fact, "betweenness" is perhaps not quite the right word for referring the work of translation as I describe it throughout these pages, even though it is not one I want to reject outright. We might think instead in more specific terms – acts, boundaries, inclinations, overlaps, uncertainties, disintegrations, snags – terms that will gain currency in their circulation herein alongside the idea of betweenness, and that will qualify that relationship differently as I seek to keep the term "translation" itself in a state of flux and indeterminacy: in a state of betweenness.

To begin, translation's relation to an in-between raises several questions that relate it back to poetry or, more specifically, to a poetics. In the work that follows, the poetics of translation is understood as that which manifests itself out of literature and a literary practice, which is as much a space of language and poetic licence as it is a theoretical and philosophical one. This encounter, between translation and poetry, is thematized as a shared relationship: both forms' ability to think and create is found within the interstices of various gaps and aporias.[1]

Characterized by motion and even as that which escapes, my point of departure in this book is a reflection on the poetic and ontic possibilities of translation. Rather than consider motion as defined by a movement back and forth, I've found it much more productive and exciting to think about what translation motions to in the haptic sense of what it might point to or bring forward, what it can make visible. Of course, to think of motion in this way, in terms of apprehension not movement, is not to argue for a reading of translation as synthesis or fixity but to gather instead some thoughts and threads on the poetics of translation as a language of inquiry and as a thinking structure.

In her book-length collection of essays, *The Language of Inquiry*, Lyn Hejinian proposes the term "poetics" for a practice that works at the interstices of phenomenological and epistemological concerns.[2] This study retains Hejinian's formulation of poetics as a "language of inquiry" that is the outcome of a relationship between formal innovation and concerns for something else: social, epistemological, phenomenological, universal, or particular claims, and so on.[3] That betweenness, between formal innovation and existential concerns, forms the basis for inquiry, for a thinking structure, by pulling the process of thought apart and working from poetical relations. These structurations, which are part of an interpretive task, require the work of construction; they require that we, readers, translators, writers, critics, cling to questions: that we activate the work and the ongoing structuring of meaning.

During the intuitive phases of this research, I was not yet aware that I would eventually start to unravel the poetics of translation as a thinking structure. I knew only that I wanted to know more about translation as a conceptual and philosophical apparatus in texts –

those by Erín Moure, Chus Pato, Fernando Pessoa, PME-ART, Gail Scott, Nicole Brossard, and Renee Gladman – that weren't necessarily considered translations in the normative sense. At the time, my thinking was heavily influenced by Nathanaël's poetically astute writings on translation, especially her seductive proposition that "to translate is to touch."[4] What emerged from these considerations was a realization that translation's touch is fleeting. By "fleeting," I do not mean to gesture to translation's relationship to impermanence, even though I embrace the notion that transience is part of translation's manifest. Translation's touch is fleeting because unlike the notion of equivalence that we might associate with the science of mathematics, for example, translation's relation to equivalence is precisely that – a matter of approximation and relation. It is an oblique gesture at best, one that attempts proximity even beyond impasse.

It is in the aforementioned sense, of translation's motion beyond impasse, that I append to translation a reading of that which escapes. Here, what escapes is not a weakness of translation but a strength. Translation demands invention. Anyone who has ever tried their hand at a translative exercise will know that translation is not an answer to the translatability of an original. The most challenging aspect of translation, in fact, is working beyond aporias, beyond those moments of impasse where differences among languages forge new relationships to language(s). While countless studies on translation express either curiosity, criticism, or delight at translation's ability to move meaning from one linguistic context to another, or at translation as a semantic piece of shrapnel cutting its losses, paying (or not) its debts for its infidelities, this study wants to know what translation, as a poetics, makes legible. What does it narrate? What does it motion towards – other than, and outside of, a *geste accompli ou raté* in the space of an impasse? What can it make visible?

The route I take is one I've learned from poetry or rather from poetic structures, for my notion of poetry is rather broad and extends beyond the poem and into those spaces of oblique relations where gaps leap towards meaning but not necessarily in an attempt to obtain certainty. Poetry, I think, thrives in the in-between and in aporetic disturbances; it is a practice that does not attempt to foreclose the object and subject of its inquiry through analytical synthesis; it embraces forms of knowing that reside outside the need for certainty as it works its way across various intervals and resonances, differences and dissonances. In short, it is a thinking and feeling structure.[5]

The links between translation and thinking, or translation and philosophy, are links that in the forthcoming chapters are constantly redrawn. One of the only constants that seems to come through each chapter is the relationship translation has to apprehension and forms of presencing. To a large degree, translation is equated with a "making visible" that grants legibility to the gaps that are woven into and between Erín Moure and Chus Pato's biopoetic text *Secession/Insecession*, Fernando Pessoa's unfinished work *The Book of Disquiet* and PME-ART's rewriting of the aforementioned book in *Adventures can be found anywhere, même dans la mélancolie*, Gail Scott's overlapping narrative in her novel *The Obituary*, Renee Gladman's beholding of *other* spaces where things impossible to fully comprehend occur, and Nicole Brossard's wager of presence and aliveness in a foreign language. Translation in the above-mentioned sense, like poetry, acts as a focalizer: a way of reading and of gaining a deeper understanding of aporetic structures, be they "real structures" or "phantom structures."[6] Throughout the chapters that follow, I locate these aporetic structures within the texts themselves, as poetic components of the work, but I also encounter aporias outside the texts as a matter of relation or of bitextual reading. Thus, translation's aporias are as much a part of the poetic component of the works I consider as they are part of what directs my reading methodology.

During the course of my research, I explored various modes of translation in which creative and critical practices intersect and thus emerge as poetics. The experimental texts herein also consist of examples wherein the poetics of translation are linked to the vocation of thinking, of processing, and of presencing –read: inventing! –new possibilities for thought, language, and poetry. The question that ignites my thinking throughout these pages, then, can be summed up as follows: what can be apprehended through the poetic and theoretical vectors of translation?

Admittedly, it is a very broad question, and I don't believe I undermine this work by suggesting that it is a question that simultaneously goes both answered and unanswered. During the course of my research, I sought to make sense of literature itself as a translation of the aforementioned intersection, which is doubled or brought to life in the act of reading. But there is a very specific conceptual knot underscoring the concerns I raise in this book, which is: what/how does translation think? Focusing on translation as a site of exchange and meaning-making seemed an intuitively evident path at first; what was more difficult to extract was not just translation's ontic contributions but translation itself as an awareness- and acknowledgment-based poetics. This sparked a new question: what could be apprehended (learned or gleaned) by reading (original) literary works through the lens of translation? And what of the reader's necessary affective presencing then?

To answer such questions, I have found it useful to bring the poetics of translation onto the side of poetry and literature, and more importantly to consider translation, as I have previously gestured to, as a language of inquiry. My thinking in this work thrives in those spaces where the work of experimental texts – whether that work is social, theoretical, aesthetic, or all of these – remains open.[7] Of course, my treatment of the term translation here is problematic since translation – as a concept or a practice – can mean a number of things. And indeed, in this book, translation is not a singular notion, as it takes many forms.

Let me begin, then, with a quick overview of what translation implies in the following chapters, starting with a reading of the poetics of translation. This will be followed by a discussion of translation's importance as a reading methodology. This double approach will allow us to better understand what emerges in the relationship between

a) what a work provokes or illustrates in its in-betweens – with the possibility of creating something new, and
b) how the poetics of translation provides insight into what eludes or escapes our grasp; how it provides the conditions for an unpredictable encounter.

In sum, this book is interested in understanding the something more that lurches forward beyond various forms of impasse, and that is akin to something like a thought process.

TRANSLATION AS A POETICS AND READING METHODOLOGY: FORGING A WAY TOWARDS A THINKING STRUCTURE

The intersection between a work of art's poetic properties and what it provokes or illustrates is partly what concerns Walter Benjamin in the opening pages of his essay "The Translator's Task,"[8] where he asks:

how can a work's relationship between information and its poetic components allow us to understand translation? In Harry Zohn's English translation, the question is articulated as follows: "If the original does not exist for the reader's sake, how could the translation be understood on the basis of this premise?"[9] By "premise" Zohn is referring to Benjamin's proposition that works of art are not intended for an ideal reader. In Steven Rendall's translation, the question is articulated as follows: "If the original is not created for the reader's sake, then how can this relationship allow us to understand translation?"[10] Rendall's recourse to the notion of "relationship" where Zohn uses the word "premise" returns us to an earlier question Benjamin asks, which, in its phrasing, suggests an entanglement between two properties of a work of art:

1 its message: what it communicates,[11] what information it supplies, and
2 its poetic properties: "what is generally acknowledged to be the incomprehensible, the secret, the 'poetic.'"[12]

In asking how the aforementioned relationship might allow us to understand translation in relation to an original work, Benjamin is not asking about a work's translation but about translation itself; he asks: "How can this relationship allow us to understand translation?"[13] In other words, we are not in the operation of the original's translation but in the very operations of translation itself within a work of art – that, I think, is a crucial difference, and it is one of the driving preoccupations of this book's interest in a given work's relationship to a poetics of translation and in translation itself as a reading methodology.

Interestingly, while it may seem as though Benjamin is suggesting that the poetic components of a work remain beyond our grasp, or that the poetics of translation themselves lie beyond our understanding, his essay remains much more productively ambiguous on this point. While "The Translator's Task" may not provide insights into how to become a more astute translator, it does touch upon the tectonics of translation by providing various visual analogies and places of assembly (vessels, dwellings, passages, etc.) where what escapes is simultaneously what survives in a relationship of "special convergence" between languages.[14]

Translation, in Benjamin's estimation, has the ability to show how languages change over time. Importantly, it is an understanding about language that goes beyond any single literary work. It is an understanding in and of language that nudges translation into a critical apparatus that is also a thinking structure. It becomes the translator's task to remain attuned to that which remains unfathomable, beyond comprehension, mysterious, and secret. In short, such a task is concerned with the poetic properties of a work of art and its motion beyond the aporia of an impasse, beyond what escapes. Not only does Benjamin give a name to this form of impossible passage, that of textual afterlife, which I shall return to shortly, but he also describes such moments in terms of the work's translatability.

It is this element of translatability within a work that I have in mind when I gesture to translation not just in terms of a poetics but also in terms of how it can serve as a reading methodology. The question of a work's translatability concerns a text's not easily assimilable qualities and whether or not – which parts – it will surrender to being translated. According to Benjamin, the most significant works find textual afterlife not because they are translated but because there is something about them, an ambivalent quality of (un)translatability, that calls for translation.[15] Such a call is precisely what motivates my thinking in the pages of this work. The conclusion I draw from the aforementioned intersection between translation as a poetics and translation as a reading methodology, one that I shall present in more detail throughout these pages, is that translatability, especially of what is left over – that something else or extra that lurches forward beyond words[16] – when understood this way, is something like a thought process,[17] and furthermore, that this intersection, as a poetic juxtaposition between what is (not) and what is left over, proposes a deeper understanding of how translation itself as a thinking structure creates halts or tensions that become entangled in a process of making visible, which is also a form of affective presencing that manifests itself in and through the act of reading. My task throughout these chapters, then, is to employ translation as a reading methodology, as a cypher, that is concerned with what can be apprehended or understood in the poetic intervals of a work.

THE POETRY OF TRANSLATION: TRANSLATION AS PROXIMITY BEYOND IMPASSE

Reading a literary text, as Paul de Man has argued, "leaves a residue of indetermination that has to be, but cannot be, resolved by grammatical means."[18] There is something that sticks to you, like a kind of subcutaneous perfume.[19] The poetic character of translation is a lot like this perfume. There is something in the openings that are created in its poetically brocaded compositions that either slips out or that we slip into as readers.[20] Each chapter in this book shapes itself around these indeterminate, over-sung notes and woven patterns in order to read into the text a husk or sheath or shell that carries something elusive, something that emerges beyond what the language of the work can hold, something not easily assimilable.

Several concepts contribute to my readings of these unassimilable qualities. What you will find throughout these pages is a literary study that foregrounds questions about translation through examples of a few textual works that espouse an innovative relationship to translation. In considering the ways in which the literary texts in question challenge our understanding of translation and its role in contemporary innovative writing practices, I show that these works are examples of translation's ontic and creative potential beyond translation as an end in itself. I argue that translation is the radiant poetic continuum that pushes the works to innovative edges; it is what makes them radical, visionary, and multidimensional works of art. I should also point out that my use of translation as a poetic framework for reading the aforementioned literary texts should not be read as metaphorical; rather, the use I make of the term subverts the idea that translation is somehow self-evident or recognizable through key concepts or configurations such as original and translation, source and target text, fidelity and equivalence. This is why the emphasis I place on the poetics of translation as a thinking structure, and thus as a language of inquiry, is so significant.

In this study, the thought process created out of the conditions of translation in a work – its poetics – is an effect of a special convergence between various forms of overlap and poetic juxtapositions that push the boundaries of poetic expression forward in the in-between of a work's becoming. In such cases, convergence is reserved not to language alone but also to formal elements of a text that carry conjunctive properties that shift parts of a work's reach across gaps and aporias and into spaces of legibility, even dialogue.[21] When brought to the side of poetry or poetic expression – as a formal feature of a work – translation becomes a way of pointing to that which – extracted from the strata of poetic juxtaposition – is (still) in process and may (partly) be eluding our grasp.[22] In this sense, translation is a poetic feature of a work as well as an effect and a function of reading for the convergences among various forms of overlap and poetic juxtapositions.

The concepts I use to describe this tectonic convergence or architectural feature of translation as poetic juxtaposition and overlap are various. These concepts serve less as interpretative grids that I apply to the texts I read than as poetic frameworks derived from my readings of the works themselves. Some of them have already made an appearance in the arguments woven above. Textual afterlife, for instance, is a term Benjamin uses to describe the circulation and legibility of original works across time and the aporias of various impasses. Similarly, translatability is an intrinsic quality of a work that finds (or not) its articulation in relation to an oeuvre whose language resists containment and in some cases even resists being translated. Regarding the notion of overlap, Benjamin's concept of the dialectical image is perhaps this book's most ardent interlocutor even though the term itself is only explicitly utilized in my third chapter on Gail Scott's novel *The Obituary*. There, the dialectical image creates the conceptual scaffolding for my reading of Scott's translanguaging poetics and overlapping narrative – its coexisting characters, voices, temporalities, landscapes, buildings, and so on – to narrate a sort of impossibility, the inability to speak obliteration.

Indeed, chapter 3 begins on the heels of Benjamin's elliptical and compact assertion in his *Arcades Project* about an alternative temporality: "It's not that what is past casts its light on what is present [...] rather, image is that wherein what has been comes together in a flash with the now to form a constellation. In other words, image is dialectics at a standstill."[23] As a type of montage, the dialectical image manifests itself as a moment of translatability of the past for a present (or a "critical now," as Benjamin often refers to it) that has yet to arrive. For instance, the predominant interpretation that historical time progresses from a chronologically linear past to a chronologically linear present no longer applies. The image as undecidable-flash-of-recognition, which gets released from the dialectical entanglement of the past and the present's encounter, disrupts the idea of any fixed order, especially temporal, as it simultaneously motions to the flickering disappearance of that which appears. Given my specific interest in the poetics of translation as a poetics of apprehension, Benjamin's concept of the dialectical image provides a useful notion for thinking about the potential continuity between poetry and translation through issues of legibility.

Even though my recourse to the dialectical image does not fully announce itself until the third chapter, the notion nevertheless gathers a kind of ghostly momentum throughout the first two chapters, where counterposed materials and their irreducible difference(s) move translation into a space beyond mediation and into something much more incalculable. I see this incalculable threshold – from one dilated and deferred space to another – as an essential characteristic of poetry and of translation as well; that is why, in this work, I regard them as coequals.[24] The approach and interest I bring to issues of legibility in the context of a work's poetics of translation is motivated by my desire to address various overlaps and phenomena of encounter in a text. This is why the dialectical image is such an important undercurrent in my thinking – it opens a line of becoming that sets in motion something we have yet to grasp. What I am after here is not mastery but translation as poetic juxtaposition, translation as a making present, translation as a form of thinking together.

Beyond Benjamin's dialectical image, all three of the aforementioned orientations find a home in the philosopher Avital Ronell's concept of inclined writing,[25] a term she has coined to describe texts that make room for a thinking-towards that involves not merely an inclination towards an other but also consists of a text's receptivity to the alterity of thinking itself.[26] Inclined writing, in other words, is a form of writing in any genre where the poetry of speculative thinking dominates the need for mastery and certitude. When we encounter inclined writing in Chapter One on Chus Pato and Erín Moure's *Secession/Insecession*, we encounter texts that perform methods of radical inquiry through equally radical methods of inscription,[27] texts that open up a space of relays, texts that embrace their own difficulties in maintaining a sense of equilibrium along uncertain and uneven ground, texts that open onto collaborative spaces in the sense that they tantalize by reaching towards spaces for thought that lie obliquely within the grasp and gaps of one text in relation to another.

In *inclined* writing – which Ronell places in contradistinction to what she terms writing on the *decline* – gaps, snags, leaps and jumps in narrative are welcomed interruptions that reconfigure the text. As faltering text, inclined writing presents disjunctions as operative parts of the text's trajectory and momentum. In contrast, a text that is written on the decline has an entirely different relationship to textual embodiment. These texts present a form of closure in relation to knowledge that does not necessarily urge or invite readers to think alongside them.[28] Translation – especially in the context of an experimentally engaged poetics – furnishes the conditions of inclined writing. Like thinking, translation's structure remains more or less open-ended, or, as I have intimated at several junctures in this introduction already, it may offer a way out of an impasse and into spaces of legibility, even dialogue. Translation, as inclined writing, is a form of thinking-towards that embraces the possibilities that may emerge in its uncertain process.

Other texts or parts of texts are even more radical in their uncertainty: they remain stubbornly lodged in a state of open-endedness and undecidability. This is the case in relation to my reading of Pessoa's *Book of Disquiet* and PME-ART's rewriting of that work in Chapter Two, where, pushing the open nature of inclined writing as far as it can go, PME-ART's performance and the book that instigated it challenge our capacity to know *how* to receive such works. These are texts or pieces of text that, as if disseminated through rumourological airs, remain volatile, hence the name Avital Ronell gives to these uneasy textual compositions – that of rumour – to account for those textually capricious instances where, for various reasons, the texts seem to stand at the threshold of time.

The concept of the rumour-text is linked to my reading of the works' poetics of translation in its ambivalent relationship to an original. According to Ronell, a rumour-text is "a widely disseminated report detached from a discernible origin or source. Inasmuch as it becomes what it is, the spreading rumour takes on the qualities of a story told, without author or term, imposing itself as an ineluctable and unforgettable account."[29] Unpredictable and seemingly unhinged, a rumour-text, like a translation, is one that travels ahead of its time; like the dialectical image, it bears deep within its structure a characteristic of errant futurity. In the sense of its syncopatious misalignment with the time of its circulation, the rumour-text is that equivocal part of a work's translatability that is riddled with unrest and possibilities for non-arrrival – or else its appearance occurs in belated or alternative channels, as through the dialectical image, for example, where the buried text may flash in the reader's mind's eye.

Benjamin's notion of textual afterlife also offers an alternative way of thinking about the rumourological quality of some compositions. In "The Translator's Task," Benjamin frames the notion of the afterlife of works of art as a feature of their translation. As he points out, in its constant renewal of an original, translation not only gives rise to an understanding of the original as a mutable form characterized by unrest, but also grants the original an afterlife. The word Benjamin uses to describe the continued life of works is *Fortleben*:

> A translation proceeds from the original. Not indeed so much from its life as from its "afterlife" or "survival" [*Überleben*]. Nonetheless the translation is later than the original, and in the case of the most significant works, which never find their chosen translators in the era in which they are produced, indicates that they have reached the stage of their continuing life [*Fortleben*].[30]

In figuring translation as an afterlife, Benjamin also points out that "the notion of the life and continuing life of works of art should be considered with completely unmetaphorical objectivity. Even in the ages of the most prejudiced thinking it has been suspected that life must not be attributed to organic corporeality alone."[31] Like Ronell's rumour-text, Benjamin's notion of textual afterlife points to occasions when texts run ahead of their author(s) – even independent of them – as they espouse a certain life of their own, an auto-mobility of sorts, that continues to circulate (even) in the absence of the subject.[32] This will become clearer with respect to my reading of the rumour-text as textual afterlife in Chapter Two and my treatment of the rumourological qualities of the (un)translability of uncertain signs in chapter 3's reading of Scott's *The Obituary*.

SHIFTING DIFFERENCES AND THE SPACE OF THE (UN)KNOWN

In the early phases of this research, my attempts at naming and defining the literary phenomenon at work in these authors' texts described their use of translation as innovative. While such an account satisfied my desire to acknowledge the originality of their approach to writing, that depiction also remained vague when I considered that innovative uses of translation could also refer to any number of approaches, not all of them grounded in literary works, that made use of translation in the manner I intended to describe; for instance, an innovative use of translation may simply refer to a creative linguistic solution that is implemented in order to overcome the challenges associated with finding an equivalent in the target language.

I also hesitated to describe the translative writing under discussion as "creative uses of translation" since the same vagueness, as with my use of the term "innovative," arises here also. For instance, one could ask: aren't all translations creative transpositions? The literary works figured throughout these pages are not so easy to characterize: are they translations or something else?[33] I would later discover that naming these works' relationship to translation was perhaps less important than being able to articulate why and how they were inciting me to think about translation in ways that were unusual. One of the driving concerns motivating my readings in each individual chapter can be more or less summarized in these two questions: What does translation make visible? And what does it allow one to touch upon?

THE (UN)KNOWN:
THINKING BEYOND THE VISIBLE INTO WHAT EXI(S)TS

What can be sighted through the poetic and theoretical vectors of translation? Each work offers more than aesthetic contemplation. Each is laden with the invitation to think beyond the visible into what exi(s)ts.

Reading the works in this book through the lens of translation – as both a reading methodology and a poetic component of the work – allows a deeper understanding of the conditions of textuality as an overlapping performance, often at the cost or expense of making something visible or invisible. Through these texts' relationship with generative overlap, they invite a poetic thinking that is otherwise a questioning about the very structures that mediate critical thought practices themselves. Such a harnessing of an "otherwise" is also true of the way I have been using translation as a cipher for these experimental texts. In allowing translation to be encountered in a form other than its regular or normative use, I am interested in discovering what translation can make visible, both in regard to the texts but also in relation to itself as a densely theoretical and politically charged concept. Indeed, this study situates translation as a form of enactment that extends beyond hermeneutics.

The implications of translation as overlap and as a form of "being with" offer various examples of the diffusion of time and temporal overlays. Working across the poetic juxtapostions within the texts, each chapter provides an opportunity to translate the various moments/vectors of alterity and tensions produced out of the crossroads between history, textuality (art), and languages. Each study seeks to explore how reading the works from the perspective of translation has the potential to create alternative connections and alignments among subjects, epistemological processes, and procedures. The works under discussion have taught me how translation can embody the poetic practice of making space: for others, for the new, for new or other ways of thinking. Moreover, the transtextual practices present throughout this study are further compounded and complexified by the vast array of ways that translation – as a poetics but perhaps especially as a reading methodology – affects the manner in which experimental and socially conscious texts are apprehended. Keeping all of this in mind, the chapters throughout this work seek to explore how translation might shift the boundaries and possibilities that initially determined its passage. My work's entanglement in various border crossings, in issues of cultural exchanges, and in diverse representations of encounters (*va-et-vient, face à face*, and *contre-face*) demands a rereading of the very horizon(s) that constitute the *work* of translation.

My examination of the ways in which translation transforms our ideas about language, literature, and writing, and how it might also work to signal or alter one's presence in the world, is neither finished nor closed. The observations and thoughts in this book offer only one permutation among others where I see this project of investigation into the ontic possibilities of translation taking root. Hopefully, this book will incite others to take up the call. Most important, for me, was to look at the ways in which translation might offer a critical lens and material conceit that invites philosophical inquiry into the very enabling properties of writing and thinking itself. My aim, then, has been to carve out a space where the poetics of translation can give way to alternative poetical-critical models for critical inquiry, hence my emphasis on translation as a reading methodology.

Translation measures the trace or the absence of something. Its consequences for thought and the way we see things – whether they are things happening in the here and now or in the space of fiction – pursue the condition of language as a thinking structure. As I mentioned earlier, translation is the expression of (two or more) things, relations, participating in one another's existence. With translation as overlap and poetic juxtaposition, aspects or outlines spring into focus to address what falls outside of language's efforts to communicate, to circumscribe. In pointing to what cannot be put into words and in assessing the counterpressure of one in relation to the other, translation's poetic expression alters aspects of a work, reroutes it, turns it into an affirmation of resistance. However indirectly, translation brings about the recognizability and apprehension of the presence of a tension: translation's unacknowledged thinking structure and ontic possibilities, especially in the reader's necessary affective presencing.

ENCOUNTER, DISINTEGRATION, AND DIALECTIC IMAGE

The authors in this book serve as a sample of people whose practices push the limits of language, or what can be done with language, into something more diffuse, more future-oriented, nudging the text and the reader's experience of it towards a potentially new territory between languages. They are formidable figures whose contributions to contemporary experimental writing and art making, whether in North America or beyond, include diverse approaches to queer and feminist experiments with narrative, difficult writing, translanguaging poetics, boundary-pushing performances, and genre-defying forms, to name but a few unifying traits. In this way, the authors who appear throughout these pages offer a fresh understanding of what Rosmarie Waldrop terms "translation's 'ultimate task': to bear witness to the essentially irreducible strangeness and distance between languages [and] to explore this space."[34] Indeed, translation's ontic possibilities are often treated throughout as spatial rather than grammatical, as a matter of contiguity, metonymy, and open form rather than as matters of fidelity, faithfulness, or accuracy.

In Chapter One on Chus Pato and Erín Moure's dually authored book, *Secession/Insecession*, translation first appears in the form of an interlingual transfer: Moure translates Pato's Galician text, *Secesión*, into the English *Secession*. This is perhaps the most straightforward occurrence of translation in this book insofar as it adheres to one of the three definitions Roman Jakobson gives to translation in "Linguistic Aspects of Translation."[35] Moure's English "interlingual translation or translation proper" of Chus Pato's biopoetic Galician text provides but one example of translation's pertinence to my study.[36] But even this clear-cut example is quickly complexified when one considers the generative opening this Galician-to-English translation provides Moure: a chance to write her own corresponding text, in English, in which she adapts, echoes, and responds to features of Pato's text and translates them from the inside out so that they now correspond to her own lived experiences. This new text, *Insecession*, is not a translation of *Secession* in the proper sense of an interlingual transfer from one language to another. Nevertheless, there is a binding correspondence between the two texts that warrants a comparative reading similar to the kind one might perform between an original text and its translation.

Such a reading is encouraged by the fact that the layout of the book recalls the *face à face* arrangement of bilingual editions, only in this context both works appear in English. As a text that is written out of her English translation of *Secession* and is therefore prompted by it, Moure's *Insecession* borders *Secession* in interesting ways. Take for example, the biopoetic nature of Pato's *Secession*. In combining the bio with the poetic, Pato partitions *Secession* into various short, autobiographical poetic-prose vignettes. Each piece offers a meditation on her life, on growing up in Galicia, on poetry, as well as on her poetic practice. Similarly, Moure's *Insecession* develops her own equivalent life narrative, echoing Pato's biopoetic meditations with her own experiences growing up in Calgary (Alberta), her work as a poet, and her views on poetry. In contrast to Pato's text, Moure's *Insecession* weaves in several reflexive musings about her work as a translator, as Pato's translator in particular, and about Pato's influence on her work. In that sense, *Insecession*'s refractive composition is just one of the ways in which Moure foregrounds translation's generative poetic possibilities. In the prefatory notes to the book, Moure calls this kind of refractive writing an "echolation-homage" that is also an "intranslation[37] of Pato's work.[38] While I shall shed more light on these terms in Chapter One, it is worth pointing out that both neologisms gesture to Moure's use of translation as a compositional mode that is also a writing alongside of – a thinking towards; this form of writing, where Pato's *Secession* becomes yoked to Moure's *Insecession*, takes the form of a positive affirmation, which I frame as an act of thinking together, a way of writing that inclines towards the other and that places translation in the purview of a poetics of friendship.

In chapter 2, I contemplate a bilingual performance by the interdisciplinary performance collective PME-ART, titled *Adventures can be found anywhere, même dans la mélancolie*, where they set out to rewrite

Fernando Pessoa's *Livro do desassossego*'s French and English translations (*The Book of Disquiet* in English; *Le Livre de l'Intranquillité* in French). Pessoa worked on the manuscript from 1912 until his death in 1935, but the book was never assembled or published in his lifetime. Not until decades later, in 1982, did the first version of the book appear. I say *first* because the book would undergo a number of mutations depending on the editors, scholars, and translators who worked to assemble it from Pessoa's archives. Four different translations (by Richard Zenith, Iain Watson, Alfred MacAdam, and Margaret Jull Costa) and numerous editions exist in the English language alone. Even while publishing work in his own name, Pessoa created a number of heteronyms to which he attributed a life distinct from his own. After crediting the book to one heteronym and then to another, Pessoa finally relinquished *The Book of Disquiet* to his semi-heteronym Bernardo Soares.[39]

Presented during the gallery's opening hours, PME-ART's performance is notable for the various ways in which the scribes transcribed, modified, and rewrote themselves into *The Book*. While it may be tempting at first to link PME-ART's rewriting of the book to Roman Jakobson's concept of intralingual translation (rewording), such a method would quickly be frustrated by the fact that PME-ART's rewrites move beyond rewriting as paraphrase. In fact, their rewrites do not set out to faithfully transcribe or reword Pessoa's text. At least not in a conventional sense. The rewrites are frequently punctuated by creative departures from the original text that attempt to render the book "a little happier" and "a little more of our time."[40] Like Moure, PME-ART treats Pessoa's work more as a pretext for writing instead of approaching it as something to be loyally copied word for word. Sometimes, for example, drawings and calligrams completely replace Pessoa's textual fragments.

Translation nevertheless remains pertinent to a reading of Pessoa's work as well as to PME-ART's performance, in that the latter highlights the residual effects of a work's afterlife. The notion of afterlife is important to my reading of Pessoa's book as well as to PME-ART's performance because one of the most significant aspects of afterlife, as I noted earlier, is not just how it challenges the linear progression of a text, from its inception to its publication or from a source to a target text, but how it questions the very idea of a destination. The term afterlife, in other words, names something about the condition of textuality itself – its rumourological qualities – rather than its (certain) arrival.

The enmeshment of Moure's text to Pato's in chapter 1, as well as my insistence on reading such moments as instances when translation takes on the form of inclined writing, allow me to read the texts' translative and differential aspects through a reading of departure rather than arrival. Working from this dislocation, chapter 2 continues the work of chapter 1 by pushing its reading of translation to the limits of a text's errant features. If bits of Pato's text ghost Moure's writing in *Insecession*, then PME-ART's performance ghosts Pessoa's *The Book of Disquiet* in a similar manner – albeit with a kind of hallucinatory intensity that gives the poetics of translation a latent quality that invites various temporalities to co-lapse.

In chapter 3, a conventional understanding of translation as either intralingual, interlingual, or intersemiotic – as outlined by Roman Jakobson – is rendered even more obscure. In other words, while in chapter 2 I demonstrate how PME-ART's rewriting of Fernando Pessoa's *The Book of Disquiet* generates what I called a perceptible encounter with a work's continuing life or afterlife, chapter 3 continues with Benjamin's notion of the afterlife of translation and explores how issues of translatability give way to the apprehension of various "sightings" or forms of presencing that suggest an emergent relationship to forms of knowledge as well.

Here, let us not think about translation in terms of a transfer from one code or language to another. The notion of translatability, as modelled after Walter Benjamin's essay "The Translator's Task," points to a more useful concept for intercepting what is not "spoken" in language yet emanates from it. I am thinking here of Benjamin's powerful yet enigmatic concept of the dialectical image as itself a form of translatability, a concept he treats in two works in particular: his massive *The Arcades Project* and his essay titled "Theses on the Philosophy of History."[41] As shall become much more apparent in chapter 3, while *The Obituary* is not a translation in the conventional sense, it modulates its narrative within different layers of poetic overlap, and this overlap – in turn – creates conditions of translatability for the reader.

Given the "slippy-slidey sentences, switching this way + that" of its multidimensional structure, a reading of *The Obituary* via translation summons various challenges.[42] This is due in part to the fact that Scott's work troubles boundaries. The novel is framed by various forms of poetic juxtaposition: philosophy and poetry, fiction and non-fiction, French and English, and so on. The layering of various forms of co-lapse, similar to what we encountered in chapter 2, is made palpable as well in the spaces between the various temporal references in which the work takes place. In light of this, it is not only the boundaries between original and translation that (en)fold (each other) but also their conventional temporal distinctions. The novel evokes an ever-changing littoral where the shores of one temporality or one narrative frame to another refuse fixity. They are ever-fluctuating. Scott's work thrives in these indeterminate states. Hers is a constantly in flux translation.

Throughout this book, I skirt the idea of eruption, of eruptive time, but I never actually name it as such. Instead, as in chapter 3, I sit with essays by Walter Benjamin, trying to gain a sense of the ecstatic lilt in perception, what he calls the dialectical image. In chapter 4, "The Snag of Translation," which includes short readings and reflections on Nicole Brossard and Renee Gladman's prose works and ruminations on the aliveness of sentences and narrative, I attempt to think *beside* the thing I want to think about, to move my perspective just off to the side, to make the *aside* the thing that touches the thing inside, the thing we might call the centre, the better to catch onto spaces of hesitancies, as Gail Scott's heroine would say, the better to keep my own thinking process alive to possibilities yet uncertain. I do this so that simultaneity layers the thought, produces the kind of nuance that catches on the loose *and* taut spaces tugging at my thinking. I encode. I fabricate. I weave it all together. Into a shaggy mess. Into sentences that I wander into. Trying to get the light and the layers just right.

What I am after in chapter 4 – and this is true of my work in this book in general – is a kind of counternarrative. Or a thought practice that is given the space and the syntax to move counter to (its/my own) narrative expectations, to short-circuit my own control over it, to allow the thought process to continue to think on the page and to reimagine its own conditions and possibilities. Renee Gladman has a useful verb for this kind of doubling: "simultanates," referring to a kind of double consciousness, "a verb that would indicate one thing causing something else to run parallel to it."[43] I'll return to this notion in chapter 4, where I bring together several concepts, some that are unique to the final chapter – like that of the snag as a stutter or hesitation that stops time – and some that find resonances in other places in this book – such as the notions of apprehension and uncertainty.

While I have outlined some of the motivations for working with the concept of translation alongside my corpus – as poetic components of the work – there is a further and perhaps more pressing dimension of the significance of translation for this book, and that is the use of translation as a reading methodology. In all the cases examined in this work, translation is present where there is a simultaneous acknowledgment that "something" isn't quite getting through, that something is defying comprehension or certainty. For example, when Erín Moure creates a companion homage-piece to her English translation of Chus Pato's text, she not only makes Pato's influence on her own work visible but also makes visible the restrictive policies of the Canada Council for the Arts, a federal granting program that supports the Canadian publishing industry and its independent publishers by offering various subsidies. In fact, the politics surrounding the publication of the translation allow one to "read" much more than the book itself. To be sure, the book translates the very conditions of its possible or impossible circulation by pointing to the fact that the book's publisher could not receive financial support from the Canada Council unless the book object contained "at least 50% Canadian-authored creative content."[44] Hence the dually authored nature of the book and Moure's generative intranslations of her English translation of Pato's work.

While chapter 1 reads translation through the conditions of a work's circulation, among other things, chapter 2 engages with translation as a reading methodology on an entirely conceptual level. For Alain Badiou, the reception of Fernando Pessoa's work is deeply coloured by philosophy's belatedness in knowing *how* to receive the work. Badiou here is referring to the idea that Pessoa's oeuvre is neither Platonist nor anti-Platonist. For the French philosopher, philosophy has not caught up to Pessoa because it has not known how to work beyond those terms;[45] it has not known how to embrace the aporias (the intangible, the irrepresentable, the void, the latent) that Pessoa's work opens and that – as a linking of both poetry and thought – still need time to be thought through.[46] In many ways, this is the challenge proposed by a work's translatability; as Walter Benjamin has asked, "among the totality of its readers,"[47] will it ever find "an adequate translator? Or, more pertinently, by its very essence, will it allow itself to be translated?"[48]

In chapter 3 on Gail Scott's novel *The Obituary*, my concern shifts from how works of art circulate and are presenced in the world to what gets translated in the in-between spaces of poetic juxtapositions. The use of translation as a reading methodology works side by side with Scott's poetics of translation as narrative overlap where both formal structures work to signal or alter the relationship between the said and the unsaid, certainty and uncertainty. In an attempt to wrestle with questions of temporal multiplicities in Scott's novel, I approach her use of narrative overlap as a dialectical image that translates the latent content concealed within the novel's compositional lines. As a thought-provoking halt caused by overlapping conditions, *The Obituary*'s relationship to the dialectical image has the potential to translate, for the reader, more than what is on the page. If we are baffled by the dialectical image's jarring ability to point to what appears as being that which simultaneously disappears from view, it is perhaps because it is difficult to conceptualize the apparition of the indeterminate or irrepresentable as a flicker of presence that vanishes at the same time that it materializes. Perhaps, then, it might serve us to remember that poetry and poetic structures excel at making images emerge from spaces that are "nothing" but in-betweens that trigger relationships into forming meaningful compositions.

In the final chapter, chapter 4, translation is the expression of two things (at least) things participating in each other's existence. In thinking through the various possible modalities for the final section, I decided that one way to frame the issue of the visible within language, and of translation within language, was to think in terms of images and invisibility. Thus, I began thinking about this book's primary works alongside other books that deal with the poetic dilemma of translating invisible structures, and found that, of all the works I encountered over the past decade, none of them reach at the "problem of the visible" as gracefully and as insightfully as Renee Gladman's deeply poetic novel *Houses of Ravicka*.

In the final stages of writing and then in the period of revision that followed, I found that reading Gladman as well as Brossard alongside the chapters I had written allowed me to access a kind of poetic juxtaposition, which I also imagined as the architectonics of poetry and thought. The more I juxtaposed my thinking and allowed it to be lighted by Gladman's and Brossard's work, the more I wondered how to allow such an oblique response to activate and make visible a productive ambiguity. In other words, my interest was in poetic juxtaposition as a methodology, as a system for reading counterposed material.

Such a form of sight is crucial to the indeterminacy of the open narrative form of the works in this book, in which each chapter suggests ways in which translation, as a reading methodology and a poetic component of the writing, can be thought of as opening onto "gestures of seeing" or "in-sight."[49] More often the fulcrum of theory rather than praxis, translation in Gladman's and Brossard's work represents an "ecology of making"[50]: a living construct and system of connectivity that fuses the process and composition of their work with a reflexive acknowledgment of that very process. Thus, their ecological impulses are not necessarily obvious at first glance. Instead, their ecological praxis happens in and through their poetics. I also draw upon translation poetics as a unique vanguard position for thinking about alternative temporalities and the interrelationship of beings and things. This is especially true in terms of thinking about the sentence as a space for living, a living space, and as an experiment of living in the present. These various forms of aliveness cultivate, for me, a curiosity about the ways in which we might approach translation differently, as "a knowledge producing, and knowledge seeking process."[51]

1

Friendship and Translation in Erín Moure and Chus Pato's *Secession/Insecession*

Writing on an Incline

The poem writes what's not yet there
Chus Pato, *Secession*, trans. Erín Moure

TESTING THE INTERVAL
(IN THE ALTITUDES OF ELATION[1])

In this chapter, I examine the space opened up by Erín Moure's translation of Chus Pato's Galician biopoetic text, *Secesión*, into the Canadian English *Secession*, which is published alongside her own co-responding homage-text in Canadian English, *Insecession*. The two texts are bound together, with *Secession* on the right and *Insecession* on the left, in a dually authored edition called *Secession/Insecession* (Book*hug 2014). *Secession/Insecession* is, in fact, a shorthand form for the title that appears on the cover of the book, "*Secession* by Chus Pato *with Insecession* by Erín Moure," a title that – in turn – is expanded between the covers of the book and reads, "*Secession* by Chus Pato the Erín Moure translation *with Insecession* by Erín Moure her Chus Pato echolation."[2]

In theorizing what emerges from the dually authored work as going beyond the normative dualisms of source and target text, I argue that, as a bicephalous text and as a text that comes to think together, *Secession/Insecession* disturbs normative translation practices by unsettling delineable patterns of categorization. There is an erotic quality to the movement of the writing as well. One that is evident in the reciprocation of Moure's text to Pato's – the way Moure writes lovingly into and out of her translation of Pato's *Seces-*

sion; how she foregrounds Pato's text as the very impetus for her own. Returning to the site of the slash in the title, I posit that *Secession/Insecession* offers a model for translation that goes beyond the realm of equivalences as it asks: what does a poetics of friendship entail for translation?

Written as a series of short reflections on the poet's life and poetics, Chus Pato's Galician biopoetic text, *Secesión*, was first published in Spain in 2009. Refracted through the poet's considerations of identity politics, places, nations, languages, ecologies, bodies, and friendships, *Secesión* opens onto a holistic literaryscape that contemplates the place of the poem in the world. In the process, Pato, like Moure after her in *Insecession*, shows how her poetic practice moves along the fault lines of subjectivity, thought, language, and love. Indeed, the work moves porously between the genres of autobiography, poetry, and the essay as each short piece incorporated in Pato's *Secesión* engages several aspects of the question *where does one write from?* For Moure, this also entails a reflection on her work as translator, which is folded into her response-text, *Insecession*.

Insecession is Erín Moure's homage and "echolation" of Pato's *Secession*, meaning that each text in *Insecession* not only attempts to answer or to respond to something in her translation of Pato's biopoetics, *Secession*, but in doing so, also produces its own accompanying/echoic biopoetic discourse. As Moure explains,

> I realized that, being the same age as Chus and having a similar position as poet in my own culture, I could write my own biography and poetics, as an echo and homage to Chus' […] In *Insecession* I talk about my own poetics, and very different experience of life (I grew up in a democracy in full postwar expansion, Chus in a dictatorship in postwar contraction), but also, more importantly, about translation.[3]

Although the work's relationship to translation is unquestionable, the dually authored nature of the book requires some unfurling, especially given that Pato's original text, *Secesión*, is not the text that faces Moure's translation. Instead, the original is replaced, in this bitextual edition, by the translator's response to her translation.[4] Thus, the work not only addresses the significance of the two poets' biographies, their relationship to poetry, and the question of *where one writes from*, but also quite meaningfully transports these concerns onto the terrain of translation.

SECESSION/INSECESSION AND THE RELATION OF THE TEXTS ACROSS THE INCLINE OF THE SLASH (/)

I am interested, in the following sections, in exploring some of the ways in which Moure's and Pato's texts break ground by treading both next to and away from each other. The titles alone already encourage the break: *Secession* and its link to *secedere* or to move apart, to break away; the *in* of *Insecession* expressing a state or condition of being both within and without, graft and graph: "Now my work haunts hers forever," writes Moure as she reflects on the fact that she has been translating Chus Pato's work for "ten years (in 2013)"[5]; "She doesn't yet speak English, though so my work remains not just inside but outside hers."[6] What is at stake, to quote another passage from the work, is "the relation of text to bodies" and one's "relation of transmissibility."[7] For Pato, the minuteness of modest, everyday gestures is encapsulated in the poet's lifetime of writing poetry: "A poet spends a lifetime writing poems, just so that some line, some tiny fragment enters the memory and dream of the language."[8] The poet's relation to language and – reciprocally – language's relation to bodies is more than just part of a gothic order, it is one already in secession: "Any language is ghostly because language is the nothingness of the living world extended in a body"[9]; she continues, still insisting on the caesura, "But my nothingness stays there, at the *finisterra* where breath fractures."[10]

Secession and *Insecession*, as texts written across the aforementioned caesura, are also texts that are literally pitched at each other and at the reader from the position of an oblique relationship – an incline that is made evident, at least on the titular level, by the slash that divides and links the two titles (as Moure's and Pato's texts tend to each other through the typographical manifestation of the slash's incline). Given the very specific kind of title Moure grants to her response-text, it is difficult to ignore that she interweaves *Insecession* with *Secession*, meaning not only that the two texts face each other but also that one is also nestled in the other:

> The slash is a graphic way of presenting a bicephalous book: our titles appear as equals. Although Pato's biopoetics *Secession*, in this edition, is interwoven with my own *Insecession*, it is in no way subordinate to my text, but is its very cause, its precursor and its most precious interlocutor. *Insecession* is my biopoetics nestled

"in *Secession*." They appear "with" each other because they are friend texts, reverberative.[11]

That graphically the incline of the slash suggests the texts are equals does not necessarily amount to an equal exchange between the two texts. While they appear together as "friend texts," it is difficult to ignore that both texts are in English and that *Insecession*, as an homage and response-text, exists in excess of *Secession* and is derived from it. As Moure herself suggests, *Insecession* is *caused* by *Secession*. But my use of the word excess need not carry negative connotations.

As the structure of the echolation-homage attests, the book is written out of a loving admiration for the work of her friend; it is about marking an address to her friend, Pato, drawn as/out of an act of humility, a mode of reception, and a way of marking/listening to the work and its impact on her own thinking.[12] Moure herself makes such a remark when she proposes that as much as translation is an act of creation, it is above all an act of humility and listening: "Translation to me is an act of creation, as engaging and strenuous as that of creating poetry. The constraint of having to try to reproduce the effects of the original poet distills the mind incredibly."[13] Moure thanks Chus Pato in the prefatory notes to the work, and she ends the book by insisting that "*Insecession* could not exist without the enduring friendship of Chus Pato, without her *Secession*, and without her willingness to let me translate her."[14] For her part, Pato has dedicated the section titled "Thoughts, Behave Yourselves," which contains five texts on the multiplicity of the "I" through its relation to "you," to Moure.[15] The evocation of friendship is important to consider here, and I will do that in relation to a poetics of translation, but first it is crucial to outline a few notes on method and to justify the trajectories of inquiry that will or will not take precedence in this chapter.

WHAT IS SECESSION/INSECESSION?
A NOTE ON METHOD

With all this time spent on the nature of the book, on the question of *what Secession/Insecession is* – a bicephalous work with an incontrovertible relationship to translation – it is useful to point out that, in asking the question *what is*, this study could have followed a rather deductive approach and been led to speculate on what it is not, or even what it is similar to, drawing historical parallels with works of a similar and dissimilar nature. The *face à face* layout of the two texts resembles the side-by-side layout of bilingual editions that enable the reader to read the translation and the original together. Except that *Secession/Insecession* is not – as I have already begun to point out – a conventional bilingual edition. In fact, it is not a bilingual edition at all, at least not in the usual sense. Pato's original, *Secesión*, has been replaced by Moure's translation into English, *Secession*, and the place typically reserved for the translation is occupied by Moure's new/"original" text, *Insecession*. To attribute the nomenclature of "original" to Moure's *Insecession* is misleading, however, for as she clearly states at the outset of the book, "each text in Canadian English responds to a Pato text."[16] *Insecession*, then, can be read in part as a text addressed to Pato's *Secesión* as well as its English translation, *Secession*. In both cases, Pato's work acts as the source text from which *Insecession* springs.

There are other avenues and venues as well – a comparative study, for instance, which would have sparked a reading that juxtaposes *Secession* against *Insecession*, meticulously marking the ways in which one text arrives at or departs from the other. While I have not completely forgone the comparative reading just described, the readings I will be performing across the divide of the slash will be done more with the bitextual figure of dual authorship in mind and its theoretical implications for literature and translation. In other words, while it will prove fruitful to mark the ways the texts respond to each other, my interest throughout this chapter will be in reading the work with a focus on what the slash in the title theoretically dis-conjoins.

With the *va et vient* of the aforementioned comparative reading in mind, another possible approach might have been to probe the significance of departedness in relation to friendship and Aristotle's view of friendship as loving the other as one would the deceased, and therefore not demanding love in return.[17] Why this quick pit stop to speak of friendship? Because friendship is significant to the space occupied by *Insecession* and *Secession*. Given that the two texts accompany and face each other, at least in the Canadian English–translated edition published by Book*hug in 2014, they are to be considered, not as mirror images of each other, but as friend or companion texts.[18]

As a philosophical backdrop for this study, then, it will prove worthwhile to bear in mind the concept of the friend/companion text and to wonder what the poetics of friendship entail for translation. Interestingly, there has not been a great deal of scholarship on the dual subject of translation and friendship. Although there are abundant theoretical resources on the subjects of alterity, ethics, and care – even questions of intimacy and love – in the politics of translation, the leap towards the friend is one that translation theory seems to have more or less ignored.[19] My aim, then, is partly to address this lacuna as well as the repercussions of models of co-authorship that give way to a thinking with and alongside the other.[20]

The question of friendship will, in time, lead this study to riff off the two-headed or bicephalous nature of the work, not necessarily taking the ancient road of mythology, the gothic, or even that of science fiction with its question *what if* and the leaps made possible there, but wondering instead what possibilities emerge from the echoes that are inserted in the structure of the dually authored work and the embedded act of thinking together that arises there. I will explore, in other words, how the two-headed nature of the work allows Moure to make visible the echo of Pato's influence on her work. In this sense, *Secession/Insecession* is an unusual text in the way it deviates from translation theory's more standard preoccupations regarding the (in)visibility of the translator, for it adds to that preoccupation the (in)visibility of the impact a work has on its translator.

In a book titled by the very complaint just mentioned here, *The Translator's Invisibility* (1995), Lawrence Venuti critiques the idea that a translated text must be delivered as fluently as possible to the reader in its new context; this, according to Venuti, implies that the translated text is received by the reader as though it were, itself, the original text, and therefore the translator must remain as invisible as possible: "The more fluent the translation, the more invisible the translator, and, presumably, the more visible the writer or meaning of the foreign text."[21] Venuti's claim that the invisibility of the translator doubly effaces the cultural and material conditions shaping the work *and* its translation has had a strong impact on translation theory's articulation of an ethics of translation. One of those effects is the attention paid to the impact a translation and its translator has on an original; such considerations – as those granted to the translator's impact – run against the grain of the idea of the translator as a marginal figure. Instead, the translator's visibility gives her authorial status.

While Moure's inclusion of *Insecession* alongside her translation of Pato's *Secesión* offers her the opportunity to make herself, as translator, visible – especially given that she includes several reflections on her work as translator – she takes the ethical injunction of visibility one step further in *Insecession* by showing how her work, as writer and translator (and as a human being), is deeply impacted by the work of Chus Pato. In *Insecession*, she writes, "ONE CAN'T in fact translate Pato without being utterly changed and challenged in one's own poetic, poeisis, that is never 'one's' own or one's 'own.'"[22] That statement, which reflects well Moure's generous poetics, also emerges out of the context of her response to Pato's text; a possible corresponding passage in Pato reads: "THE POEM doesn't fit in the poem, nor in the entire language, nor in the shadow of the language."[23] In that moment, the standard conception of the visibility of the translator, as one who impacts the original through her translation, is turned into an even more generative figure, as Moure shows how the impact works in both directions. Whether or not Pato's passage on the poem is the originating germ that prompted Moure to respond with a passage about translation is not as important as the fact of the passages' enmeshment with each other. As the reader passes from one to the other, the authority and authenticity of the original text ceases to exist as space is opened for a lively bitextual dialogue. Moreover, while it is usually accepted that translation changes something in the nature of the original, *Secession/Insecession* suggests that the translator herself is affected and changed in the process.

Finally, what I propose to do in the following pages – and this I believe is not contrary to the possibilities I have been pinning to this study's diverging lines of inquiry – is follow the inclinations of literary translation as a form of "speculative inventiveness"[24] and "poetic probe" and "think small, preferring the spec over the spectacular,"[25] which is a posture of thinking I will develop shortly and that I am borrowing from the philosopher Avital Ronell.

WRITING ON AN INCLINE: INCLINATION AS POETIC APPROACH

In an interview with the philosopher Diane Davis titled "Breaking Down 'Man': A Conversation with Avital Ronell," Avital Ronell suggests that the prizing of "scientific objectivization" comes at the cost of inducing a kind of phobic reaction to the philosophical modesty of more poetic approaches in a scholarly work.[26] Her own work champions such "modest" poetic approaches; of course, the measure of modesty is to be read, in part, under the scope of irony here, as Ronell's work is constituted through a poetic approach to thinking that is not at all moderate or unassuming. Her work, which is always delivered with layer upon layer of densely poetic and theatrical material – never straightforwardly – opens philosophy's viewfinder to marginalized, unexplored, or overlooked territory: stupidity, addiction, complaints, the telephone – these are but a few of philosophy's "modest" refuse items, which are given refuge in Ronell's work both through the hospitality of a densely philosophical and poetic thinking and her own modest posturing of embracing (poetic) undecidability over certainty. As Diane Davis remarks,

> this interruptive force [in Ronell's work] – inasmuch as it does indeed startle, irritate, illuminate – takes a certain swipe at certitude, prompting rigorous hesitations that open the conditions of possibility for what Ronell's works are always after: an ethics of decision in a postfoundational whirl(d) [...] That is, she takes on the role of gracious host to anything that must be evicted/evacuated for a discourse of mastery and certitude to sustain itself. And why host such a radical party/text? Because it's within the space of certitude's withdrawal that the possibility for what she calls "responsible responsiveness" becomes available: the possibility, that is, for an ethics of decision after the so-called "death" of the humanist subject.[27]

Ronell's work, in its engagement with what she terms "responsible responsiveness," like Moure's relationship to Pato, begins with her transformative reading practice and her production of "genre-busting texts," a practice that does not attempt to foreclose the object and subject of her inquiry through analytical synthesis but rather aims to keep the text open even as she works with and alongside it.[28]

For Moure, Rancière and Pato provide such a model of responsible responsiveness:

> THE "EXCLUS" or excluded is a conflicted actor, in Rancière's notion of the political; she is a figure who does not try to smooth over that cut or blow of the scinding or secession; the scimitar slash

between law/fact, right/death. In Chus Pato's work, this figure would be the poet, who excludes herself or admits to being excluded, and who therefore speaks.[29]

In Pato's *Secession*, the figure of excess and undecidability is embodied in the poetry that is intermixed with the prose on the page as well as in the (thinking) poet:

> THUS language, that up to this moment has done nothing but communicate, realizes: that it transfers. It realizes that it speaks where there is a world to speak of [...] It sings what never happened, or will ever happen and what always occurs in the poem: strangeness, surprise at being human and speaking, at being similar and strange to ourselves.[30]

In both cases the writer's work breaks with the instrumentality of language to focus instead on that which remains eccentric to language, poetry for example, for "the poem writes what's not yet there."[31] Poetry, according to Pato, is "the hardest zone of a language."[32] For poets/thinkers such as Pato, Moure, and Ronell, poetic approaches embrace forms of knowing that reside outside the need for certainty, for poetry – to echo the aforementioned quote by Chus Pato – is that part of language that resists absorption.

The philosophical modesty of Ronell's poetic approaches, and her inclination to "think small" and to read for the "spec rather than the spectacular," is further explored in a talk the philosopher gave in the context of a lecture series offered at the European Graduate School in 2014. Titled "Walking as a Philosophical Act," Ronell's lecture examines a series of (small) steps and missteps taken by Jean-Jacques Rousseau in his *Les Rêveries du Promeneur Solitaire (Reveries of the Solitary Walker)*. In the talk, Ronell explores the relationship of knowledge to transcendence, suggesting not only that the grammars of epistemological trajectories are wholly unstable but also that the supposed unity and rigour of certitude and mastery over various objects of attention are but romantic ideals that "presume a level of understanding."[33] Ronell in her essay is critical of the figure of the sure-footed philosopher who comes down the mountain to share *his* enlightenment[34] – a discourse that is exclusionary as it requires mastery and certitude to sustain itself.[35] During the opening remarks of "Walking as a Philosophical Act," Ronell states:

> I want to consider simply in terms of philosophical tracts [tracks] and literary tropologies, the history of coming down the mountain. The lawgivers, the light-bearers, the phallus-wielders, the world-class illuminated came down the mountain. Socrates, Moses, Nietzsche and Zarathustra [...] fatefully came down the mountain. They delivered. Rousseau, for his part and parts, came crashing down a hill. So I think the fact that he traces and tracks the way he falls on a hill also pushes against a whole tradition of philosophical and literary positing. Rousseau makes us ask about postures and figures of thinking on the move, our relation to the path – remembering that in Greek *methodos* is path – so what's our relation, our method, what it might mean more precisely to write, as Rousseau says, on the decline. He's actually, in the second reveries, walking down and writing on the decline [...] So what it means to write on the decline, on an incline, only to lose one's standing.[36]

Working on the metaphorical register of philosophical "tracts" as ways of "making tracks," Ronell suggests that, at least in "Western" philosophy, there is a tradition of "doing" philosophy, of walking the philosophical walk and, by implication, of talking the talk that suggests a "certain" relationship to knowledge and transcendence. In light of these remarks, Ronell asks: what does it mean to perform a series of missteps, to stumble, to depart from an established course, and to lose one's grounding? What is the responsibility of the one who writes (on the decline or from an incline), and what is her relationship to the mirage effect of certitude?

Inspired by Ronell's critique of the sure-footed philosopher and her reading of Rousseau's *Les Rêveries* as a text that breaks new ground by questioning the very grounding of the ground, I am interested in the following sections in tracing how *Secession/Insecession*, as a dually authored book with a dialogical form[37] and as one that falls in "sharp contrast to romantic images of the writer as an autonomous and heroic thinker or creator," is an example of inclined writing – one that, among other deviations from the figure of the sure-footed philosopher, dwells in opposition to the tradition of the solitary, illuminated walker coming down the mountain to share *his* enlightenment.[38]

Such moments of deviation from certainty are thematized across the misaligned echoes that traverse the response-structure of the two works. There, the reader's dialogical reading of the juxtaposed texts fractures the work into smaller echoic assemblages, unfinishing what was once finished as he or she parses the texts for their various resonances. These resonances range in style. Some form a kind of *mise en abyme*. For example, where Pato's text reads, "I turn around, go with you; wherever you want to go, I'm going too,"[39] Moure's text responds, "And then she opened the book. *Oh poetry.* May I translate? Wherever you are going, dear poem, dear Chus, I am going too."[40] Other resonances have a furthering effect that reterritorializes an idea from one text and expands upon it in the other; the following passage, from Pato's *Secession*, "for some time, I considered my texts to be hybrids, but writing is a mutant, a territory," is expanded upon in *Insecession* so as to read: "for years I considered myself the author of my texts, then the texts mutated and the territory became open, like snow."[41] In the previous example, Pato's reflection on the hybrid aspects of her poetry is self-reflexively absorbed in *Insecession*. While the term "hybrid" in *Secession* could be referring to a number of constraints, in *Insecession* it becomes a comment on authorial originality.

Ronell's resistance to certainty as a form of "responsible responsiveness," it should be pointed out, especially when read in relation to the modest approaches presented above, is not merely a question of working against the attainment of assurance or truth about a given subject. It is also about turning our attention to philosophy's modest refuse items, those undecidable, marginal subjects that do not figure or are disfigured in discourse; such an inclination asks that we remain attentive to various modes of address, to what might be and is often considered small, minute, or trivial, and to those modes of address that, for whatever reason, refuse to address, overlook their address, or are hurtful in their mode of address.

In light of the emphasis placed on various relations of address, it is useful at this juncture to return to the significance of friendship that was hinted at in the beginning of this chapter with Moure's claim that *Secession* and *Insecession* are to be considered as "friend" or "companion" texts. Moreover, friendship is significant to this study not just because it is a subject that is itself one of those modest modes of address that is frequently either left untouched and uncharted in philosophical discourse, or because it is just as often euphemized, subsumed, and translated into other philosophical concepts – ethics, alterity, or hospitality, to name only a few – but also because friendship, even by another name, is important due to its ethical and political address and consequences, as that which unites or divides two or more individuals. Friendship is a relation characterized of "betweenness," and it is with this "betweenness" in mind that I explore translation's relationship to friendship in the following section.

FRIENDSHIP AND TRANSLATION: INCLINED WRITING AS A MODE OF ADDRESS

In his essay "Politics of Friendship," Jacques Derrida asks how it is that the great philosophical and canonical discourses on friendship – from Aristotle to Montaigne, and from Kant to Hegel, among others – have not accounted for friendships between two women or a man and a woman.[42] The open call at the end of Derrida's essay is towards a "coming" friendship – *une amitié à venir* – that interrupts models that are premised on an alliance between brothers.

In *Secession/Insecession* such an interruption is identified with the proleptic powers of poetry on one side and translation on the other. As I have already pointed out, Pato declares the poem to be that which writes what is not yet there.[43] A few pages later, at the close of the book, Pato's *Secession* ends on the idea that the poem, as an invocation of love, coaxes forward an undecidable future: "The poem is an intelligent fissure, it's love that persuades time to exist, time that implants itself into what is to come, primogenital."[44] Elsewhere, Pato writes, "the poem is the politics of the future."[45]

In another text in *Insecession*, such fissures in time are expressed in the undecidable temporality of translation that coaxes the poem both forward and back and forward yet again: "I translate Pato's work from the state of the finished or co-finished, in which I as translator interfere. I unfinish what she has declared finished, to finish it again in English."[46] As Daniel Aguirre-Oteiza remarks, "in Jacques Derrida's terms, *Secession/Insecession* is an address 'without the least assurance,' a 'harzardous' plea to a future utopian community that differs from itself, and is deferred, in every present difference of the poem."[47] Although love would seem the ideal gesture for working against principles of exclusion, beginning with the creation of new models for friendship beyond fraternity and a new conception of time, Aguirre-Oteiza nevertheless warns against this much too narrow reading of the work: "this poetics of love cannot be separated from a rhetoric of violence. *Secession/Insecession* interweaves personal family histories, instances of collective violence around issues of national identity and reflections on the Final Solution and ecological devastation."[48]

Although Aguirre-Oteiza does not continue to cite Moure, it seems significant to add that, a few lines later in *Insecession*, the reader encounters echoes of Emmanuel Lévinas when she writes, "I believe in a responsibility to the unknown in the other who faces me or faces away from me."[49]

For her part, in an exchange with Davis, Ronell captures well the stakes of the modest friend in philosophical discourse: "what does it take for scholars to sustain friendships – does the institution disrupt or block genuine friendship, should such a thing or practice or gift exist? That's another storyline."[50] In a more recent book-length publication on the subject of friendship, Ronell continues to wage a complaint against what she calls philosophy's "unreadable calling cards of relatedness," of what can and cannot be considered friendship material, on the one hand, and what can and cannot be considered a serious subject of philosophical debate, on the other:[51]

> As Derrida has argued, friendship serves as the blueprint for political discernment and for amorous cleaves. On this stagnation and related tropologies, women, for the most part, have been assigned to the historical sidelines, even though they prove adept at traumatically intrusive break-ins and manage to achieve a modicum of social rewrites. One thinks of Antigone, of Heinrich von Kleist's feminine figurines that shoot out counter-memory to block historical narratives of entitlement; one continues to be struck by the howls of one-woman-lone-warrior types like Valerie Solanas; one continues to stress over the seething deflations of Ingeborg Bachmann and the ongoing peel-down of Sylvia Plath.[52]

The place literature makes for friendship, as subject, is often generated out of elegiac circumstances. If not through death, the friend remains an arguably marginal figure, one relegated to a role of secondary importance, as sidekick or confidante.

Often written in the high style of philosophic homage to the deceased, these texts cite and recite the verses of the elegized writer, turning the gesture of citation – but most importantly the gesture of reading – into a generous homage. Maurice Blanchot's work on friendship, although similar to that which emerges from the slash in *Secession/Insecession*, situates its homage for the friend on the terrain of the elegy. For Blanchot, friendship requires us to cultivate "an infinite distance, the fundamental separation on the basis of which what separates becomes relation."[53] That ethical distance forms a "movement of understanding" that demands "discretion"[54]; we are not to speak *of* our friends but *to* them.[55] Speaking thus, there is an acknowledgment that emerges for the "fundamental separation" between one friend and another – a "pure interval" that, for Blanchot, "measures all that is between us ... [that] brings us together in the difference and sometimes the silence of speech."[56] In *Le Dernier à Parler*, a text written shortly after Paul Celan's death, Blanchot produces a text that illustrates the measured interval referred to above by working beyond the register of commentary on the work of his admired friend. He cites Celan's work, but does so without specifying the specific source of the work such that his text is double: his commentary is translation and his translation is commentary.[57] In this double movement, Blanchot, like Moure, dramatizes translation as the site not just of reading but of homage to his friend.[58]

Under the guise of an ethics of translation, the relation between friendship and translation is neither original nor difficult to grasp when we consider that the question and practice of an ethics of translation is deeply concerned with how to respectfully receive, approach, and accompany the other – the friend text – across languages and cultures. From Lawrence Venuti's seminal work on the invisibility of the translator to Gayatri Spivak's view that the translator must be the text's most loving and intimate reader,[59] an ethics of translation is also an ethics of care where the translator must negotiate issues of hospitality and address, of ways of being with the text, the other, to be translated. As Spivak remarks,

> To surrender in translation is more erotic than ethical. In that situation the good-willing attitude "she is just like me" is not very helpful. In so far as Michèle Barrett is not Gayatri Spivak, their friendship is more effective as a translation. In order to earn that right of friendship or surrender of identity, of knowing that the rhetoric of the text indicates the limits of language for you as long as you are with the text, you have to be in a different relationship with the language, not even only with the specific text.[60]

As theoretical texts that underscore an ethics of care in translation practices across cultures and the various axes of power this entails, these same theoretical texts also offer examples, at least in a transversal sense, of friendship's pertinence to translation. Here is Moure again:

> It is difficult to duplicate or ignore this process [of breathing], as it is difficult (breathing) to ignore the relation with the friend, the one outside the skin tent (breathing) but similar, she who disagrees and looks differently, and contributes this different seeing to the texture of space-time, to an afternoon, for example.
> We have an argument, briefly, over words and sentences.
> Who we are:
> Me along with you:
> What do I/we mean by me/you here?
> Poetry, it is said by this me which is not *me*, is a conversation, or a texture like a shawl and each one of us weaves our own particular corner, or the bit where we gently hold its edge, aware that others are pulling gently as well on the surface of the textile, contributing their own gesture to the whole. And none of us produce this whole, not on our own, not with our friends alone. None of us are this whole nor can any of us speak for this whole that is poetry, we can only bring our hands' work into the conversation, and raise not just our voice but our ears to it, to listen [...] Translation is about this too, this listening.[61]

Even though the question of friendship is not one that is explicitly broached in translation theory's dedication to an ethical practice, asking about the significance of friendship for translation seems to derive naturally from the emphasis on the care the translator must take in approaching the task of translating the other.[62]

Up until this point, I have floated above textual examples and a kind of theoretic grid grounded in an ethics of translation that can only begin to point to the various instances where translation is deeply affected by friendship, both real and textual. What I have thus far failed to convey is the important affective dimension of friendship as an encounter – real and textual – that can be so powerful, so influential, so electric, that it can change the course of thinking of a writer, translator, or reader. This is precisely the poignant anecdote recounted by Erín Moure in regard to her encounter – textual at first – with Chus Pato.

LITERATURE AND TRANSLATION: THE UPWARD FALL

In "Walking as a Philosophical Act," Avital Ronell suggests that it is not only *how* we walk along the philosophical path that is important in relation to how we approach a given subject of inquiry; we should simultaneously not be afraid to take into account various forms of interruptions that affect which steps to take next.[63] As Ronell herself cautions, "we should not be afraid to look at so many archives of missteps. Taking a first step does not amount to following a prescriptive logic. Sometimes, thinking makes itself unavailable to cognitive ledgers and complexity overruns our ability to see straight."[64] Remaining close to the idea of overrunning, Ronell goes on to suggest that various forms of movement are important to the philosophical walk and that stumbling is equally important. Recalling what she terms "a very Hölderlinean landscape," Ronell goes on to suggest that it is even possible to experience an upward fall; we can also fall upward, she insists.[65] This upward fall is akin to an ecstatic or manic overreach. Certain interruptions, she suggests, occur in moments of textual excess, like those of Barthes's text of bliss or *jouissance*,[66] which can be likened to a kind of "affirmatory crash" and the "joy of losing one's bearing and bounds."[67] For Moure, poetry enacts such a fall.

In an essay on medieval Iberian troubadour poetry, Moure begins with an invocation of such a disruption: "*O cadoiro* is, literally, *the place where falling is made*. In Galician, *cadoiro* is one word for waterfall. *Cataract*, perhaps. Thus, *the fall*. This to me is the place of poetry. For whoever writes poetry must be prepared, ever, to fall down."[68] There are many ways to interpret the fall evoked in the preceding passage. For example, Moure narrates an instance when that great, unexpected fall takes place in the form of an encounter with the medieval Galician-Portuguese songbooks of troubadour poetry known as the *cancioneiros*[69]: "And in 2004 I did fall. Having already fallen into Galician and then Portuguese, I had one of the founts of lyric in Western Europe, the troubadour poetry of the medieval Galician-Portuguese songbooks, the *cancioneiros*."[70] The love poems of the troubadours are ecstatic poems mixed with existential meditations. "In this verse, the speaker's own subjectivity, own feelings, are the poetic 'substance,' yet these are quite consciously *constructed* by the poet, never 'unmediated,' always social, intended, and profane: directed toward another human, not to God."[71]

Poetry is also the place of dis-junctions. From the brief suspension of enjambment to the breath or pause initiated by the caesura, the rhythmic exigencies of a given line are often a complex, choreographed stutter; places where moments of faltering, of causing the reader to stagger, are where, simultaneously, a line comes undone – perhaps even desires to become undone.

In a book-length collection of essays on translation, the prolific writer and (self-) translator, Nathanaël, writes of translation, of the "failure of translation," in a manner that is strikingly similar to Moure's evocation of poetry, especially as it pertains to the lyric and to Ronell's ecstatic upward fall:

> Here, then. What I call here shall be 'the failure of translation'. A place, liminal, interstitial, abyssal – all of these – into which we fall, as one might fall in love, breakingly, or else fall apart, devastatingly, catching on the pieces of our own ruination, jaggedly, tearingly, seemingly (seamingly?). Fall away imperceptibly.[72]

The emphasis on "here" spurs me to hypothesize that *here* is the indeterminable, because invisible, place of translation.

To translate is to enact location or, better, a series of locations – those moments, according to the American experimental writer-philosopher, Renee Gladman, when the expression comes into being.[73] Although Gladman is not writing specifically about translation, her pursuit of the variables "acts and locations" in her book of essays, *Calamities*, provides a useful poetic juxtaposition through which to consider the "here" that both records and fails to record a (linguistic) boundary crossed by a body. In all three writers – Moure, Nathanaël, and Gladman – the fall allows us to understand something, to borrow a phrase from Gladman, "that had always eluded us"[74]: (love) poetry, (the failure of) translation, acts of location.

For the writers mentioned above, the "leurre of falling," as Nathanaël so aptly calls it, is never unmediated.[75] For Moure, the lure of poetry spurred her to travel to Lisbon in 2004, "after years of dreaming,"[76] to read the medieval *cantigas* – the poems "de amor," "de amigo" and "de escarnio e maldizer."[77] In Lisbon, she wandered through the city and its archives, following the trail of inscriptions, falling into what she calls "tapestries of word and sound, the 'wallpaper' – repetitive sonorities of, yes, an unrequited love."[78]

In 2001, three years earlier, Moure had experienced such an upward fall. That time, it was upon the poetry of Chus Pato. As Moure herself recounts in her book of essays, *My Beloved Wager*, during a visit to the Andel bookstore in Vigo, Spain, on 20 March 2001 with her Galician language teacher, translator, and friend, María Reimóndez, to buy dictionaries and books to help her learn Galician, she stumbled upon –

and fell, interminably and irremediably, in love with – the work of Chus Pato.

> I saw on the counter a large book with an incredible knobbly cover, bright orange, bearing the inscription: *m-Talá*, and below that, the words *Chus Pato*.
> I had no idea what it was, or what those three words meant, but I could tell it was a special artefact. It was a book that refused the standards of book marketing, that made itself into a stunning object [...]
> I picked up the book and opened it.
> My story ends here. All the story of the *before* and *prior* ends right here.
> For from this point onward, it's no longer a story. The prior and before are annulled, and a new anterior, interior, posterior, exterior, polyterior are opened. An entire life changed right then: mine.[79]

Ecstatic over "the torrents of words," and although she barely knew Galician at that time, Moure made up her mind: she would translate the poetry of Chus Pato.

> *It's impossible to translate*, María said. *I can tell*, I said. *That's why I want to translate it*. We both bought copies.
> I carried it with me everywhere, this book *m-Talá*:
> I underlined in it, highlighted in it, read it aloud, wrote notes in it. I googled things in it. I was in the heat of Babylon, on the steppes in the cold, listening to a radio show in Galicia, in the belly of the whale with Jonas, in the river with Ophelia.[80]

In *Secession/Insecession*, Moure references her encounter with the poetry of Chus Pato: "And then she opened the book. *Oh poetry*. May I translate? Wherever you are going, dear poem, dear Chus, I am going too."[81] She also celebrates translation specifically for its impossible nature: "If translation is impossible (my mother's ashes) then impossibility is the only thing that can occur."[82] That the English Canadian edition of *Secession/Insecession* is woven out of ecstatic circumstances is useful to keep in mind as we turn to questions of the texts' intimate relationship to each other.

(IN)VISIBILITY:
LE CERCLE D'INTIMITÉ OF THE THIRD TEXT

I now want to pursue a new question, one that I find myself asking over and over again: how or where, under which circumstances, do texts meet and collide? How or with whom do they move? When I ask these questions, I have in mind something of translation. For instance, when I open a recent book-length essay on translation by the experimental feminist and Québécoise writer, Nicole Brossard, I stop at the very first sentence and the very first question she poses: Why translation?[83]

In reality, the sentence does not in fact end where I pretend it does. Instead it has a much lengthier itinerary: "Why is translation a subject unlike any other? Why is it so conducive to a genuine fervour of meaning that can sometimes turn argumentative, as though every word contained a life challenge, a miniature vision of the world within it?"[84] What I retain from the full-length question is that whatever translation reveals, it seems it has less to do with translation itself than with an internal agitation in words, as though each were a keeper of a secret whose visibility (or secret life) is sometimes glimpsed in translation. In that sense, we might add that whatever is revealed in translation, or whatever translation grants to vision, it is that something of translation is always also necessarily invisible.

For feminist writers and critics like Nicole Brossard, who began working on questions of language and subjectivity in the 1970s, the question "why translation" became intrinsically linked to issues of (in)visibility – morphing the question of "why" into the question of "how": how can we rethink the role of translation, writing, and reading? How can language and literature alter or mark one's presence in the world? The critique was directed towards patriarchal language and its effacement of women's realities. This led many feminists to work on language-focused texts of a highly experimental nature.

In their desire to mark the gendered spaces produced in both linguistic and social contexts, these women turned to literary translation, for it offered a potentially empowering form of writing where women's experiences could find their anchorage in the agency of their reading and rewriting of texts, often by other feminists.[85] In so doing, they created and appropriated for themselves an "écriture au féminin" that echoed the post-structuralist "écriture féminine" of Julia Kristeva, Hélène Cixous, and Luce Irigaray, all of whom placed theory at the centre of their writing. "Do the translations seek to hide the work of translation and appear as naturalized in the English language, or do they function as texts, as writing, and foreground their work upon meaning?"[86] That is the distinguishing question posed by the late Barbara Godard, whose work, both as a feminist translator and as one of its most eminent theorists, not to mention her various editorial contributions in promoting bilingual feminist literary production across Canada,[87] helped establish and legitimize a highly experimental feminist translation practice and poetics in English Canada and Quebec.[88]

With resort to feminist theory on the one hand and to a distinctly feminist poetics on the other, Godard helped theorize translation as a site of exchange and collaboration. Thinking of these collaborations as double movements between "re/reading and re/writing" practices, she argues that the presence of the slash in re/reading and re/writing both demarcates and blurs the boundaries between reading and writing, writing and translating. Pointing to the example of Nicole Brossard's *Le Désert mauve* (*Mauve Desert*), Godard describes translation[89] as a "dialogic moment [...] underlining the double activity of women's writing as reading/writing, as the re/reading of the already-written followed by the divining/writing of the unrecorded."[90]

Shifting her attention to reading and writing as acts of production and therefore as performative, Godard views translation as an act of "transformance,"[91] a term she uses to "emphasize the work of translation, the focus on the process of constructing meaning in the activity of transformation, a mode of performance."[92] In transformance, translation becomes an active site of exchange, a place for (writing as) thinking, where the translator is an agent and the translation is an act of production rather than simply the site where equivalencies are maintained or where a copy or reproduction of an original takes place.

Transformance is, in many ways, a useful neologism for reading the attention granted to issues of (in)visibility in *Secession/Insecession*, but it is still too narrow in terms of accounting for the gesture of reception and address that Moure wants to grant to Pato through the publication of *Secession/Insecession*. Moure, in my view, goes further than the early utopic feminist translation project of making woman, as subject, visible, for her work as translator and poet is fractured and multiplied by her intimate relationship with Pato's work – and more importantly, it is this mark on her work and thinking that *Insecession* attempts to make visible. As literary scholar Daniel Aguirre-Oteiza explains, "Moure, a 'Montreal poet,' 'born the same year as Chus Pato,' who is writing a 'biopoetics,'[93] casts her voice into sharp relief as a differentiated poetic voice, albeit one mediated by another poet's voice."[94] The *in* of *Insecession* is one visible manifestation of this intimate "sharp relief" as Moure folds her text into Pato's without suggesting that both uniformly come together. The in of *in secession* illustrates how her text will always exist in proximity to Pato's text while simultaneously remaining in excess of it.

Although the bicephalous quality of the book rewards a reading that notices the ways in which one text arrives or departs from the other, if the titles appear "with" each other, as Moure suggests, and if the relationship between the texts allows her to make herself visible (as writer, reader and translator), then the cut implied by the slash in the title also opens onto a third text: "there is a new space of thinking that emerges which is neither the thoughts of one nor the other, nor the reader, but arises between and among ... I have been known to call this 'the third space.'"[95]

Moure's suggestion of a third space resonates with the fact that Pato begins *Secession* with a quote by Roland Barthes on the *unreaderly* third text, which he refers to as "the receivable":

> A *readerly* text is one I cannot rewrite (can I write today like Balzac?); a *writerly* text is one I read with difficulty, unless I completely transform my reading regime. I now conceive that there may be a third text: alongside the readerly and the writerly, there would be something like the *receivable*. The receivable is the unreaderly text which catches hold, the red-hot text, a product continuously outside any likelihood, whose function – visibly assumed by its scriptor – would be to contest the mercantile constraint of what is written; this text, guided, armed by a notion of the *un*publishable, would elicit the following response: I can neither read nor write what you produce, but I receive it, like a fire, a drug, an enigmatic disorganization.[96]

Moure, for her part, under the heteronym "Ruin E. Rome," an anagram of her name, playfully alters Barthes's passage in *Insecession*, allowing the quote to traverse her *corp(us)s*, not unchanged, and not unlike her "e(ri)nigmatic disorganizations" of Pato's text:

I now recognize a third text alongside the readerly and the writerly: let's call it the *intranslatable*. The intranslatable is the unreaderly text which catches fire, burns in the mouth, an instance continuously outside any likelihood, whose function – ardently assumed by its scripter – is to contest the mercantile constraints on what is written. This text, guided, armed by a notion of *material*, prompts me to redact the following words: Dear Chus, I can neither read nor write what you produce, but I can *intranslate* it, like a conflagration, a drug, an insecession, an e(ri)nigmatic disorganization.[97]

Moure, like Brossard and Godard with "transformance," invents a neologism, "intranslation," to account for this process of simultaneous proximity and excess.[98] It is also worth noting that despite their mediated appellations, both terms – Barthes's *receivable* and Moure's *intranslation* – gesture towards a fictitious third text that dwells in between or rather alongside the readerly and writerly one.[99] This leads me to gesture to the symbol of the slash as a visual manifestation of what would otherwise remain invisible as it can only be received or in-translated.

Put another way, regarding the third text that exists alongside the readerly and writerly ones, both Barthes's "receivable" and Moure's "intranslatable" register what is produced in the reader: a desire, a tiny shock, an entire world (moving) – in short, a thing in perpetual becoming. The fact that the book is divided into two parts, which are signed by two authors, invites certain reading modalities, such as a move back and forth, that modify the more linear practices of reading called for by other works and other book formats. As Moure remarks in *Insecession*, "translation ('the poetry of Chus Pato') is a way of bringing – into the secession or cut – another voice, her human voice, markings in words from a culture across a far border, to mark these words (her words) into new ears and onto new bodies."[100] This is one of translation's most generous attributes, that it does not act alone: "[Translation has a] double personality of sorts," writes Brossard in relation to literature's (not psychology's) dream of being another. "I read you in a foreign language; I will take you with me into my mother tongue. I is always an other in the act of becoming."[101] Given that the resulting texts are "armed by a notion of material," the writing of *Insecession* with or alongside Pato's *Secession* marks a space of friendship, both real and textual – one that materializes in the intranslatable text.

Intranslation is the invisible third text or body that materializes between the reader and the work. It is not an argument for transparency; rather, it is a way of acknowledging the various texts, quotations, dialogues, friends, and forces that shape and entwine the (intranslatable) text. Viewed in this light, *Insecession* is the body-text that hosts the intranslatable echolations that bring the author–translator–reader into "a differential logic."[102] This differential logic, as much as it offers a model of co-authorship applicable to both literature and translation, also evokes and revokes the stable identity of the writer/translator. It is in this further sense that Moure's "intranslation" project differs from earlier feminist models of experimentation, such as transformance.

The liminal space of differential logic, proposed in Aguirre-Oteiza's reading of *Secession/Insecession*, has further implications for a reading of Moure's intranslation, for, according to Aguirre-Oteiza, it "also catches up to and mediates 'Erín', the seemingly original and immediate proper name that identifies the translator."[103] Moure's description of intranslation as an "e(ri)nigmatic disorganization,"[104] Aguirre-Oteiza points out, exemplifies the split – not just in Pato's choice of title, *Secession* (and its connotations of a cut, withdrawal, or breaking apart), but also in the conception of the poet's identity.[105] Responding to the question regarding the meaning of *Secession*, Pato explains in an interview that its significance "brings [her] immediately to the notion of caesura in Hölderlin [...] Here caesura is also distance, cut, secession; it is the consciousness of the empty space between one exhalation of the voice and the next that makes writing possible."[106] The address and space made for the other, then, is not simply an ideal feature in Moure's annexation of *Insecession* to *Secession*; the consideration of the other is already deeply embedded in Pato's own poetics.

> Perhaps (psychology?) being a poet means assuming the caesura, constituting oneself in secession, in the very impossibility that languages might link words and things. A poet assert *I I* is a deserted site, a silence, a cut, a distance [...] A poet he remembers the writings that preceded him, those to come, those not yet born [...] No poem will ever be its own master, nor master of the language, nor of the world.[107]

In Pato's conception of *Secession* as a generative opening towards the other, and in Moure's mirror gesture towards Pato, the dominant model of individualistic authorship, to borrow a phrase from Lawrence Venuti, that continues to dominate the publishing industry, at least in an Anglo North American context, breaks apart in neologisms such as intranslation and e(ri)nigmatic disorganization, as do notions of original and transparent self-representation.[108] To borrow a phrase from Moure, "the I of a poet torques in translation, is a constructed I, a social spacing. To secede from this social spacing and speak a located body, corpuscles, the poet secedes from the I."[109]

THE BICEPHALOUS TEXT: AN INVENTION DRAWN FROM THE PRECLUSION OF SUBSIDIZATION

For Nicole Brossard and her early feminist collaborators, authorial originality was a myth to be debunked. Transformance, in that sense, is a neologism meant to counter the prevailing conception of the translator as a passive instrument or vessel through which the original moves while remaining intact. For Brossard, as with Moure and Venuti, the translator is also – among other things – a writer. To quote Brossard writing about the work under discussion here, "in fact, Erín Moure lays bare what until now has remained in the subtext: me, translator, poet, I live, I hear, and I respond at many levels to what I translate; in short, in every translation, I respond to my own life of reality and thought."[110] Indeed, for Brossard, the why and the how of translation soon overlap with the "emotional and associative circuits" of writing: the considerations I project onto translation stem from thinking about literary creation."[111] And shortly thereafter the question of *how* also becomes a question of *whom*: "Every translator is a reader first and foremost – that is, someone who takes into their inner world another world along with its mysteries, ambiguities, dazzlement, and danger zones."[112] This attention to the reader and to what or to whom enters is where I wish to continue thinking about how, and on what poetic terrain, the translative act might constitute itself (or not).

Marking as it does the exchange between her own work and Pato's – making Pato's influence visible in her own writing by enabling Pato's texts to circulate among readers who cannot read Galician – *Secession/Insecession* sets an example for a greater opening up of the literary spaces that shape writers and readers alike so as to enlarge what Brossard calls "the circles of intimacy present when working on a translation."[113] Yet when Moure enlarges her "circles of intimacy" by bringing her own work and Pato's into the fold of the slash, it is not simply a way for her of confirming what Brossard describes as "the encounter produced by an intense reading [that] alters, confirms, regenerates how we see and feel reality."[114] What I have not yet begun to touch upon are, in fact, the restrictive funding policies that make it impossible for Canadian publishing houses to receive subsidies to publish translations that do not stem from Canadian authors. My reading of the generative aspect of the work has, up until this point, been sparked by its creativity and ardour; I have not yet addressed a crucial aspect of the book: Moure's insistence in the prefatory notes that each text in *Insecession* "responds to a Pato text, with one added Chinook wind."[115] I now want to address that claim.

THE CANADA COUNCIL FOR THE ARTS AND CANADIAN-AUTHORED CREATIVE CONTENT: ERÍN MOURE'S CHINOOK WIND

Chinooks are warm winds that blow where the Canadian prairies and Great Plains meet. In relation to *Secession/Insecession*, these winds blow the reader all the way to the Canada Council for the Arts, a federal granting program that supports the Canadian publishing industry and its independent publishers by offering subsidies. Publishers, like *Secession/Insecession*'s Book*hug in Toronto, can receive support for publishing books in translation as long as they fit the following criteria: "[For publishers] this program provides grants for the translation of literary works written by Canadian authors."[116] To be eligible, a book must "contain at least 50% Canadian-authored creative content; have at least 48 printed pages between the covers [... and] be published principally in English, French or one of Canada's Aboriginal languages."[117] Publishers, then, cannot receive financial support from the Canada Council for the publication in Canada of international translations done by Canadian translators.

Of consequence, here, is how the funding policies partly explain the dual-author nature of the book. For her desired Canadian publisher to receive financial support to pay for the costs of publishing her translation of Chus Pato's text in Canada, Moure had to transform her translation of *Secession* into "Canadian-authored creative content." This is because even though, technically, it was not Pato who wrote *Secession* – Moure's English Canadian translation – funding policies do not make these distinctions, so Moure had to invent a new book to accompany her translation of Pato's work. She did this, not only by writing her own accompanying text, which acts as an echo and homage to Pato, but also by making *Insecession* one text longer than *Secession*. That way, the now bicephalous title, *Secession/Insecession*, would qualify as Canadian.[118] The Chinook, then, is the text that appears at the end of *Insecession* – the one titled "48, OR 49" – and that doesn't share a corresponding text with Pato (remember that to qualify as Canadian, the book had to "have at least 48 printed pages between the covers"): "I still owe 48 words, 47+1 so the book will be Canadian +1 missing from 'Lgiht's End.'"[119]

Prior to the publication of *Secession/Insecession*, Moure had published her English translations of Chus Pato's *Charenton* (2007), *m-Talá* (2009), and *Hordes of Writing* (*Hordas de Escritura* in Galician) in the UK with a publisher called Shearsman. *Flesh of the Leviathan*, another title from Pato's oeuvre translated by Moure (*Carne de Leviathan* in Galician), would appear a couple of years after *Secession/Insecession*, in 2016, from the US publisher, Omnidawn.[120] As a note at the end of the book suggests, Moure has translated Chus Pato since encountering her work in 2001, but while *Secession* is her fourth translation of the author's work, it is the first to be published in Canada.[121] The material conditions shaping *Secession/Insecession*, then, are also embedded in a material solution of finding a way to bring her English translations of Pato's work into Canadian circulation.

Those familiar with Moure's oeuvre will recognize in *Secession/Insecession* her generative practice of inclusion, whether through the incorporation of collaboration, intertextual references, and quotations in her poetry or through her prolific practice of translating other poets: French (Québécois/e), Spanish, Portuguese, and Galician into English. In her desire to make Pato's work and her influence on her work visible for a Canadian readership, Moure created the appropriate textual apparatus to accompany her English translation of her friend's text across the Canadian border, hence the creation of her own response-text, *Insecession*.

The dually authored book that is *Secession/Insecession* represents Moure's brilliant and ingenious attempt to bring Pato's work into the Canadian literary context by inventing a book-form that would allow her to do so; simultaneously, Moure's *Insecession* is transformed into an occasion to pay homage to Pato's work and influence on her thinking and poetics:[122]

Reading and translating Pato has decidedly affected my own poetry (I have often written and spoken about this). And I would say that the fact of being translated into English and thus into cultures outside of Galicia (of many languages that also read in English) has changed Chus' sense of address – her work by and large addresses the Galician nation, but I think she realizes more that her work has reverberations for us all, for other nations, and for those of us in marginal or differential "nations," such as that of women, of queer life, etc.[123]

There is a loving quality to the expansive movement of the writing – one that points to a space of friendship (real and textual) that is further entwined in the correspondence Moure's text keeps with Pato's: the way Moure writes into and out of her translation of Pato's *Secession*; how she foregrounds Pato's text as the very impetus for her own; how she acknowledges the marks of Pato's words on her own. By creating a space where both texts appear together, as companion or friend texts, Moure not only gives Pato's *Secession* a new (Canadian) address but also offers readers, like me, who cannot read Galician the gift of Pato's writing. Interestingly, it is through this generative aspect of friendship that while Pato's arrival via Moure's English translation of her work has done something to mould and morph *Secession/Insecession*, the book as object, it also makes visible the Canada Council's restrictive funding policies regarding the financial support for publications of translations of foreign literary works by Canadian translators.

The sense of address, of a new address, that Moure grants to Pato, in the sense of *Secession*'s new circulation in Canada and also in the sense of Moure's address to Pato in a text derived from translating her work, surpasses the earlier feminist experimental project of "transformance" and the attempt to make the translator visible as a creative collaborator. Instead, the bitextual nature of *Secession/Insecession* exists so that Chus Pato's work can be made visible in a literary context that, at least from a mercantile standpoint, is steeped in the very impossibility of her circulation in that context. If, as Derrida contends,[124] translation is both a necessary and impossible task, then Moure's translation of Pato's work is, without her own accompanying text, marked by a double-impossibility.[125]

Thus, in pursuing the inclined (dis)position of Moure's translation of Pato's *Secesión* into *Secession* alongside her own homage text, as

Moure's text tends towards Pato's text through the figure of the slash (a typographical manifestation of the incline), I remain close to Brossard's suggestion that in translation one lets the other in, so that framing the response, reciprocation, and resemblance of one text to another, to borrow the language used earlier to describe Moure's relationship to Pato's text, I echo Brossard in asking: "What will I do with you once you have entered my universe? Will we go some of the way together? How far?"[126]

TRANSLATION AS THINKING TOGETHER

In countering the uni-directionality (from source to target text) that is often employed to describe the movement of translation, I have, up until this point, attempted to show how translation is, first, an encounter on both sides, and second, how it opens a space of loving correspondence that is akin to the space of care in friendship. I dedicate the remainder of this chapter to the relevance of translation to thinking and to the following questions: What kind of intellectual history would the slash of *Secession/Insecession*'s title open onto, especially considering that the slash is a way of representing the fact that the texts are presented, in this translated edition, as *with* each other, as friend texts? And what are some of the links that might be drawn and redrawn between translation and philosophy? Between translation and thinking?

In her essay, "Deleuze and Translation," Barbara Godard points out that, for Deleuze,

> questions are important [...] because through them the outside works from within an enunciation ("machinic assemblage") to set in motion a process of transformation, a line of flight [...] This relay of questions, a recursive chain of chance, responds to "the outside" or force in a line of errant or "nomadic distribution." Questions, then, are one way to think about translation which, loosely speaking, might be called *an art of approach* to an outside involving a repetition with a difference.[127]

Translation, like Deleuze's questions, as Godard points out, is also an art of approach to an outside involving a repetition with a difference. Such an approach in *Secession/Insecession* is visible in the inclination of the slash in the title as well as in the preposition "with" that dons the more descriptive version of the long title.

In her essay collection *My Beloved Wager*, Moure weaves her thinking about a space of approach, an "aproximação," around Hélène Cixous's writing on the Brazilian writer Clarice Lispector, "wherein touch and meeting do not appropriate or domesticate but co-occur in the space of an encounter. A zone of overlap."[128] According to Moure, it is "a spacing, neither outside nor inside the organism."[129] In other words, an approach creates a space of hospitality; non-absorptive, the approach as overlap makes space for the asymmetrical, for alterity, thus allowing difference to prevail over assimilation.

Moure's recourse to an added text at the end of *Insecession* to ensure that the book would qualify for subsidization offers a telling example of the ways in which receptivity doubles as response-abilty. This "responsible responsiveness," to return to a notion coined by Avital Ronell in earlier parts of this chapter, captures well what Moure, in *My Beloved Wager*, describes as a matter of acknowledging that we are "incorporated beings" in a "provisional theatre":

> Thinking about and in spacings, placings, stagings, and how to think and be in such spacings – a thinking always in language and always spatial, physical, as well, because we are sited, incorporated beings. The purpose of this thinking is to learn how to be able to act and enact (and this is an emergency, how to emerge) in the world in a way other than that which hegemonic politics today would construct for me […] We urgently need thinking that pushes the boundaries of spacings.[130]

Secession/Insecession embodies a form of enactment, an act of thinking that exceeds (because it subverts) hegemonic policies that would otherwise curtail it. The fact that Moure appends *Secession/Insecession* with one added text on the side of her *Insecession* renders the book asymmetrical, and that very asymmetricality registers what Aguirre-Oteiza, paraphrasing David Damrosch, refers to as the "linguistic and poetic difference of the foreign text," which punctures the text with the aforementioned quality of overlap and pushes the boundaries of what is possible.[131]

A similar performance of difference is registered in the poets' biographies at the close of the book, where the political background of both poets' upbringing is explicitly stated: "Montreal poet Erín Moure was born in 1955 in a Canada governed by the Liberals under Louis St. Laurent," while Pato's biographical note reads:

> Chus Pato (María Xesús Díaz) was born in 1955, when Galicia was in the grip of the Franco dictatorship in Spain. Today a central and iconoclastic figure in Galician and European literature, Pato relentlessly continues to refashion the possibilities of poetic text, of words, bodies, political and literary space, and the construction of ourselves as individual, community, nation, world.[132]

The mark of difference between both poet's backgrounds is not simply relegated to the space of the poets' biographies, of course; *Secession/Insecession* is a biopoetics after all – a blend of each poet's biography with her poetics. This blend of bio and poetic opens towards a space of difference that archives, not memory, but dispersion.[133] Citing Derrida's *Mal d'archive*, Moure goes on to explain that what is archived moves in multiple diffuse ways, for the time of the archive – like that of poetry and friendship, as I have previously argued – opens onto a time to come.[134]

Although mainly written in prose, the work is nevertheless densely poetic. If Moure declares in *My Beloved Wager* that she desires a poetry that refuses erasure while it simultaneously elucidates the manifold voices and subject positions that compose the bio or poetic *I*, a poetry that, as she states, "could not be simply ingested. Not a consumer poetry [... but a] poetry that lets us think," then *Secession/Insecession* could certainly be viewed as one potential response.[135] Moreover, difference is also made clear throughout the work, starting with Moure's choice of the title *Insecession* – an asymmetrical slippage from *secession* to *in secession* – that inscribes her response to Pato's own title.

Building on this idea of asymmetrical slippage alongside Moure's notion of approach, as being neither outside nor inside the organism, the title's use of the preposition "with" continues to register a critical practice of difference and diffusion that is made even more apparent in *Insecession*'s self-reflexive insertions of parts of Pato's text into its own. In *Insecession*, for instance, we read: "'With love all this is bearable,' writes Chus Pato. Or, more accurately, *Con amor* ... for it was me who wrote 'with love all this ...'"[136] For readers of Moure's English translation, *Secession*, the passage Moure is citing can be found inserted a few pages earlier, where the "original" reads "With love all this is bearable."[137] There is a playful subversion at work here, however, for even my aforementioned parenthetical information – in wanting to point out that the passage belongs to Pato – attributes the English words to a poet who does not know the language. Retrieving the Galician text, the reader realizes that Moure's citation of it, in *Insecession*, has altered the passage slightly, for the Galician original reads "por amor" instead of "con amor."[138]

For Deleuze, terms like "with" and "and" give way to a "disjunctive synthesis" that is "neither conjunction nor disjunction, but both." Here is Godard again:

> At stake in translation, as in philosophy, has long been a concern with meaning separated from language, with dualisms, in short. Departing from an idealist philosophy of certain meaning anchored by the unity or totality of either a transcendent Idea or a generalizing *Aufhebung*, Deleuze replaces it with a singularity or differentiating event, with the hesitancy and stuttering of the atom, the particle, the zigzag, the flux. "Intermezzo," he writes, is the only way out of dualisms, the in-between, the passage. There is no teleological progression, no final emancipation, but only an endless, irregular, diffuse movement of becoming. Diffusion accelerates in the middle, spreading rhizome-like and branching out along the surface rather than putting down arborescent roots.[139]

When read alongside *Secession/Insecession*, the slash that simultaneously stands in for the term "with" is reminiscent of the singular multiplicity of Deleuze's atom, which is continuously splitting and branching out into an endless progression of slippages.

In one of the book's prefatory insertions, such a slippage is registered in *Insecession*'s playful rephrasing of Pato's text. Where, for instance, Pato's text reads "We recognize altitude from elevation, we call the most extensive prairie: Ocean," Moure's echolation responds: "We recognize altitude as we ascend, we call the ocean that unfolds below: Canadian Rockies."[140] The slip from "elevation" to "ascendance" might not seem significant, nor might the slip from "prairie" to "ocean" or from "Ocean" to "Canadian Rockies" lead to an apparent political intervention in the foregrounding of difference. When read against a reading of translation theories' concepts of arrivals and departures, however, the slippages that suddenly interrupt both texts mark translation as the site of a fruitful *dérive*[141] that is akin to the process of thinking itself.

The result of the generative drift and echoic design of Moure's response-text to Pato's biopoetic is a work that, far from attempting to sustain a one-to-one correspondence with Pato's text, rather serves as an example of "oblique intimacies," a term I am borrowing from Nathanaël:

> My geographies being inherent to my languages and my body being ensnared in each, I will eschew the inclination to make separate the very ensconced Cartesian divide, and will borrow instead from Claude Parent and Paul Virilio's architectural vocabulary, to posit translation as an *oblique* relationship, the oblique intimacies of which entail the touching of texts in parts and the gaping misalignments in others, the *partitioning* of bodies of text precisely where they touch, which is to say in *imperfect translation*, in other words, catastrophically misaligned.[142]

The idea of translation as a series of oblique intimacies, like the notion of an asymmetrical slippage or that of *dérive*, interests me primarily because the concept provides a key for reading Moure's *Insecession* as an imperfect translation of *Secession*, but a form of translation nonetheless. Such gaping (mis)alignments, for example, are expressed in moments when the texts nudge each other in complicity. In the following example, from the prefatory notes to the book, a delightful crossover is being staged: Pato writes "when you make love, where are you?,"[143] to which Moure's *Insecession* responds, "when you translate Chus Pato, where are you?"[144] Linking lovemaking to the gesture of translating Pato, *Insecession* does not repeat Pato's utterance but rather perversely translates her response into a space of erotic intermittence.[145]

Such an approach recalls Sherry Simon's neologism, "perverse translation,"[146] for describing those acts of translation that become enmeshed with the creative interference, excess, and deviance of creative writing.[147] Were we to seek to attribute a one-to-one relation of equivalence between the sentences from both texts mentioned above, or to think of Pato's text as source and Moure's as target text, the aforementioned lines would lead us to conclude that Moure's *Insecession* is a deviant translation of Pato's text. Of course, Moure herself, with her use of the prefix "in" in "insecession," already foregrounds the fact that hers is a derivative text. As such, the slash between Moure's *Insecession* and Pato's *Secession* embodies a dis-conjunctive approach. Transposing Godard's reading of Deleuze's metaphor of the stuttering atom onto Moure's dis-conjunctive approach, the dominant abyss-in-need-of-a-bridge model is replaced, in *Secession/Insecession*, by a flow of intermingling relations that is both an "and" and a "with":

> The "middle" is where things "pick up speed" *in a sideward movement* that "sweeps away the one and the other" in the "logic of AND." In the "entre-deux," the "in-between," the one intertwines with, embraces, the other. Thinking takes place in this interstitial place of crossover, thinking the outside as time within the fold, the outside-force as shared limit *both joining and separating*.[148]

Moving in a "sideward movement" that "both joins and separates" and that provides the opening where "thinking takes place," the inclined symbol of the slash in *Secession/Insecession* allows the texts to drift, to approach each other, to intertwine, to think (each other), and to respond without necessarily becoming a blur. Translation is thus transformed into a space of thinking that is simultaneously a space of address and an apostrophe.

THINKING IN THE APOSTROPHE

Given the intimate frame of address in *Secession/Insecession*, it is difficult to ignore the generous poetics that materialize between the two texts: "What counts for me, and what materializes in my reading," notes Moure in an essay on the book in question, "is the <u>one</u> that arises between <u>two</u>, the life that emerges between two lives."[149] The one that arises between the two, like Deleuze's singular multiplicity, enacts a plural poetics where, as Moure points out in an essay on the work under discussion, "what arises isn't a desubjectivization or a resubjectivization, but an emergent in(tra)subjectivity that surges from reading itself, and thus is situated, strangely, in proximity to the reader, in the very act of reception."[150]

The question of how to re/write Pato's text does not simply implicate Moure as a translator, it also implicates a great deal of care and recognition of the vital contamination of Pato's work in relation to her own. In the following example, Moure makes this affective relation clear by pointing out that the encounter is not merely textual and that it involves other kinds of bodies as well: "TRANSLATION ("the poetry of Chus Pato") is a way of bringing – into the secession or cut – another voice, her human voice, markings in words from a culture across a far border, to mark these words (her words) into new ears and onto new bodies."[151] Reading these scenes alongside Godard's reading of Deleuze, this space of encounter or middle ground is introduced as the site of relation that goes beyond the intersubjective and that moves or folds out of collaborative and perpetual becoming. The example given in Deleuze is that of the French conjunction "ET" which is also "E(S)T." As Godard points out, "ET" (and) slips beyond the relation of what's between the conjunction and rather addresses the ongoing fixation, especially in idealist philosophy, of the subject as the centre of being.[152] This is true too of the way Moure deploys *Insecession* so as not to make it or herself the centre of the work.

The slash, then, like Deleuze's figure of the middle, is a way, a method, of pursuing writing/philosophy as a "transcreative process of becoming," one that privileges a lively (and living!) process – a conversation – rather than a fixed product: "This logic of the AND AND AND, the logic of the series or 'geography of relations,' works against the politics of incorporation, whether of communion or cannibalism, as both 'multiple affirmation' and 'stuttering.'"[153] This idea, that one thing is not hierarchically absorbed by another, is crucial to the precarious relationship of *Secession* to *Insecession* where the "transversal" that "cuts across binaries" is suggestive not just of the slash in the title but also of the nestling of *Secession* in *Insecession*.

> Translation is possible, I think, along with Beckett and Borges, because the original, any original, can never be finished. Because a linguistic act must be *received* to be an act (ink and paper are not acts) and because the recipient is not "one" either. The recipient changes (and is changed, constantly, by differential forces of time that construct it), even in a single language.[154]

In the section "Ruin E. Rome," Moure poses and re-poses the question "must someone think," this time addressing it to a long list of friends through the formula AND, AND, AND:

> Dear Hannah Arendt, I write [...] Dear Lisa, dear Kim, dear Carla, dear Karis, dear Chus, dear Gail, dear Oana, dear Judith, dear Rachel, dear Anna, dear Martha, dear Christa, dear Claire,

dear Anastasyia, dear María, dear Bélen, dear Nicole, dear Angela, dear Oksana, dear Uljana, dear spook, dear ghost.[155]

Just as the slash is a conventional symbol for line breaks in poetry, here it also marks the break or rather the (ex)change – the metamorphosis – that takes place in the space of encounter and reception lodged between the works. As Aguirre-Oteiza remarks, "through a seemingly endless set of apostrophes, Moure posits a dialogical form of difference which interpellates past and future readers and writers."[156]

Such a hospitable space of encounter is evident in sections where Moure addresses Pato directly: "In trying to parse spatiality and corporeality, I think of the prosthesis, yes, of poetry as prosthetic gesture, and of poetry as conversation. How performativity is also material gesture, something I learned from Chus Pato in translating the *razó* of her poems."[157] In both instances mentioned above, the slash transmits the conversation the poets are speaking into: "I hesitate to say anything about poetry except: it is a conversation we speak into, and our consanguinity in words (material effect) matters."[158] Interestingly, the use of consanguinity comes from Pato, who in turn is quoting the dialogue between Karoline von Günderrode and Kleist: "I underline," Pato writes, "*Consanguinity as a good* [...] *no one had ever considered this. The kinship that attenuates the distress felt before that alien sex to whom one can never surrender.*"[159] The potential of poetry's consanguinity is perceptible in Moure's inclusion of *Insecession* with her translation of *Secession*. Situating one's reading practice in the in-between of the two biopoetic texts serves as a tantalizing experience for the reader, who, reading in the back and forth of the slash's inclination in *Secession/Insecession*, reads in the space of alternating caesuras. The caesura as breath, to echo Pato, opens the act of reading to the space of echoes on both sides of the texts – echoes that inflect the texts with difference as well as sameness; echoes that capture the poetic bond between texts, between poets, and between poets, texts, and reader(s). The potential of translation's consanguinity is perceptible in *Secession/Insecession*, where the desire to reach the unrepresentable – a prominent feature of my discussion of Fernando Pessoa's *The Book of Disquiet* in the chapter that follows – dis-conjoins both texts together. Even more persuasively, *Secession/Insecession* is an example of writing that is inclined towards future possibilities for poetry.

CONCLUSION

My interest in translation as a form of thinking together, and, more specifically, my devotion in this chapter to the task of reading *Secession/Insecession* as a book whose structure enacts the dynamics of a thinking together, is not just a simple matter of reciprocity or textual companionship. The dually authored book, as one that embeds several moments of correspondence and refractive echoes through Moure's echolation-homage, delivers its full resonance in a reading of slippages performed across and between texts.

In *Secession/Insecession*, translation affirms the new by placing the work of Chus Pato in a new context, making it available to new readers, in a new language. Through the inclination of the slash that positions both works as "with" each other, Moure's translation of Pato's text has turned the impossible (her circulation in Canada) into an actuality. The dually authored book mutates what is impossible (an aporia) into a possibility. As Moure herself notes, it is crucial to acknowledge that her own text would not exist without Pato's.

The model proposed in *Secession/Insecession* makes the process of writing, reading, translating, and thinking a continuous, open, and generative model: one that is reverent to the point of exuberance and that makes the homage the poignant subject, not just of friendship, for it is not uncommon for poets to elegize the dead friend, but of translation as well. What *Secession/Insecession* makes abundantly clear, moreover, is that the contingent circumstances shaping the book – in terms of geographical, cultural, and political forces – are impossible to ignore, and that they are among the most important aspects of and contributions to the transversal connection between thinking and translation, a connection that, in turn, gives way to the dually authored format of the book.

2

Rewriting Fernando Pessoa's *The Book of Disquiet*

PME-ART and the Afterlife of Translation

Everything depends on what we are and, in the diversity of time, how those who come after us perceive the world will depend on how intensely we have imagined it, that is, on how intensely we, fantasy and flesh made one, have truly been the world. I do not believe that history, and its great faded panorama, is any more than a constant flow of interpretations, a confused consensus of absent-minded witnesses. We are all novelists and we narrate what we see, because, like everything else, seeing is a complex matter.
    Bernardo Soares, *The Book of Disquiet*, trans. Margaret Costa

PREAMBLE[1]

The first time I saw PME-ART – a Montreal-based bilingual (French/English) interdisciplinary performance collective – was, I think, in Montreal in 2011; it was in the bilingual show *The DJ Who Gave Too Much Information / Le DJ qui Donnait Trop d'Information*, where the performers took turns playing vinyl recordings as they recounted an anecdote related to each record. A few years later, when PME-ART occupied the Leonard & Bina Ellen Art Gallery for eight consecutive days with *Adventures can be found anywhere, même dans la mélancolie*, a show where they transcribed and radically rewrote Fernando Pessoa's unfinished work, *Livro do Desassossego*, from its English and French translations (*The Book of Disquiet* and *Le Livre de l'Intranquillité*), I saw in PME's multilingual rewritings of the book not only the melding of the language of the visual and literary arts but something of the work of the translator as well. Fascinated by this *lieu de rencontre* – between languages and between versions of the book – and by the overlaying of Pessoa's Lisbon over Montreal, I was struck by the way the scribes,[2] in their creative echoes of the original, made palpable a quality not necessarily new but one already inherent in the work itself: its defiant nature.

Composed of well over four hundred fragments that fall roughly into the categories of philosophic meditations, dreamy Symbolist texts, and diaristic passages (influenced by Edgar Allan Poe, Charles Baudelaire, and Walt Whitman, among others), and described as an anti-book of sorts, *The Book of Disquiet* was never finished in Pessoa's lifetime (1888–1935). To offer a sense of the book's unwieldiness, four different translations and numerous editions of the book exist in the English language alone.[3] Given the book's unique history, which I shall outline below, the act of rewriting its fragments and thereby changing them – something like what PME-ART has done – could be interpreted as an active contribution to the book's (un)making. Reading the performance in the aforementioned light makes the act of rewriting the book less a gesture of appropriation of a found object than a way of activating, and of being hospitable to, the book's open-ended, plural, and elusive nature.[4]

Signed by his semi-heteronym, Bernardo Soares, rather than by Pessoa himself –not an unusual gesture for this author, who created various alter egos for his oeuvre – *The Book of Disquiet* has a long and slippery history that is worth being briefly sketched here, beginning with Pessoa's creation of heteronyms. But first, a few notes on the trajectory of this chapter.

CHAPTER OVERVIEW: THE QUESTION OF THE BOOK'S ORIGINATION

In this chapter, I consider the propulsive nature of Fernando Pessoa's *The Book of Disquiet* in relation to PME-ART's bilingual performance at the Leonard & Bina Ellen Art Gallery in Montreal titled *Adventures can be found anywhere, même dans la mélancolie*. In the performance, scribes undertook the task of transcribing and creatively rewriting fragments from Pessoa's unfinished work, *Livro do Desassossego*. Producing rewrite after rewrite of fragments from the book's English and French translations, *The Book of Disquiet* and *Le Livre de l'Intranquillité*, this co-authored performance not only merged performance art and literary creative practices but also summoned several questions regarding the propulsive nature of the work – its particularly melancholic quality, suggested in the "disquiet" of the title as well the work's posture as the diary of the recluse Bernardo Soares. Having offered a reading of the previously mentioned work, I then turn to PME-ART's attempt to place *The Book of Disquiet* in a gallery setting in an ongoing way, through the performance of rewrite after rewrite of the book.

I should point out at this juncture that my intention is not to read and compare the various versions of *The Book*, nor is it to perform a close reading of *The Book* and PME-ART's rewrites, but to use the example of PME-ART's performance to better understand and illustrate the condition of a text's unrest or afterlife. In what follows, I am basing my reading of PME-ART's performance on my own memory of it as a spectator. Aware that this might be viewed as a flawed approach, because too subjective, I embrace the *trou de mémoire* and possible inaccuracies of my memories because they represent what I still retain from an event that was held four years ago, an event, moreover, that seems pertinent to the present study's interest in the reach and continued life of works of art. I should make another point, however, regarding the partly subjective dimension of my methodology in relation to *The Book of Disquiet*'s afterlife: while I refer mainly to my own memories and experiences of PME-ART's performance, I do not maintain that a work's afterlife is necessarily contingent on human reception. I shall clarify this point as the chapter progresses.

As I highlighted in this book's introduction, for Walter Benjamin, the task of translation is to provide the possibility of an encounter where "the most intimate relationships among languages" can emerge.[5] Benjamin argues in his essay that this "special convergence" between languages, where the relationship between one language and another is at stake, makes new knowledge possible in the in-between of language's becoming. Benjamin gives translation's epistemological vocation a name, that of afterlife or the afterlife of translation.

Textual afterlife can be thought of in terms of a text's experiential aspects rather than an innate truth concealed within it. While it may be tempting to locate these experiential aspects in a reader or spectator, this is not what Benjamin suggests in "The Translator's Task." In fact, Benjamin is quite clear on this point: "certain concepts gain their proper, indeed their best sense, when they are not from the outset connected exclusively with human beings."[6] For Benjamin, a work's afterlife is not contingent on our experience of a text, for the work has a life and a history of its own. In that sense, afterlife is an innate feature of a work, but it is not one that can be distilled to the text's essence or truth. Afterlife, then, refers to a text's ability to evolve and change; that is why categories such as "truth" and "essence" are misleading.

In this way, in its rearticulation of an original, translation provides insight into the conditions of textual mutability. Translation is not purely an attempt to represent an original; it is also bound to a critical interpretation of the work. Even as a creative practice and a mode of critical interpretation, translation's relationship to an original is necessarily characterized by unrest by the very fact that it is impossible for the translator to keep the original exactly as it was; put another way, it is impossible in the act of rewriting a text to keep the original completely intact. Shifting a text from one context to another inevitably changes something in the work. This is true beyond translational operations, and it is an especially salient feature of the act of reading as well. In the context of translation, a comparative reading can reveal something about the text, and about language, that a reading of a single text cannot; for example, a comparative reading reveals the irreducible nature of the original; it reveals language itself as a living, thinking structure.

Deeply suspicious of the teleological movement of "progress," Benjamin does not situate the original and the translation on a linear continuum. Instead, the translation and the original can be viewed as engaged in a relationship of metamorphosis. In other words, the original is not what was; the original is what continues to change and evolve alongside the translation in a process of becoming. What is most interesting in Benjamin's assessment of afterlife is that it is not just the translation that is transformed and that gives new life to an original. Rather, the original itself is affected by this mutation, "which could not be so called if it were not the transformation and renewal of a living thing, the original is changed."[7] A work's afterlife, then, can be thought of in terms of renewal and transformation.

This chapter uses the notion of afterlife as a means of thinking about the various forms of textual unrest or disquiet in Pessoa's *The Book of Disquiet* and PME-ART's rewriting of that work. I propose, then, to consider the work's relationship to disquiet as an utterance of unrest or afterlife – one that exceeds a knowable origin or destination and that is situated at the cusp of a private and public discourse. I am suggesting that PME-ART's *unmöglich Aufgabe* (impossible task), in *not* replicating a word-for-word transcription of the book, involves responding to the text's unrest by continuing to exhaust its indeterminate possibilities through rewriting. The scribes accomplish this, I argue, by inserting themselves into the work as heteronymic mutations of Bernardo Soares. In this way, through PME-ART's rewrites, the book thus continues to be overcome by an amorphous writing subject. Pessoa's fragmented and unfinished text, then, as I show in this chapter, weaves back and forth between everyone and no one, public and private discourses, heteronymity and anonymity, effacement and radical inscription,[8] as well as inside and outside death. In a later section of this chapter, I borrow Avital Ronell's terms "post-autobiographical utterance" and "rumour-text" to name the "after-my-death report" that characterizes parts of *The Book of Disquiet*.

Moreover, as I shall show throughout these pages, Pessoa's *The Book of Disquiet* thrives in this form of excessive undecidability and nomadic unfinishing, for not only was Pessoa himself a great shape-shifter – he dispersed his oeuvre across more than a hundred heteronyms – but the autobiography that constitutes *The Book of Disquiet* recounts the life of a man, Bernardo Soares, who never existed ouside Pessoa's fiction sentences. Furthermore, considering that *The Book* was never published or assembled by Pessoa or, indeed, during his lifetime, and that it was collated by several editors, translators, and scholars into different versions, the question I pose is not which one is the truest *Book of Disquiet*, or even whether there such a thing as Pessoa's *Book of Disquiet*, although the question is certainly valid, but rather, how are we to tell whether or not, in its itinerancy or anti-trajectory, *The Book* has actually arrived?

Thus, the wandering nature of Pessoa's *Livro do Desassossego* – as it is performed by the Montreal artist collective PME-ART and its scribes through their rewrites of its English and French translations – serves as my testing ground for thinking about experimental and creative translational practices in relation to Benjamin's stance on the afterlife of works of art.

PESSOA'S HETERONYMS

In Pessoa, selves multiply. Bernardo Soares, Alberto Caeiro, Ricardo Reis, Álvaro de Campos – these are only some of Pessoa's heteronyms. In other words, they are all Pessoa and not Pessoa. What makes Pessoa's heteronyms distinct from pseudonyms has to do with the autonomy Pessoa ascribed to them, in that he created intricate back stories that attributed a life to them distinct from his own. For example, the heteronymous Alberto Caeiro is a shepherd whose poems are written in free verse; Ricardo Reis is a doctor whose oeuvre emulates classical forms; Álvaro de Campos, who invokes the expansiveness of Whitman's poetry, is also a naval engineer; and *The Book of Disquiet*'s Bernardo Soares is an assistant bookkeeper. Soares, unlike Caeiro, Reis, and de Campos, is considered Pessoa's semi-heteronym:

> [Bernardo Soares is] a semi-heteronym because his personality, although not my own, doesn't differ from my own but is a mere mutilation of it. He's me without my rationalism and emotions. His prose is the same as mine, except for a certain formal constraint that reason imposes on my own writing, and his Portuguese is exactly the same.[9]

Heteronyms – which were his own invention – allowed Pessoa to recast his words and thereby disembody them into other author-characters. Note that his surname, Pessoa, means *person* in Portuguese. In French the inflection is slightly different: a *personne* can be someone or no one depending on the grammatical context. This ambiguity is important. Pessoa's creation of heteronyms, four of which are mentioned here although there are around one hundred others, formed a coterie of writers who often interacted with one another's work in the form of criticism, interviews, or exchanges of letters.

THE BOOK OF DISQUIET IN PREPARATION

In 1913 an exiguous part of *The Book of Disquiet* arrived on the scene with the publication of a piece of writing called "In the Forest of Estrangement" ("Na Floresta do Alheamento"). The piece was published in the journal *A Águia (The Eagle)*. This time, almost uniquely, Pessoa not only signed the text in his own name but also framed it in a letter to a friend as an excerpt "from *The Book of Disquiet*, in preparation."[10]

By the early 1920s, the book had still not fully materialized as a finished product; it would instead remain adrift. Richard Zenith, in his introduction to his 2002 English edition and translation, points out that "[as] Pessoa worked on it for the rest of his life, the more he 'prepared' it, the more unfinished it became."[11] Eventually, in a kind of manic surrender, Pessoa began scribbling the letters "L. do D." (*Livro do Desassossego*) on various texts, even those predating 1913. As Zenith argues, these indexing scribbles were added somewhat precariously, "sometimes as an afterthought, or with a question mark indicating doubt."[12] Noting how Pessoa struggled to maintain a uniform voice or style for the work as a whole, scholars have tended to divide the writing of the book's fragments into three phases.

The first phase, which is attributed to the heteronym Vicente Guedes as early as 1913, is written in a style similar to that of *fin de siècle* semi-Symbolist prose pieces. The texts offer meditations on various states of mind, imaginary dreamscapes/landscapes, and advice to dreamers/lovers. The second phase of the book's development, beginning around 1920, is characterized by a near ten-year pause that places the book's writing in a state of limbo; finally, sometime around 1929, when all the other heteronyms have gone silent, Pessoa introduces Bernardo Soares, the semi-heteronym and humble assistant bookkeeper who eventually becomes the sole author of the work, even though his arrival post-dates the book's inception. It is believed that Soares wrote more than half of the book between 1929 and 1934.[13] In Pessoa's lifetime, only twelve fragments from the book were published in Portuguese periodicals,[14] leaving close to four hundred fifty. Some are marked "L. do D." in the margins, to be puzzled over by scholars and editors long after Pessoa's death.[15]

THE BOOK AS AN ANTI-BOOK

The first published edition of *The Book of Disquiet* appeared in 1982, forty-seven years after Pessoa's death.[16] "It was a heroic effort," writes translator and editor Richard Zenith, "since Pessoa's archives are notoriously labyrinthine and his handwriting sometimes almost illegible, and it was doomed – for these very reasons – to be seriously flawed. Subsequent editions considerably improved the readings of the original manuscripts and added new material, at times a little recklessly."[17]

Zenith notes that if Pessoa had accompanied *The Book of Disquiet* through to publication, it not only would have been a different book than the one assembled posthumously by various editors, but also would have been a much smaller book.[18] It is not clear exactly what Zenith has in mind when he applies the adjective "smaller." It's possible he is making a point about the triage of fragments that Pessoa would have performed versus the one done by editors who began with nothing but a vast and unwieldy collection of unbound fragments turned editorial project – a manuscript or a book that, to quote Zenith, "multiplied without ceasing, being first one book and then another, told by this voice and then that voice, then another, still others, all swirling and uncertain."[19] On my desk alone there are four different editions of the work: three are in English, one in French.

With many texts existing prior to *The Book of Disquiet*, and Pessoa's post-dated annotation of *L. do D.* in the margins of certain works, *The Book of Disquiet* is a book that continues to rehearse itself, that continues to be reassembled and, in that sense, continues to be rewritten – first by Pessoa himself as well as his heteronyms, and second by countless editors, translators, and scholars who have arranged and continue to rearrange the book posthumously. *The Book of Disquiet* can thus be approached as an authorial project on the one hand and as an editorial construct on the other – features I shall soon return to specifically in relation to PME-ART's performance.

REWRITING AS A *LIEU DE RENCONTRE*

The literary texts produced out of PME-ART's rewriting of the fragments from *The Book of Disquiet* and *Le Livre de l'intranquillité* assumed various shapes and tactics. Some transcriptions actively deviated from the source text, using Pessoa's fragments more as a prompt for their own echo-fragments. As Jacob Wren recalls,

> while previous experts and translators sought to work toward some definitive version of *The Book of Disquiet*, here we clearly find ourselves drifting toward the distant other end of the finished/unfinished spectrum [...] When nothing is finished, everything remains possible. At least for a while. Or at least within a work of art. This is one of the paradoxes that art can scratch away at and evoke: sometimes a job well done is a job partially undone, to make room for the future. Pessoa never finished his masterpiece, *The Book of Disquiet*, and neither does *Adventures can be found anywhere, même dans la mélancolie*. One can gaze at a fragment and fear its implicit sense of failure. Or one can glance at a fragment and think: this is only the beginning.[20]

While some rewrites contributed to the book's endless drift between becoming and unmaking, other transcriptions remained more faithful to the task of rewriting the book, changing only a few words here and there. In some cases, however, even minor modifications were enough to completely alter the destination (the mood and tone) of the fragments. In an article in *Canadian Art*, Wren points to the freedom the scribes afforded themselves as they rewrote the work:

> Sometimes we did simply copy out the page, or a section of the page, and this act of transcription significantly changed it. Or we copied it out making only small changes. Sometimes these small changes, altering only a few words, in fact did the most to make the page a little bit happier."[21]

Far from reticent about their intention to intervene and insert themselves into the work, even rendering it a little bit "happier," PME-ART's creative manipulators, who overlapped Pessoa's work with their own, fabricated new lines of inquiry in what was already a deeply introverted and philosophically inflected work.

INTRODUCING PME-ART'S PERFORMANCE

Imagine a large gallery space that has been divided into two sections. In the first section the walls are white and bare. There's a table in the middle of the room where six scribes are seated with their books and sheets of paper of various colours. You can walk around the scribes, trying to catch a glimpse of the passages they are transcribing, how they are modifying them to render them "happier" and "more of our time," but you soon notice the lack of intimacy the setting affords ... or is it too intimate?[22] The onlooker either ghosts PME-ART's process of rewriting as a marginal onlooker, or accepts his or her position as a figure of excess in the performance. When you enter the gallery, you are immediately drawn to the middle of the room, where the scribes are busy at work, but upon entering their "inner circle" or "workspace," you quickly realize you will not be invited to partake or participate in the work's rewriting. In fact, there is an overwhelming sense that your presence as an observer could obstruct the scribes' creative process. Sensing the disquiet brought about by how the performance is structured, the way it incites an uneasy interaction between private and public spaces, the viewer feels drawn to explore the rest of the gallery, if only to leave the scribes to fully concentrate on the demands of their task.

In the second section of the gallery, a long shelf runs the length of the wall, where the scribes place their transcriptions once they are done, page by colourful page. There's a camera too, mounted above a plinth that serves as a broadcast podium where scribes go to read their rewrites and that initially captures the image of the transcription and projects it onto the wall. When each performer is done with his or her rewrite, he or she walks over to this section to project the newly transcribed text. They read it to themselves, silently at first, then they read it a second time, out loud whether or not there is actually a spectator present. Again, there is this double play of intimacy ghosting the process of rewriting. On the one hand the aforementioned gesture is a private one: the scribe reads the passage to him or herself. On the other hand, what is interesting is that the gesture then morphs into a public one as the scribe reads the transcription aloud. Of course, to interpret the gesture as one that moves from a private to a publicly broadcast discourse is misleading, for the nature of the performance itself already situates the gestures of the performance within the public space of the gallery, which is free to all who wish to come and witness it.

In a more logistical sense, to evoke the idea of work or the work – whether of a public or private nature – is also to take note of the fact that the performance unfolded, over the period of eight days, during the gallery's regular working hours. Between 23 October and 1 November 2014, PME-ART's rewriting of *The Book of Disquiet* occupied the space of the gallery from Tuesday to Friday from noon to six p.m. and on Saturday from noon to five p.m. It makes sense to link this idea of "work" to the durational nature of the performance. Setting aside the implications of their working schedule, each rewrite of a fragment was reminiscent of a task on a factory assembly line. As each scribe or performer finished his or her rewrite of a fragment, and before that person undertook another one, it was broadcast in an adjacent room with the help of a microphone and a projector, then placed on a wooden shelf about three feet off the ground running the length of the gallery. Over time, as the pages multiplied, the horizontal tablet was virtually transformed into a conveyor belt. In a piece of criticism by Nayla Naoufal on the performance, published in Montreal's *Le*

Devoir, the headline aptly reads "la fabrique de littérature," recalling not only PME's transformation of the language of the gallery space into the language of the studio space where one makes works, but again suggesting that the performance was situated between public and private gestures. The performance's finale – with the creation of an unreadable "Monster Book" – further maintained the blurring of the aforementioned edges, for, as Jacob Wren explains, the object in the gallery was perhaps more the scribes themselves and their transcription work than the work itself:

> On the last day of the performance/exhibition, for the finissage, we stapled all of the rewritten pages back into a copy of the original *Book of Disquiet*, reading each one aloud before we did so, creating what we called the Monster Book. I did not expect the finished Monster Book to be so aesthetically compelling, so like an art object, the kind of physical object we had never really made before. All of the colourful pages jutting out at every possible, origami-like, unseemly angle. A record of our work together crammed into a somewhat unreadable package. Something I could imagine seeing in an art gallery, if the object in the gallery hadn't actually been us and our ongoing performative work.[23]

While a book is generally intended to be read and circulated, the final public reading of the fragments, before they were stapled into a copy of *The Book of Disquiet*, can be interpreted as a last gesture of homage directed at work (and at a work) that in many ways eschews progress; it is work whose end is done for the work itself, Pessoa's, and therefore done for no one. PME-ART's rewrites, which doubled *The Book of Disquiet* by producing a text upon a text, also multiplied the site of reading into a unreadable object where something more or less, or both, coalesced around and was unleashed from the work.[24]

To think in terms of public and private discourse is somewhat useful in considering the rewrites themselves. PME-ART's mandate may have been to transcribe a book that had been in public circulation since 1982, but the interventions they performed on the text – the diverse ways their rewrites departed from the source text – were of a more private than public nature; admittedly, "private" in this context is perhaps not the most precise term compared to, say, "invisible." This is because, in terms of the transcriptions, there may have been some signs of intervention – especially when drawings and calligrams replaced a standard paragraph – but generally speaking the scribes' modifications were invisible. A spectator who did not already have intimate knowledge of *The Book* – most of them? – would have found it often impossible to tell which were the scribes' and which were Pessoa's words. In terms of the private nature of the rewrites, to return to the term I had temporarily replaced with the idea of the invisible, the rewrites were expressing the private thoughts of the scribes who had replaced Soares as diarists. Whether or not those private thoughts stemmed from art or from life is another matter; however, that does not concern me here. What does interest me is the idea that the rewrites suggested a productive tension between art and life, public and private, the seen and the unseen – all of which remained in keeping with the spirit of Pessoa's unfinished project.

Of all the studies on *The Book of Disquiet* I've come across, Paulo de Medeiros's *Pessoa's Geometry of the Abyss* is by far the one that grants the most attention to the visual aesthetics of the work. "Throughout the *Book of Disquiet*, visual elements are made key to any form of thought," writes de Medeiros, "hardly any fragment is without some reference to seeing, watching, looking, the eyes, or the gaze."[25] With the book's emphasis on visual elements, it is equally noteworthy that PME-ART's performance took place in a gallery space rather than a library or even a theatre, to name but two other possible settings.

The performance's divide between two sections allowed the performance collective to incorporate, in the first section, the immediacy of a creative process through performance (like the one afforded by the conditions of a theatre or theatrical space). In the second section, the long shelves recalled the archival practices of an institution – a library, for example. The first section also reminded the spectator of the authorial project the book represents, while the second section hearkened back to the editorial project that has preoccupied so many editors and scholars since Pessoa's death. It is fitting too that at the end of their performance, PME-ART transformed Pessoa's original book into a "Monster Book" – a hefty, colourful, protruding, and unreadable art object – that would not only replace the original but also remain in keeping with its itinerant and unfinished publication history.

THE BOOK OF DISQUIET'S SECRET RENDEZ-VOUS

In a talk on the nature of the test or testing, the philosopher Avital Ronell points out that

> we do not always know how to calculate the importance of a work. In some cases there is nothing even to guarantee that the work will arrive. Some works seem to set an ETA – there is a sense that it will take them years to make their arrangements, overcome the obstacles of an unprotected journey, get past the false reception desks blocking their paths. In the more assured and seductive version these works follow the itineraries of Benjamin's "secret rendez-vous," targeting "the secret rendez-vous" that a work has made with the singularity of a destination in the form, perhaps, of a future reader. The reader or receptor from the future assumes the responsibility of being addressed, of signing for the work when it finally arrives – helping it originate. Yet little tells us how many hits a work will have taken on its way, or whether we will be there to receive it [...] Perhaps the work will be prevented from showing up at the appointed time. On the other hand, some works barrel toward their destinations, causing a lot trouble for a lot of daseins. Heidegger once said that it can take two hundred years to undo the damage inflicted by certain works (I think he was evaluating Plato, so thousands of years).[26]

Ronell's intimation that a work carries its own in-built and fluctuating temporality – depending on the reader who is there (or not) to receive it – is well illustrated in a book that has not one but multiple versions. In the introduction to his book-length study of *The Book of Disquiet*, Paulo de Medeiros echoes the undecidability captured in Ronell's statement:

> If one adds to the editions in the original Portuguese those appearing in translation, also diverging from the Portuguese editions, one can imagine an infinite multiplication of books that in itself would already contribute to an annulment of the very idea of a single book, as if the text, in its publication history, would also represent a form of incessant disquiet."[27]

There is, in de Medeiros's assessment, a pellucid relationship between the scattered fragments, as they were being written and recuperated by Pessoa over time, and future manuscript versions of the work by editors and translators, which have been characterized as impossible tasks to complete. Although his own articulation of the book's unwieldy nature is less metaphysical than Ronell's, de Medeiros echoes the seemingly infinite ontological possibilities of the nomadic book-object.

Recently, Tim Hopkins of the London-based publisher Half Pint Press has produced one of the most unique book-objects in his attempt to embody *The Book of Disquiet* in the form of ephemera. This particular edition, published in 2017, of which only eighty copies exist, is composed of handmade pieces of ephemera ranging from a matchbook to a string of unused bus tickets, a map, gift tags, office stationery, and so on. As I write this, New Directions Press has released a revised English translation by Margaret Jull Costa, who had translated the work once before for Serpent's Tail.[28] Her new translation is based on the 2013 Portuguese edition assembled by the Pessoa scholar Jerónimo Pizarro. In Pizarro's latest edition, the fragments are organized in the presumed order in which they evolved; thus, the book has two main sections, the first representing the Vincent Guedes phase, the second embodying the work signed by Bernardo Soares.

The American publisher New Directions is marketing Costa's book as "The Complete Edition." The paratext is interesting, considering that the introduction, which is signed by Costa, is far from reticent about the fact that the book must remain an impossible task, a work in progress: "Pessoa never understood this rigorous process of selection and adaptation. The 'book' thus remained forever a work in progress."[29] Costa ends her introduction by invoking the freedom that the book, regardless of the edition or translation, affords the reader:

> In a way [the book's] very incompleteness is enticing, encouraging the reader to make his or her own book out of those fragments. What awaits every reader of *The Book of Disquiet* is the sheer serendipitous pleasure of opening the book at random and reading whichever fragment you happen to alight on.[30]

For the French philosopher Alain Badiou, the reception of Pessoa's work is characterized by philosophy's belatedness in knowing *how* to receive the work. He asks: "Has the philosophy of this century (that of the past decade included) been able to – has it known *how* to – put itself under the condition of Pessoa's poetic enterprise?"[31] "We must therefore conclude," Badiou continues, "that philosophy is not – at least not yet – under the condition of Pessoa. Its thought is not yet *worthy of Pessoa.*"[32] Badiou's use of "at least not yet" suggests that Pessoa's work is syncopatiously misaligned with the time of its being written. In other words, his writing – as de Medeiros points out in his brief reading of Badiou's assessment of Pessoa – belongs to a readership of the future that must accept contemporaneity with Pessoa.[33] Badiou's claim, that philosophy has to catch up with Pessoa, hinges on the new pathways through art and thought that his work carves out. Such a focus offers some insight into the nomadic and promissory nature of the future-oriented work as one lighted by philosophy and lyricism on the one hand and by history and experimentation on the other. But what is this "condition of Pessoa" that Badiou understands as being ahead of philosophy?

Perhaps we can begin thinking about this condition of failed or misaligned contemporaneity by considering the formal aspects of *The Book of Disquiet* – a work that was conceived and composed in fragments and that continues to circulate through the editorial efforts of various scholars, editors, and translators, albeit in various (imperfect) iterations. Indeed, as I have intimated throughout these pages, the book's disquieting publishing history suggests that *The Book of Disquiet* is riddled with a material quality of untranslatability that destines it for a state of fragmentary incompletion.

The book's incompletion, as a feature of its untranslatability, reminds me of the figure of the Tower of Babel. To understand the reference to Babel, it is useful to examine it in relation to Derrida's essay on Walter Benjamin's "The Translator's Task," where he provides an insightful interpretation of the fragmented nature of the tower, which he views as not only instigating disquiet but also remaining forever in the process of being constructed: "The 'tower of Babel' does not merely figure the irreducible multiplicity of tongues; it exhibits an incompletion, the impossibility of finishing, of totalizing, of saturating, of completing something on the order of edification, architectural construction, system and architectonics."[34]

The logic of disquiet in *The Book of Disquiet*'s mutating form across editions and translations – its edification – matches the confusion of Babel itself: "[The word] Babel, as a proper name, should remain untranslatable, but, by a kind of associative confusion that a unique tongue rendered possible, one thought it translated in that very tongue, by a common noun signifying what *we* translate as confusion."[35]

Like Babel, *The Book of Disquiet* remains not only fundamentally *im*possible in its unfinishedness but also impossible to finish; it also claims its own diffusion of the proper name – naming the (anti-)book-object itself as well as titling the book so as to disquiet it at a material as well as a hermeneutic level; put another way, *The Book of Disquiet* is a largely (un)nameable thing.[36]

With these considerations in mind, the eponymous quality of disquiet that is proper to Babel and its parallels with *The Book* are based less on conditions of confusion than on an ambivalent relationship to translatability, for the (un)nameable that teeters between ideas and things – their untranslatability – is simultaneously that which calls for translation. In the same essay as the one quoted above, Derrida aquiesces to a similar idea in relation to Benjamin's poetics of translation when he states that the paradox of translation – the very confusion of translation – is a condition of the multiplicity of language(s): "From this limit, at once interior and exterior, the translator comes to receive all the signs of remoteness (*Entfernung*) which guide him on his infinite course, at the edge of the abyss, of madness and of silence [...] and madness waits on both sides" (203).[37] It is worth noting, as well, that as Soares explores the world as it comes to him through his thoughts and senses, in shards or fragments, the book too can be described as an improvisation that defies lucidity. Indeed, in a letter to a friend, Pessoa admonished the fragmentary nature of the work: "My state of mind compels me to work hard, against my will, on *The Book of Disquiet*. But it's all fragments, fragments, fragments."[38] Unlike most manuscript versions of the book, which attempt to present a uniform product, PME-ART's rewritings on loose sheets of variously coloured paper echo Pessoa's fragmented compositional process; he wrote it piece by scattered piece on napkins, envelopes, and whatever materials he had on hand at the moment of the fragment's spontaneous recording. PME-ART's performance, too, contributes to Babelian features of *The Book of Disquiet*, perhaps most poignantly by making those incomplete and fractured features a notable part of their own work.

Indeed, as concerns *The Book of Disquiet*'s fleeting nature, it is difficult to ascertain whether it ever really "took off," at least in terms of being an unfinished anti-book of sorts. For de Medeiros, that *The Book of Disquiet* is an anti-book of sorts has less to do with the editorial history of the work than with its fragmentary nature "and its refusal of systematic thought."[39] Then again, assuming that Pessoa was not done collecting and preparing the book – taming its restless spirit – there is a sense in which he was writing beyond his time,[40] that the book had never fully arrived on Pessoa's doorstep to begin with, and that it was in motion well before Pessoa ever caught wind of it. In this less assured version, the book is replete not just with uncertainty but with untraceable origins, which is why it can be read as bearing the traces of disquiet and, what is more, of afterlife.

THE TIMES:
BECOMING CONTEMPORARIES WITH PESSOA

In a retrospective glance at PME-ART's twenty-year career as a performance group, Jacob Wren summarizes the 2014 performance in the following manner: "to see what happens when a door long assumed to be locked is partially reopened, when fragments left unfinished seventy-nine years ago are mischievously treated as if they still remained unfinished today, as if one could simply continue working on them."[41] Wren also concedes that, in attempting to render *The Book of Disquiet* a little happier, the question of one's own time and contemporaneity with the work was never far from mind nor method[42]: "What might it mean to rewrite these fragments today?," he asks. "What shades of early twenty-first century emotion might be woven into Pessoa's unfinished twentieth-century elegy?"[43] PME-ART's engagement with the affective dimensions of "the times" in which they rewrote the book suggests that they were attempting to give the work a temporary destination, a time stamp. Could their performance, then, be read as an answer to Badiou's provocation about our (and philosophy's) inability to catch up to Pessoa? And if so, how were the scribes attempting, through their rewrites, to bring Pessoa's book into the present moment?

Assuming that the unfinished book will continue to float through the flux of time – from Pessoa's twentieth century to PME-ART's early twenty-first century and to readers beyond – the book is not just one that moves through time; it is also one that changes depending on its temporal and perhaps even geographical coordinates. As we have seen, the book is continually mutating, barrelling towards an unknown destination where editions will continue to vary in their contents and in their orderings of those contents.

Indeed, the book's mutability is exemplified in PME-ART's brief eight-day intervention. Their approach ran counter to the usual one, which is to dutifully transcribe a work in order to preserve its authority; instead, they endowed the work with new references, alternative entries, and fresh interpretations. Their rewrites, in other words, were both deliberate and spontaneous. Moreover, PME-ART's interrogation, "What does *The Book* feel like today?," and "What is 'my' relationship to *The Book* in this present moment?," certainly contributed to a reading of *The Book*'s disquieting ontology. I am curious now to explore how it might simultaneously respond to Badiou's quandary as well.

PME-ART's mandate was to render the book more of our time by inserting themselves and their experiences into the text; yet the book that PME-ART decided to transcribe represented Bernardo Soares's diary and autobiography – his melancholic and fragmented day-to-day reflections on life and art. Is it paradoxical, then, that Soares's diary, an intimate and inwardly directed (narcissistic) gesture, was transformed into an outpouring of outward connections? Can the conflation of the diary of one person and that of another offer a way into what Badiou terms "the condition of Pessoa's poetic enterprise"?

PME-ART's scribes all performed (and broadcast) an outward gesture of thinking's inwardness. The fact that the diary's mostly undated fragments treat Soares's day-to-day is nevertheless what offers spectators, readers, and scholars an opportunity to contemplate the book's relationship to time and PME-ART's rewrites of the work in the twenty-first century. What I mean by this is that their performance drew attention to the links between Pessoa's "now" and our own "now." Tinged with the marks of "reportage," in the journalistic sense of "reporting on the times," PME-ART's deliberate insertion of the present moment into their rewrites and their embrace of textual variants made it close enough to the original to highlight parts of it; at the same time, the mix of "fidelity" and "departures" from the original did something to heighten features of the text as well. In this case, Badiou's provocation that Pessoa was writing beyond his time, and that we should concede to the prerogative to become his contemporaries, turns Pessoa and his heteronyms into messengers in the sense that the word bears in another essay by Walter Benjamin – his "Theses on the Philosophy of History," where the "messenger" or "reporter of the times" is embodied in the figure of the angel of history.[44]

In that essay, Benjamin borrows an image from a painting by Paul Klee titled *Angelus Novus (Angel of History)*. According to Benjamin, the angel of history is a messenger who gazes towards the past as he is simultaneously blown towards the future by a storm that brews in the present. "The angel would like to stay," Benjamin writes, "but a storm is blowing from Paradise [...] This storm irresistibly propels him into the future to which his back is turned, while the pile of debris before him grows skyward. The storm is what we call progress."[45] In the angel's witnessing of the storm and in his desire to awaken the dead, he becomes a messenger of the times: those before, those of the present moment, and presumably those to come as well. Time, in this sense, is not just a temporal matter, but like PME-ART's performance mandate to render the book more "of our time," it can be understood in the sense of "the times" as "news."[46]

The Book of Disquiet, in the sense afforded to it as "reporting on the times" and as "news," becomes an open letter: a private utterance made public where Soares's diary is overtaken by a certain kind of journalism. Quite apart from being a literary object that appears at a crossroads between "journal" in the intimate sense of a diary[47] and news in the public sense of an open broadcast, the utterances that compose *The Book of Disquiet* participate in a double hermeneutics – double because the work is situated in between public and private discourses. Is the overlap in discourse, then, what allowed PME-ART to reach the text with a certain sense of contemporaneity?

For the philosopher Avital Ronell, the intersection marked by public and private discourse is characterized by a rumourological quality that, in Walter Benjamin, takes on both an internal and an external function. In her essay "Street Talk," Ronell explores the rumourological quality of works by Martin Heidegger, Walter Benjamin, and Jean-Jacques Rousseau. As Ronell unfurls one philosopher's rumour-text and enmeshes it with the other two, a common thread is visible that runs through all three: the conception of rumours as stray utterances that run ahead of their author – even independently of them – as they espouse a certain life of their own, an auto-mobility of sorts, that continues to circulate (even) in the absence of the subject.[48] As Ronell points out, the disquieting function of the rumour is thematically anchored in the writing itself, internal to it, while it is also that which is ex-centric to the work (thus it is external to it) and which appears to have a "decisive rapport to [an] 'after-my-death' discourse."[49] Indeed, there is much to unpack in Ronell's suggestion that the blurred edges between private and public discourses are similar to those of a rumour. Even more perplexing is the link Ronell makes between the rumour and what she terms an "after-my-death" discourse.

In one example Ronell provides, Jean-Jacques Rousseau has just survived an accidental encounter with a carriage and a Great Dane. While Rousseau keeps "face" in the literal disfiguration of his accident (his body is mutilated by his fall in several places), and while he maintains authority over his "physical and textual body," such a form of control soon eludes him.[50] The news of Rousseau's fall travels quickly through the streets of Paris, where it takes on a life of its own. According to the news, Rousseau did not just fall; he died. After reading of his death in the obituaries, Rousseau states that he was mortified to learn that the state had given itself the right to publish any manuscripts found in his apartment. The falsely interpreted posthumous publication of his work carries a double consequence: not only does the rumour of his death outlive him but so too does his textual body; as Ronell points out, "worst of all, however, he also will have witnessed himself after his presumed death, in his afterdeath, being buried alive."[51]

Part of what can be gleaned from Ronell's reading of Rousseau is the idea of the rumour as afterword: as a genre of writing that has an *après ma mort* (afterlife) structure that can be likened to what she calls a post-autobiographical utterance.[52] Reading Ronell, the definition of rumour I propose is that a rumour is a floating discourse; it is one that suggests instability as it is situated on the edges of a private and public discourse that becomes indistinct, even interchangeable. To understand *how* rumours move, then, we must also understand the temporality of the rumour, as an utterance that "runs ahead of its author." What I extrapolate from Ronell's temporal treatment of the rumour is that it is characterized by an eruption: a moment of creative flight where the coherence of an origin(al) is called into question. But what does this mean for Pessoa and PME-ART? Referring back to Badiou, Pessoa's "after-my-death" discourse is one that still bears to be understood.[53] My proposal is thus to continue throughout this chapter to situate *The Book of Disquiet* on the terrain of the rumourological and to continue to envision the work's relationship to disquiet as an utterance of unrest – one that exceeds a knowable origin or destination.

BETWEEN EDITORIAL AND AUTHORIAL TASKS

The Book of Disquiet exposes the limitations of dividing the book between an authorial project on the one hand and an editorial construct on the other. These categories might be useful in some instances, however. For example, Pessoa eventually authorizes Bernardo Soares to pen the unfinished *The Book of Disquiet*, even though traces of Guedes's signature still stand out in relation to the fragments signed by Soares. Soares's authorial project, in turn, cannot be apprehended without considering the diffusion of subjectivity at work throughout the text. As Pessoa's semi-heteronym, Soares is not just any other authorial figure derived from Pessoa's cast of heteronyms. He embodies a double of Pessoa himself and thus overlaps Pessoa in ways that the other heteronyms, as supreme fictions, do not.[54]

To complicate matters further, Soares can also be viewed as an embodiment of all the other heteronyms, for as Pessoa's doppelgänger he holds within himself the inscriptions and voices of Pessoa's palimpsest and limitless universe.[55] Further unrest causes the distinctions between the categories of author and editor to blur when Pessoa decides to attribute *The Book* to Bernardo Soares and hatches a plan to edit Guedes's previous sections, thus volleying the project between an authorial impetus and an editorial one:

> The organization of the book should be based on as rigorous a selection as possible of the various existing texts, adapting older ones that are untrue to the psychology of Bernardo Soares [...] Apart from that, there needs to be a general revision of style, without losing the personal tone or the drifting, disconnected logic that characterizes it.[56]

While such a project was never brought to completion, it does problematize the distinction between the task of the writer and that of the editor as it confuses the two.

Tim Hopkins's handmade collection of ephemera for Half Pint Press provides another lucid example of the melding of the two projects. As a result of the process of transforming the book into a collection of ephemera, the reader's notion of what the book is, its established norms and bound forms, finds itself sharply questioned. Hopkins's immanent signature looms over the box set. Such a halo of immanence is also undeniable in the work of the book's countless editors and translators. Margaret Jull Costa, for example, makes the enmeshments between the editorial and authorial projects visible in her introduction to the New Directions Press edition when she prefaces the difficulties in translating Pessoa: "I was reminded just how difficult it is for the translator to find meaning in those 'meaningless' sentences – which can often be oblique or enigmatic – and, at the same time, reproduce that same languid fluidity in English, that seductive voice."[57] Of course, writing and translating are both forms of editing. And obviously, the enmeshment of translation as writing and of translation or writing as editing is not news; yet the ways in which *The Book of Disquiet* invites various forms of intervention into its conception are far from conventional.

The book, to name just one possible iteration, could have existed exclusively, or at the very least primarily, as an archival artifact rather than any kind of editorial or authorial construct at all. But that has not been its fate, and we have to wonder why not:

> What would have been Pessoa's influence in modernism, had his texts been known, in translation, across Europe and the United States? What would have been the reception of *The Book of Disquiet* had it been published and translated immediately after Pessoa's death in 1935 or even a few years later, after World War II for instance, instead of languishing until 1982 to be first edited, and even later to be translated into English and thus finally receive world-wide recognition of its significance?[58]

De Medeiros's question about the text's belated reception is unanswerable. Yet it is precisely that unanswerability that continues to enmesh the various editions, translations, and versions of the book together into an impossible object. Insofar as the book remains adrift, inexhaustible in a sense, it will continue to yield invitations unto its (un)essayed finitude. Signed by the semi-heteronym, Bernardo Soares, a figure who is both Pessoa and not Pessoa, the book holds within its atomized structure – the undated fragments of a purported (fictional) diarist, the autobiography of a melancholic recluse – something rumourological.

THE RUMOUR

After Pessoa's death, the book hit a literal dead-end. It remained entombed in trunks that held twenty-nine notebooks and around 25,000 texts/sheets of paper and envelopes containing essays and criticism, poetry and plays, translations and linguistic theory, and so on, all written in French, English, or Portuguese. Some texts were typed, many were written by hand and recorded on napkins, envelopes, loose sheets of paper, others were kept in notebooks or in the margins of earlier texts.[59] *The Book of Disquiet* is an example of textual afterlife, then, in the sense of its perpetual (semiotic) restlessness. Long after Pessoa's death, the book was given "another topography of circulation," as Avital Ronell puts it in another context.[60] Always destined to be elsewhere, *The Book*'s restless qualities certainly justify such a reading, of afterlife, as does the fact that its disquieting publishing history stems from its author's ultimate departure: death.

Taking into consideration its fleeting nature, as though it arrived from a secret source of scrambled origins, only to always be getting away, and, in a sense, always on its way out, *The Book of Disquiet* can be read as a rumour-text: a post-autobiographical utterance marked by an "after-my-death" report or afterlife. Readers who are familiar with Walter Benjamin's notion of afterlife (*Fortleben*) may start to intuit a connection here between the continuing life of works through the original's relationship to translation and Ronell's concept of the rumour-text as that part of a work that lies outside anyone's control and that takes on a life of its own. In its renewal of an original, translation not only gives rise to an understanding of the original as a mutable form characterized by unrest, but also grants the original an afterlife. As Walter Benjamin writes,

> a translation proceeds from the original. Not indeed so much from its life as from its "afterlife" or "survival" [*Überleben*]. Nonetheless the translation is later than the original, and in the case of the most significant works, which never find their chosen translators in the era in which they are produced, indicates that they have reached the stage of their continuing life [*Fortleben*].[61]

For his part, Derrida explains that afterlife or *Fortleben* in German, what Gondrillac translates as *survie*, implies an extension of the life of the original rather than life after death or *post mortem*. "Such sur-vival gives more of life, more than a surviving. The work does not simply live longer, it lives more and better, beyond the means of its author."[62] In figuring translation as an afterlife, translation participates in the un-rest and continuing life of artworks.[63]

Both Ronell's rumour-text and Benjamin's textual afterlife offer examples of how works take on a life of their own, how they survive their authors and surpass their readers. Like Benjamin's notion of textual afterlife, the rumour does not have a fixed boundary except perhaps for the fact that its imprint is future-oriented. In translation, the original does not lag behind the translation, nor does it have a fixed temporality; it too continues to evolve. In that sense, the rumour, like the afterlife of translation, cannot be fully anticipated; and like a fragment from a larger vessel, to echo Benjamin, it comes to us as incomplete, ongoing – as though its business lay elsewhere. Perhaps there is a bit of an echo of Badiou's reading of Pessoa here as well, and a suggestion that the rumour-text and textual afterlife are somehow linked to possible entries into the text's errant futurity.

I believe that a further potent link to describe the rumour's relationship to language is to understand it through the concept of "afterlife" and "translatability" found in Benjamin's essay "The Translator's Task." In terms of "translatability," the relationship between original and translation does not depend upon it actually being translated. Instead, translatability is an intrinsic part of the work that exists independent of the translator. According to Benjamin, "the question of a work's translatability has two senses. It can mean: will it ever find, among the totality of its readers, an adequate translator? Or, more pertinently, whether by its very essence it allows itself to be translated."[64] These questions recall Badiou's comment that philosophy has not yet known how to catch up to Pessoa. Moreover, it seems to me that this is a problem summed up in Benjamin's first question – regarding our ability to receive the work being translated – as well as in his second question, which has to do with that which may resist translation. In both cases, Benjamin's notion of "translatability" works well to help us understand how textual afterlife troubles the very idea of a destination. To borrow from Benjamin, "[translatability] would merely be a demand to which human beings had failed to respond."[65]

The notion of afterlife is important to my reading of Pessoa's book as well as to PME-ART's performance because one of the most significant aspects of "afterlife" is not just how it challenges the linear progression of a text, from its inception to its publication or from source to target text, but how it questions the very idea of a destination. The term afterlife names something about the condition of textuality itself rather than its arrival. According to Benjamin, the most significant works find textual afterlife not because they are translated but because there is something about them, a quality of translatability, that remains latent. To understand these matters from another angle, it is helpful to remember that earlier in his essay, Benjamin proposes that a work's translatability opens onto two questions: the first has to do with finding an adequate translator; the second question Benjamin poses in relation to a work's translatability has to do with whether or not it allows itself to be translated.[66] Textual afterlife, as a condition of a text's translatability, then, has precisely to do with Badiou's preoccupation with contemporary philosophy's failure to know how to receive Pessoa. Put another way, Badiou's provocation is related to the question of the work's afterlife and philosophy's inability to know how to respond.

CONCLUDING ON ERRANT FUTURITY: PME-ART AS A READERSHIP OF THE FUTURE

Since Pessoa's death, the book that is not one has held a kind of quantum superposition. With his death, the work has hit a literal dead-end on the one hand, but on the other it has continued down several forking paths, with no observable in-betweens. As versions of *The Book of Disquiet* multiply, it has become the ultimate orbiting text. It is a book situated on the very outskirts of itself.

> What we have here isn't a book but its subversion and negation: the ingredients for a book whose recipe is to keep sifting, the mutant germ of a book and its weirdly lush ramifications, the rooms and windows to build a book but no floor plan and no floor, a compendium of many potential books and many others already in ruins.[67]

Picking up on the groundlessness of the ground – recall Zenith's observation that *The Book* lacks a floor – further encourages us to read *The Book of Disquiet* as a rumour: "a widely disseminated report detached from a discernible origin or source. Inasmuch as it becomes what it is, the spreading rumour takes on the qualities of a story told, without author or term, imposing itself as an ineluctable and unforgettable account."[68] The idea that *The Book* is somehow detached from a discernible origin or source is, I think, most compellingly located in the figure of the semi-heteronym, Bernardo Soares, the assistant bookkeeper in the firm Vásques & Company, whose factless autobiography is the horizon of *The Book of Disquiet* itself.

In the disfiguration of the writing – which is expressed in Pessoa's changing figures, from heteronym to heteronym, but most poignantly in Pessoa's semi-heteronym, Bernardo Soares, who represents a mutilation of Pessoa's personality – there occurs a literal and a figural defacement. As Pessoa relinquishes his name and the names of several other of his heteronyms to Soares, I cannot help but wonder what, in a rumour, one has to lose but one's (good) name.[69] Is Soares, the assistant bookkeeper, to blame for the book's rumourological quality? Or is he, as the keeper of all records, keeping tabs on the rumours, transforming the book into a kind of "rumour control centre," "capturing stray utterances," as the fragmentary nature of *The Book* might suggest, thereby constructing a catalogue of moments about to lapse into oblivion?[70] What better than a factless autobiography to frame the rumour, after all.

For de Medeiros, the assistant bookkeeper Bernardo Soares houses the spectral qualities of the text.[71] "Soares uses the terms 'phantasma' and 'espectro', ghost, spectre, phantom, to refer both to himself and to others he encounters or imagines encountering," de Medeiros points out, and "in its form, fragmentary, obsessive, constantly returning to the same topics, with great intensity, the text itself should be seen as a form of haunting."[72] I agree with de Medeiros. To the degree that *The Book of Disquiet* persists on a certain level of "fantasmic transmission," it continues to roam "afterworldly in-the-world," restless as a ghost.[73] How many editors have received the psychic call, played the role of *The Book*'s amanuensis, taken its dictation, arranged its "post-autobiographical utterances," listened to its archival cues, Pessoa's trail of clues – in the form of letters or notes, multiple prefaces – as though he too was constantly rehearsing the book, trying it on. The act of close listening, as though to a rumour, sent Richard Zenith in 2001 to review his own edition and translation, published in 1991, in order to redress the rumour, as it were.

> Soares, the bookkeeper and thus keeper of all records, can be likened to a crypt: If one is still to see in *The Book of Disquiet* any survival of the heteronyms then, it is already as a phantasmagory of the name of the author, here condensed in that of Bernardo Soares, even though that other one, of Vicente Guedes, though replaced is never quite annuled, surviving under erasure as it were,

a sort of trace, visible only in its signature and the minimal biography the text still retains among a few references.[74]

The logic of the crypt is, in fact, one that de Medeiros develops over the course of an entire chapter. While I won't invoke all of de Medeiros's arguments in the space of this conclusion, I do find it useful, in terms of my reading of the rumourological qualities of the work, to highlight certain aspects of his account especially with the goal of capturing how, as a rumour-text, *The Book of Disquiet* continuously confounds public and private discourses, rest and unrest, and the overlap between a closed and an open letter.

In his chapter on *The Book of Disquiet* as crypt, de Medeiros usefully points out that for Derrida as well as psychoanalysts Nicolas Abraham and Maria Török, the crypt not only houses a desire but also implies a division of the self into a simultaneous process of introjection and incorporation such that the expansion of the self as well as the creation of the other involves a multiplication of the self[75]: "In this process a part of the Self is assumed then as Other, but kept inside the crypt and dead, in a specular effect of topographic definition in which inside and outside reflect each other while simultaneously separating and excluding themselves."[76] In its conflation of interior and exterior, this passage bears a striking resemblance to Ronell's description of the architectonics of the rumour-text, which – like Walter Benjamin's glass arcades, examined in the next chapter – bear a permeable relationship between the vectors of an inside and an outside.

This element of co-presence was exemplified in PME-ART's approach to the book: their rewrites – including their visual and material poetics – existed in a material reality that was neither beyond nor completely intrinsic to the text. In other words, they entered into the textual reality of the work and at the same time escorted it towards their own. And because each scribe came to the text with a different subjective state, the "essence" of the rewrites was never locatable, which was perfect for a book lacking a clear beginning and certainly lacking a discernable end. In a similar sense, the gallery setting gave the work a visual/textual topography that floated between the vectors of ideas and processes as well as between the viewable art object and its impossible completion. If, as Jacob Wren insists, PME-ART's performance dislocated the work – both in the textual sense of the book but also conceptually in the sense of their task to rewrite it – so that "the work" became associated less with the book than with the scribes themselves, it was partly due to the book's ongoing transformation and the errant dimensions of PME-ART's role as future readers.

The slow and contemplative pace of the performance, as the viewers or readers waited for the rewrites to materialize, never allowed for a complete view of the work, nor did it grant the viewer a greater understanding of the rewriting process. What came to be transferred – from Soares to the scribes and then to the reader/viewer – was the time of the rewrites themselves, which was as enigmatic as it was fleeting. In this sense, the performance simultaneously gave and enacted a visual and a spatial trajectory for the book that was impossible to translate yet was among the performance's most prominent features.

If PME-ART's interrogation, "What does *The Book* feel like today," and "What is 'my' relationship to *The Book* in this present moment," highlighted *The Book*'s disquieting ontology, it also granted its destination a supposed "happier" end. Without articulating a final or definitive version of the book, the resulting Monster Book (like the scribes themselves) invited a temporary co-presence with the work. Their rewrites coincided with the objects and things of Soares's universe in an emphatic exchange that was future-oriented. The "adventure" in PME-ART's performance title was, it turned out, this errant futurity.

3

Standing in Translation's Wake

Gail Scott's *The Obituary*

One has, I am now certain, to be a little mad to see into the past or the future, to be a little abridged of life to know life, the obscure life.

Djuna Barnes, *Nightwood*

... disappearance is not absence

Fred Moten, *Black and Blur*

In this chapter on *The Obituary* I want to explore how issues of translatability give way to the apprehension of various "sightings" or forms of presencing. These sightings vacillate between a state of indeterminacy and a shape- or meaning-making whose contours are indicated in the tension between the poetic juxtapositions of one signifying surface and another. In time, the emanating and flickering properties of the aforementioned proposition will become clear, especially when I begin to read Scott's novel in relation to Walter Benjamin's concept of the dialectical image, which he treats in two works in particular – his massive *The Arcades Project*, and his essay "Theses on the Philosophy of History."[1] In the sections that follow, I also retrace Gail Scott's creation of a porous and sutured subject in her novel *My Paris* and consider Sherry Simon's reading of the aforementioned novel's "comma of translation" alongside Walter Benjamin's poetic understanding of the dialectical image as an explosive site of connectivity that, like his view of translation, opens onto a play of dis-conjoined and overlapping surfaces that link together various threads (histories, languages, referents, etc.).

While traces of Benjamin's influence may have shaped *My Paris*'s comma of translation, spurring Sherry Simon to propose a parallel reading between the play of surfaces suggested by Scott's comma of translation and the figure of the translator/historian found in Benjamin's "The Translator's Task," in its palimpsest depiction of past, present, and future, *The Obituary* furthers this emergence of presence by shifting its focus to overlapping time frames and to "buried speech."[2] As Simon explains, regarding Benjamin's essay and in relation to Scott's *My Paris*,

> both translator and historian rely on the unexpected encounter of objects and words, the confrontation of languages and temporalities, to jar us into a renewed understanding of the present. The work of translation, like the work of history, provides *forms* through which the past and present 'flash' into uneasy constellation.[3]

This interval between translation and history made visible in Benjamin's dialectical image is the space where the project of *My Paris* is carried over into Scott's *The Obituary* – and this is precisely the space I intend to explore in this chapter.

Proceeding with the above-mentioned dimensions in mind, I consider various forms of overlap in *The Obituary* – the drift of meaning from one site to another, Scott's signature translanguaging poetics, and the narrative's deployment of translinguistic misapprehension – focusing mainly on the impact of these overlaps on narrative diffusion: their creation of alternate yet simultaneous temporalities and their influence on the opening of a space of translation through the intralingual qualities of her experimental composition, its plurilingualism and polyvocality. This attention to what is overlaid leads me to consider the novel's palimpsest portrayal of time where what has been coexists with the time-space of the now, giving way to a provocative indeterminacy in the form of irruptions, discontinuities, narrative ruptures, lags, crossed-out words, and so on.

Such indeterminate traces abound in *The Obituary*. The novel's emphasis on delays, uncertainties, gaps, and repetitions crystallizes in a porously phonic telling; the indeterminacy of these radical poetics produces a constellation of multiple and multidirectional meanings. As readers we are constantly reminded of the edge of the incommunicable. What interests me is *The Obituary*'s ability to make visible/audible what has been made eccentric to language, not just in its fiction sentences, and what has undergone a process of erasure in (everyday) speech. In *The Obituary*, linked stories of dispossession are embodied in the text by *une négativité fuyante*[4] that points, for instance, to a lack of recognition of shared historical responsibilities for the forced assimilation that led to the genocide of Indigenous peoples.[5] This fleeting quality of negation in the novel begins with an oneiric fragment that consists in a tale the protagonist's grandfather won't tell. Although I shall return to the significance of *The Obituary*'s multiple references to an unspeakable tale, I gesture to it here in order to begin flagging ways the novel frames the dilemma of ~~how to represent~~ the ~~irrepresentable~~ not represented.

Various "translation" strategies in the novel contribute to making these erasures visible/audible over and through time. Voices float through the novel. There is no master narrative or single narrative voice. Instead, the narrative is consistently kept off-balance. Although there is the semblance of a forward-moving narrative, it is one that drifts between languages, scenes, characters, voices, locales, temporalities, even genres. If voices emanate along the corridors of the novel's elusively dis-conjoined structure, the reader also floats through various quotidian scenes, trying to make sense of the pieces of the tale even as they overlap – or perhaps especially because, like the dialectical image, they overlap in temporally diffuse ways.

Aspects of coexistence and narrative overlap are also refracted in the shards of perspective that compose the narrative, as the main protagonist, Rosine, is fractured into several forms of embodiment: she is the shadowy figure and face haunting the triplex at 4999 rue Settler-Nun (variously referred to as I/R/Rosine, daughter of Veeera or *Face*), and she is embodied in an erotically fixated fly-on-the-wall figure (called *I/th' fly*), as well as the writing subject/historian who provides the story with historical factoids and meta-commentaries that are mostly relegated to the subterranean level of the text – footnotes – which are demarcated by a "♥" symbol (she is referred to as the lezzie ~~Basement~~ Bottom Historian).

Other speaking subjects, both named and unnamed, contribute to the plurality of voices that meld the narrative together. Those subjects include the late nineteenth-century Shale Pit Workers!, Rosine's grandfather, her uncle Peeet, Aunty Dill, her mother Veeera, a Parisian gendarme called Casse-Noisette and his rookie Québecois assistant and hacker Jean-François Jean, a voice on the radio called Celia Raw Raw©, Shakespeare's Macbeth playing Rosine's and her neighbours' psychoanalyst, as well as Rosine's neighbours, who often appear alongside narrative reports from The Street and The Triplex – structures that, in *The Obituary*, witness and record the city around them.

As they merge together, the diffusion of temporality as well as the incorporation of various speakers into a palimpsest narrative "construction" – a word that, as shall become apparent, acquires architectural significance – create the conditions through which ghostly voices emerge from various time frames into a situation of perpetual translation.

It is in this sense, that of a potential flicker of presences made possible through formal narrative torques, overlaps, and residual temporalities, that I situate *The Obituary* within a poetics of translation. Such a feature becomes evident in the link I establish between Scott's representation of the triplex – a quintessential architectural signifier in the Montreal landscape – and Benjamin's use of the arcades as a visual analogy for thinking of translation as a play of dis-conjoined surfaces.[6] Most importantly, I examine how the voices and stories that emanate from and around the triplex where Rosine lives offer clues to an unspeakable past. In so doing, I consider how various forms of narrative and material overlap in the novel are linked through the figure of the triplex as a space of translation where, I suggest, additional forms of meaning/signification can emerge. Moreover, I argue that – like the triplex – the character of Rosine, too, houses secrets from the past. The content of these "secret transmissions" varies from personal memories to collective histories. From trauma to desire, the narratives that are set in motion emerge as voices that all seem to be running along the axes of their own time. These voices emerge in the narrative, often as disembodied and ghostly, as though they had been floating in the air for decades, even centuries, and as if they had been pushed by the winds of changing weather systems.

From a formal perspective, Scott overlays these voices across sentences that, from one to the next, interrupt, extend, and perform simultaneously. In its various forms of narrative overlap – through either the palimpsestic characterization of Rosine or the three-storied triplex where she lives – the pull of the past into the present and the ghostly stories that circulate within the novel's pages provide a tantalizing opportunity to analyze the prevailing spectral qualities of the novel, which, as I will argue, calls for a reading of the novel's poetics of translation as a translanguaging poetics to narrate a sort of impossibility, the inability to speak obliteration, buried speech.

Scott's layered multilingualism creates a dynamic through-line that connects the novel's hybrid and ever-shifting language and narrative features with the subject of architecture. The novel weaves translation and architecture together, namely through the figure of the Montreal triplex. Language is a structure, it takes on many forms, is unstable, towering, shape-shifting, taking on a kind of spatial existence. It wafts, transits, moves through the city's neighbourhoods and histories in simultaneous and relative recombinations. "The novel introduces the experience of existential translation into the dynamics of discommoded narrative," notes Andre Furlani.[7] Its narrative is one of excursus, he adds, "a spatial rather than temporal organization that better admits the city's heterogeneity."[8] This quality of Scott's prose owes a lot to how her sentences are grammatically inflected by the elision of its *gérondif*.

As I indicated in the introduction to this chapter, before I develop the central arguments further, I want to first add a few thoughts on Sherry Simon's influential reading of the poetics of translation in relation to Scott's *My Paris*, and how my own work on *The Obituary* has been inspired by the terms Sherry Simon puts forward in her study of *My Paris* – namely her references to Benjamin's arcades as a visual analogy for translation. Doing so will allow me to draw links between what I understand as *The Obituary*'s spectral, overlapping qualities and these qualities' relation to a poetics of translation. I then want to briefly consider Benjamin's concept of the dialectical image and how it relates to my understanding of *The Obituary*'s relationship to translation. Of course, my summary understanding of Simon's and Benjamin's arguments will undergo development as the chapter progresses. What follows, then, can be considered an extended prefatory note.

WALTER BENJAMIN AND SHERRY SIMON: STRUCTURES TOWARDS AN UNDERSTANDING OF THE POETICS OF TRANSLATION

In her article "The Paris Arcades, the Ponte Vecchio, and the Comma of Translation," Sherry Simon explores the space of cultural difference opened by Gail Scott's incorporation of "the comma of translation"[9] in her highly experimental novel *My Paris*. The comma of translation refers to Scott's use of this punctuation mark to join French expressions to their literal English translations: "*Écriture blanche*, white or neutral writing," "*femmes-cuir* (queer), leatherwoman,"[10] "*Comme si de rien n'était*, as if nothing happening earlier,"[11] "*C'est si peu dire que je t'aime*, it's so little to say I love you."[12] Except when they are used as markers of difference, commas in the novel appear more or less sparingly. Instead, *My Paris* is constructed of small syntactical units – associational shards written in the present participle and gerund forms – which are separated by periods.

Simon points to Scott's adherence to a "rigorously modernist style, made up of sentence fragments separated by periods." Simon further maintains that although Scott's novel is "imbued with the ghost of Gertrude Stein,"[13] Scott goes against Stein's dictum to eradicate the comma from the sentence in favour of imbuing *My Paris* with the heteroglossic sounds of the city where she lives.[14] Hence, according to Simon, the comma allows Scott to permeate her Paris-based novel with the sounds of a multilingual Montreal.[15]

My Paris is also haunted by the ghost of Walter Benjamin, particularly his *Paris Capitale du XIXe Siècle* (*Passagen Werk* in German and *The Arcades Project* in English), a copy of which has been left behind by the previous occupant of Scott's studio. *The Arcades Project* is Benjamin's monumental, unfinished study of Paris' glass-housed arcades – the mid-nineteenth century equivalent to present-day shopping malls. Composed of notes, essays, and an assemblage of archival materials, *The Arcades Project*'s montage is organized around twenty-six "convolutes" – literally "bundles" – which are alphabetically and thematically ordered as subjects/objects, such as "Arcades" and "Catacombs," "Fashion," "The Collector," "The Automaton," "Boredom," "Baudelaire," "Dream City," "Photography," "Advertising."

In his attempt to create a dialectical image of time, where what is past and what is present are recognized as mutually imbricated rather than successive, Benjamin's *The Arcades Project* aimed to create a "flash of illumination" in the reader – a flicker of awareness that would reveal as much as critique the consumer culture that defined the bourgeois experience flourishing in the nineteenth and twentieth centuries.[16] Writes Benjamin:

> The dialectical image is an image that emerges suddenly, in a flash. What has been is to be held fast – as an image flashing up in the now of its recognizability. The rescue that is carried out by these means – and only by these – can operate solely for the sake of what in the next moment is already inetrievably lost.[17]

Seizing the reader with a flash of recognition, Benjamin was convinced that "behind the facade of the present, these otherwise forgotten moments could be recovered from oblivion and reintroduced, shoved in the face of the present, as it were, with devastating force."[18] Such a form of critical interruption emerges from Benjamin's materialist critique of historical time and the predominant interpretation that historical time progresses from a chronologically linear past to a chronologically linear present. *The Arcades Project*, then, would infuse the detritus or trash of history that was disappearing underneath the heap of the "new" with life again.

The Arcades Project's method of montage – especially its capacity to stage an overlap between what has been and what is now – dismisses the idea that the past and the present are part of a linear continuum known as "progress."[19] In "Theses on the Philosophy of History," Benjamin calls this form of imbrication "now time" or *jetztzeit*. In his essay, Benjamin illustrates the concept of *jetztzeit* by invoking the image of an angel moving towards the future with his back turned as he gazes towards the past. As I noted in chapter 2, this image is borrowed from Paul Klee's painting *Angelus Novus (Angel of History)*. Meanwhile, a storm brews in the present. It is the storm of historical wreckage, and it is gathering at the angel's feet: "Where we perceive a chain of events," Benjamin writes, "he sees one single catastrophe."[20] He continues:

> The angel would like to stay, awaken the dead, and make whole what has been smashed. But a storm is blowing from Paradise [...] This storm irresistibly propels him into the future to which his back is turned, while the pile of debris before him grows skyward. The storm is what we call progress.[21]

As the angel is blown towards the future, he simultaneously cannot stand outside the heap of histories that are blowing all around him.

Progress in this case, with the angel's back to the future even as he moves towards it, does not necessarily entail a morally or ethically superior view of the present or the past. With his depiction of the swirl of debris like a tower accumulating at the angel's feet, Benjamin gestures to history as a discourse that is partly unspeakable – presumably because the ideology of progress itself irrevocably dictates forward movement. That tower of debris is also embodied in Scott's *The Obituary*, where the reader encounters the figure of the triplex that is built on layers of history that have not simply disappeared to make room for the future of this new construction. The latent layers of history housed on the site where the triplex is built erupt across the narrative to form ghostly pockets of narration within the novel's depiction of "now-time." This ghostly or latent content participates in the translatability (or not) of the novel's insinuation of unspeakable tales, which like the storm of progress that blows the angel of history toward the future accumulate around the site of the triplex.

This very storm blows us now through the pages of Scott's novel: "Here, Reader, in this storm – snow to rain back to snow again – driving North, here, let us [in interest of dénouement], follow silhouette dégageant from wind-battered crowd + turning West twoard parc, thin + bright as high winter air, ringing with echoes of those going before."[22] With its ubiquitous attention to meteorological conditions – mostly freezing rain and snow – and its insertions of a few weather reports by the voice on the radio, Celia Raw Raw©, a critique of progress slyly makes its way into *The Obituary*'s animate weather conditions. Wind currents are described as carrying fallen (dead) yellowing autumn leaves and blossoms across the city as well as pages from the torn *Book of Genocides*. The novel's emphasis on the weather is also accompanied by subtle yet persistent reports regarding the ever-changing effects of light and its fleeting shadows throughout time. As I shall address in the section on the rumour as well as in the final section on ventriloquism, the storms that brew in *The Obituary* bear the trace of a subversive impersonation of Benjamin's storm of progress, which carries the detritus (or shadowy figures) of history across the blur of time.

To desire to be translated, to invite not synthesis but a coming into existence, to allow relations to be perceived even if they defy structures of argumentation – this is the invitation I receive when I sit down to read *The Obituary*. But the call of translation is not just one that wants to manifest itself in the ethos of the reader. At the heart of *The Obituary*'s complex style of composition, a fossilized secret lies deep within the narrative's élan. As I have already begun insinuating, such a secret takes the shape of a transgenerational secret that is inherited by the subject, Rosine, and her various permutations. This phantom kernel within the subject's psyche acts like a ventriloquist, splitting the subject's interior even though its presence and meaning are not fully understood. This kernel is referred to by psychoanalysts Maria Török and Nicolas Abraham as the crypt that houses family secrets. The loss or trauma the crypt conceals cannot be accessed or spoken by the subject that is haunted by it.

In proposing that *The Obituary* is a novel that wants to be translated, I am primarily gesturing to its relationship with the ineffable and to the stratified layers of meaning that conceal the trauma deeply embedded in the novel's telling. In attending to the persistent mystery or gap that haunts not just Rosine but *The Obituary*'s narrative, Benjamin's concept of the dialectical image – and my own treatment in this chapter of translation itself as dialectical image – is useful to keep in mind. As spaces of poetic juxtaposition, translation and the dialectical image both operate within a set of relations that lead not to certainty or truth but to a gesture that points to the gaps that emerge everywhere in the narrative: from its overlapping structure to its depictions of various forms of erasure, *The Obituary* points to clues and traces of an unspeakable past, a form of negated enunciation that is fossilized within – within the subject, within the novel's depiction of a transtemporal Montreal, and within narrative itself. The project of the dialectical image, then, is to translate the unspeakable tale into speech. Here, I consider translation as a language of inquiry that, like poetry, operates within the gaps of signification and the knowledge of that which eludes our grasp.

FROM *MY PARIS* TO *THE OBITUARY*: THE PLAY OF SURFACES OF THE POROUS TEXT

In *My Paris*, Scott's inclusion of the comma of translation decomposes the narrative into an assembled, porous telling. As does the influence of Gertrude Stein, Walter Benjamin's influence on *My Paris* emerges in the formal qualities of the novel, especially in terms of experiments with non-narrative forms, such as montage. The partly associative as well as cumulative effect of *My Paris*'s experimental sentences disperses the continuity of the narrative in ways that welcome gaps, fissures, and indeterminacies into its telling. The result is what Scott calls "the porous text."

Such gaps and fissures in the diffusion of the narrative allow what is outside the narrative – for instance, the soundscape of Montreal in a Parisian landscape – to slip inside the frame. Consequently, when Scott includes a comma between a French expression and its literal English translation, she allows the mostly English-language narrative to be punctured by a disruption from the outside. Scott's break with the homogeneity and smooth continuity of the sentence's linguistic and syntactic unravelling gives her sentences an undeniably localized register, out of which springs, among other things, Quebec's multilingual and multicultural heterodoxies.[23]

In its mark of cultural difference and its incorporation of an outside turned inside, the porousness stemming from the comma of translation blurs the distinction between inner and outer, centre and margin. Such a quality of porousness also creates a sculptural relief in the narrative – a play of dis-conjunctive surfaces where the punctured narrative accentuates the porosity of the subject in its suspension of closure. More than a relay between Paris and Montreal, or a question of opposing the English language to the French language, the comma of translation allows for a play of differences that, according to Sherry Simon, gives physical form to the third space opened between the language of the original and its translation:

> The "comma of translation" leads us directly to Benjamin's reinterpretation of the role of the translator where he suggests that translation is less about transmitting a message than it is about revealing differences. The task of the translator, he suggests, is not to neutralize the difference between the original and the translation through the replacement of one with the other but to display the complementarity of languages and texts. The space between one language and another opens up a "third space" between original and translation, a utopian space that no longer means or expresses anything, but refers to a "reine Sprache," a pure language, an expressionless and creative Word. Benjamin gives a physical shape to this space: the shape of the arcade.[24]

In giving physical form to an otherwise elusive and "expressionless" (translative) space, Benjamin transforms the arcades into a three-dimensional analogy for translation:

> True translation is transparent, it does not obscure the original, does not stand in its light, but rather allows pure language, as if strengthened by its own medium, to shine even more fully on the original. This is made possible above all by conveying the syntax word-for-word, and this demonstrates that the word, not the sentence, is the original element of translation. For the sentence is the wall in front of the language of the original, and word-for-word rendering is the arcade.[25]

Piecing out the translation word-for-word, Benjamin suggests that a "literal translation" does not obstruct the original but that it provides a new vantage point for the original instead.

Benjamin's ecstatic reinterpretations of the interrelation and temporality of translation and its original are part of a cluster of metaphors he puts forth for the apprehension and seizure of a much larger poetic understanding of translation as affecting not just the original but language itself (*reine Sprache*/pure language).[26] For her part, Sherry Simon sums up Benjamin's architectural and refractive interpretation of translation in the following manner: "The glass roof allows light to flow through matter, just as the literally translated text is a transparent surface which allows the light of the original to fall on the new version, creating an interplay of surfaces."[27] The relationship established here, between original and translation, exceeds a mere "mirroring." For Benjamin, the original (what has been) and the translation (the shape of the work in the now) shed light on a "critical now" not because they necessarily illuminate each other but because they are mutually imbricated in a play of surfaces.

In particular, I have in mind a passage from *The Arcades Project* that resonates with the refractive reading of translation in the previously cited passage from Benjamin's "The Translator's Task." In the following passage, moreover, Benjamin's understanding of the dialectical image can be read, at least transversally, in relation to translation: "It's not that what is past casts its light on what is present, or what is present its light on the past; rather, image is that wherein what has been comes together in a flash with the now to form a constellation. In other words, image is dialectics at a standstill."[28] Interestingly, there's another passage in Benjamin's "The Translator's Task" where the relationship between languages creates a productive overlap out of which the original too is changed: "no translation would be possible if, in accord with its ultimate essence, it were to strive for similarity to the original. For in its continuing life, which could not be so called if it were not the transformation and renewal of a living thing, the original is changed."[29] Instead of a series of events, the past and the present reveal something of each other in much the same way that Benjamin proposes that translation should reveal rather than conceal elements of the original. In other words, the present does not obstruct or occlude the past. Instead, their interrelation allows the time-space of history, as a dialectical image, to refract and thus illuminate parts of the past in the present. In that sense, the original is changed.

Like Scott's porous subject, who floats across a landscape only to discover that in her porousness she both haunts and is haunted by it, the use of "among languages" in the aforementioned quote suggests that the original permeates and pokes holes in the translation as much as the translation permeates and pokes holes in the original; hence the image of the glass-roofed arcades, an image that has a distinct quality of permeability with regard to an outside/inside, also becomes the symbol through which the time of the original (what has been) and the time of the translation (now) overlap. Theirs is a relationship of asymmetrical reciprocity that makes the flash of recognition in the dialectical image possible.

In my reading of Benjamin's dialectical image, oppositions such as past and present or original and translation become modes that mutually inflect each other and whose overlap gives rise to a critical space as well. For Benjamin, the distinct feature of the dialectical image is its ability to produce a "shock of recognition" in the reader through its startling use of juxtaposition, and this is as true for history as it is for translation. It is a profoundly revelatory relationship: the idea that in the defamiliarized context of translation, certain elements of material signification in the original are reframed, hence rendering the dialectical relationship between the original and its translation visible and meaningful. The same can be said of the dialectical image in a materialist view of history. Through the critical tension of the dialectical image there is a critique of modes of historical interpretation that, if we recall the pile of detritus blowing in the storm of progress, suppress time into ahistorical bits of alienated trash. To borrow from Benjamin, "nothing that has ever happened should be regarded as lost for history."[30] The productive force of the dialectical image is embodied in these contradictory poles – between blindness and sight, erasure and legibility, victor and loser, and so on – hence Benjamin's insistence on the dialectical image's potential flicker of recognition within the reader. It is my contention that *The Obituary* offers a structural critique of the progress of history by dramatizing the overlapping contradictory poles in an illuminating play between emergence and submergence, acknowledging the flicker of visibility and invisibility as it illustrates that there are those who keep moving in time and those who are buried along the way (some without a burial place).

COMPOSITION AND TIME

To illustrate the form of critical arrest that the dialectical image provokes in the reader, it is helpful to return to Benjamin's "Theses on the Philosophy of History," in which he assembles a series of short passages that critique the certainty of narrative historical development according to which history is apprehended as a continuous series of events. Instead of viewing history as progressing from one set of events to another, Benjamin contends that it is impossible to access the past as it really was since "history" is comprised of different moments – some recounted, some not – that (in)form the story of the present. He writes,

> The true picture of the past flits by. The past can be seized only as an image which flashes up at the instant when it can be recognized and is never seen again [...] For every image of the past that is not recognized by the present as one of its own concerns threatens to disappear irretrievably.[31]

Readers of Gertrude Stein may hear some resonances to her essay "Composition as Explanation" in the passage just quoted. In that essay, Stein treats legibility and time, among others things, as a matter of composition. Since composition defines the experience of what is seen, the angle of vision through which we see the subject or object changes depending on how it is framed.

Such a difference in perspective must take into account the compounding of times. Hence, Stein writes: "There is singularly nothing that makes a difference a difference in beginning and in middle and in ending except that each generation has something different at which they are all looking."[32] This melding of times, between the beginning, the middle, and the ending, is in many ways quite similar to Benjamin's concept of "now time" or *jetztzeit* where "history is the subject of a structure whose site is not homogeneous, empty time, but time filled by the presence of the now."[33] To return to one of the Stein's text's signature phrases, such a notion of time is summed up as follows: "The only thing that is different from one time to another is what is seen and what is seen depends upon how everybody is doing everything."[34] Along this visual line of thinking, Stein's emphasis on composition as what is seen takes into account the space of multiple vanishing points: "Nothing changes from generation to generation except the thing seen and that makes a composition."[35] For Benjamin, such vanishing points must provoke the shards of historical materialism to explode "the continuum of history."[36] He contends that in doing so, such an interruption would liberate "the oppressed past" by granting the image of what has been a flickering presence in the dialectical now.[37] For Stein, it is those moments that do not become assimilated into (victorious) "instant classics" that remain illegible:

> That is the reason why the creator of the new composition in the arts is an outlaw until he is a classic, there is hardly a moment in between and it is really too bad very much too bad naturally for the creator but also very much too bad for the enjoyer, they all really would enjoy the created so much better just after it has been made than when it is already a classic, but it is perfectly simple that there is no reason why the contemporaries should see, because it would not make any difference as they lead their lives in the new composition anyway, and as every one is naturally indolent why naturally they don't see.[38]

Benjamin makes a similar claim in his "Theses on the Philosophy of History" in relation to a dialectics between revolutionary and conservative voices. He writes that "there is no document of civilization which is not at the same time a document of barbarism."[39] In the aforementioned quote, civilization and barbarism are tinged with ambivalence. They are "so-called" civilization and "so-called" barbarism because they are documents narrated by the ruling class. Benjamin's critique, then, regards what such a narrative process erases: "Nothing that has ever happened should be regarded as lost for history. To be sure, only a redeemed mankind receives the fullness of the past – which is to say, only for a redeemed mankind has its past become citable in all its moments."[40] Like Benjamin's method of montage, Scott's method of overlap emphasizes the legible over the threat of its disappearance in a way that makes the dialectical tension between them apparent. Such a method also locates the writing subject within her moment in time, which is a task that translation too both permits and undoes. The task of the following section, then, will be to examine some of the structures of this dialectical tension that allows the subject of *The Obituary* to become legible and located.

WALTER BENJAMIN'S FLICKER OF PRESENCE: MONTAGE AND THE DIALECTICAL IMAGE

a) *The Cut-Up as Caesura* (Le Cadavre, Exquis Signifie?)

Much like *My Paris*, *The Obituary* is written using the "old surrealist trick"[41] of montage, which points back to Benjamin but also to avant-garde writers, namely William S. Burroughs and André Breton, who appear in *The Obituary*, where they serve as models for Jean-François Jean's surveillance assignment (Jean is a rookie hacker and student of *techniques policières*) – an assignment he is tempted to subtitle "Dreamland."[42] Segmented into various "frames," the surveillance materials include chat logs, police cams, and diary and email entries, as well as "phone tabs," all of these looped together, "disappearing/appearing in no fixed order. Creating nifty multi-flash effect."[43] The cut-up form of the student's final police assignment is in many ways a parallax version of *The Obituary*'s own form.

Divided into poetic units that are spliced together with periods, and drawing from Breton's "hazardous selection method," the porous construction of *The Obituary*'s narrative, with its accumulation of culled materials, also echoes the towering collage of Benjamin's *The Arcades Project* – not to mention the pile of detritus that is accumulating at the angel's feet in "Theses on the Philosophy of History." Such a parsed style of writing, "[its] incipient integration of life + art," has an important hallucinatory side effect.[44] Although sewn together, the dis-conjoining of these compositional remnants creates fissures – portholes![45] – where the potential for additional meaning emerges.[46]

In poetry, this "additional meaning" often resides in the caesura – that leap, or gap, or space, or breath line – where the poetic image becomes unhinged. Viewed in this way, *The Obituary*'s compositional parsing turns the sentence into a poetic structure rather than a grammatical unit. Reading into, over, or between enjambed lines in poetry, where leaps play a quintessential material role in contributing to the poem's meaning, *The Obituary*'s poetic compositional lines privilege the indeterminacy of the poetic image over narrative acumen (sharpness). In fact, it is in the gaps in the narrative, where the poetic image becomes unhinged, that we can come to recognize the flickering presence of an unknown.

In her introduction to her book-length collection of essays, *The Language of Inquiry*, Lyn Hejinian writes:

> Poetry comes to know that things are. But this is not knowledge in the strictest sense; it is, rather, acknowledgement – and that constitutes a sort of unknowing. To know *that* things are is not to know *what* they are, but to know *that* without *what* is to know otherness (i.e., the unknown and perhaps unknowable) [...] This acknowledging is a process, not a definitive act.[47]

Here, the caesura of Hejinian's known–unknown need not be reserved exclusively for the space or gap between the lines. If we compare *The Obituary*'s indeterminacy, as poetic overlap or caesura, to Erín Moure and Chus Pato's relationship to scission as a strategy against invisibility and the instrumentality of language, it becomes clear that the process of making visible is also a process of knowing through the entanglement of difference.

Such a process of incorporation and layering runs counter to forms of knowledge production that presume a fixed form of understanding over the subject. Instead, *The Obituary*'s experimentally overlaid structure – its outstanding translanguaging poetics, porously assembled voices, and narratives, as well as counternarratives – sutures these aforementioned features together to create a narrative brimming with ontological possibilities. Put another way, Scott's porous structure in *The Obituary* allows for subjects to be sighted rather than recited by the certainty of an omniscient narrative superstructure. There, in the very fissures of indeterminacy, they emerge with at least the possibility of the freedom to speak – and speak they do, although such a form of presence does require the reader to participate in, to listen closely, and to surrender to the complexity of the text, which is its defiance of translatability itself.[48]

If we recall the fragile ecosystem of reception made clear in Moure and Pato's *Secession/Insecession*, then we will equally recall that such a gesture is also based on an ethics of address in a call-and-response structure that demands "responsible responsiveness." The gesture of responsible responsiveness is helpful to keep in mind in relation to *The Obituary*'s insistence that "remembrance concerns not the dead. But what is alive + speaking within us."[49] Such a form of remembrance is lodged in a kernel of unspeakable truth that, as I've begun to suggest, pokes holes in the narrative's certainty. Gaps or unknowns, as I have previously elucidated, create temporal ruptures that overlap one another in a play of dis-conjoined surfaces, much like a caesura might break up a line's certain progression in poetry.

But a line can also refer to a family line, and in *The Obituary* such a line is also characterized by gaps and uncertainties:

> *The Man from Glengarry* went to the stove: Veeera knew the score. People sans possibility of origins, losing links. In the wake of Others. Was not 'Grandpa', as she calling her father, known back in Pincher Creek for hawking diamonds + reading tea leaves, saying certain individuals [~~her beloved dying mother~~ his wife] bearing the Seal of the ancestors? ♥ He saw it in a teacup. Where, one day long ago, also seeing his favourite granddaughter, Rosie. Black eyes, blonde curls, skating on future ice of big dark city. Something happening but winter keeps her warm. Entirely my sentiments, old man thinking. When alas beholding, in bottom of cup, time going on back. Out Room door. Stairs. Yellow leaves, also exiting court. What alarming Grandpa most: his little Rosie casting no shadow.[50]

If secrets cannot be spoken of in the present moment, the dialectical tension between the known and the unknown nevertheless gives way to a flicker of presence that haunts the narrative and its temporal warps.

The rupture from a known family lineage, the rupture in narrative (continuity), and – consequently – the rupture of the site of reading (where are we? when are we?) all contribute to the legibility of various unknowns, or at the very least to the presencing of a secret:

> Grandpa, for us you were the future [+ the future tale within]. Which tale's omissions contributing to succeeding generations' inability to communicate with open-mindedness, understanding, steadfastness of principles, consequently, always putting up defence walls of near paranoia. To Wit: your story of Great-Grandma at the ranch.[51]

These unknowns, which are figured in the novel as "[the future tale within, which is the realm of the ancestors],"[52] are dis-conjoined in *The Obituary*'s promise of a future novel: "Rest assured, dear X, a tale's encrypted mid all these future comings + goings of parlour queens, sweet 70s chicks, telephone divas, Grandpa's little split-tailed fis'. A tale unspeakable as owls in ceaseless vigil staring from eyes round + amber as that cat Etta's [more on whom shortly]."[53] But as scholars Kate Eichhorn and Angela Carr contend in their queer reading of the novel, the yet unspeakable novel, the one to come, is nevertheless already inscribed in the encrypted narrative: "Our future novel is already here, even if we (readers) have not quite yet arrived and even if its preoccupations are with the ~~past~~ present secrets."[54] The narrative dispersion of the story is, in fact, overtly announced by one of its many narrators, who proclaims,

> Oh darling X. Is not our future narrative to keep us moving forward? Bus, bicycle, cinema streaming up du Parc, in three, four different measures, for avoiding paranoia. Stay put *[Face]* + keep an eye on things while we go to get th' story. Yes. We disperse. Often. Dissociation oblige! When certain members behavin'. Inappropriately.[55]

The composite nature of the speaking subject and the de-composition of a smooth and singular narrative line are crucial to *The Obituary*'s project of co-lapsing various "perspectives" and moments together. It is within these overlaps that Scott inscribes her narrative with additional meanings, new frames of thought, and new possibilities for "seeing/apprehending" that which is unspeakable.

b) Sight and Insight

What I want to examine now is the way in which the composite representation of *The Obituary*'s sutured narrative is assembled through the shifting borders delimiting the past from the present so as to form a critical and insightful "now." The narrative's permeability is thus expressed in terms of a dilation where the porous boundaries between an inside and an outside remain productively ambiguous.

One of the ways *The Obituary* extends the structural work of *My Paris* has precisely to do with how different layers of time work together. In bringing the past into the present, Scott inscribes various temporalities and their subjects against the grain of their potential disappearance. Compared to *My Paris*, however, where the narrator finds a copy of *The Arcades Project* in her studio, *The Obituary*'s engagement with Benjamin's compositional use of montage, free association, and juxtaposition is not as explicit. Yet *The Obituary*'s narrative drifts, its poetic use of narrative structure, its juxtaposition of images, and its palimpsest displacement of chronological events all suggest a line of continuity with the experimental narrative qualities of *My Paris* and Benjamin's *The Arcades Project*.

Thematically, Scott's engagement with Benjamin's theory and method of montage in *My Paris* and *The Obituary* also represents a shared concern for the spectacle of history. More precisely, as Dianne Chisholm notes in regard to *My Paris*, "the concern that Scott shares with Benjamin is the problem of representing the spell-binding effect of capitalist phantasmagoria wherein 'real' history is obscured."[56] As I have previously pointed out, rather than reading history as a linear progression through time, Benjamin's montage technique critiques the notion of progress while also providing a depth model of reading. Montage, then, supplants "the fairy tale of progress – with a concrete object, the arcade, that resembles the city in miniature and embodies the Ur-form of capitalist modernity. In montage, the object appears as an image: a primary dream image of the city's dreaming collectivity."[57] Such a mode, Chisholm notes, creates a technology of perception, a way of "seeing"[58] contemporary urban reality.[59] This form of sight is crucial to the indeterminacy of *The Obituary*'s open and heterogeneous narrative form. This method of writing does not present a totalizing view of the subject, nor of the story through the omniscience of an all-knowing narrator; rather, it shatters the perspective into several composite perspectives; in this way, the juxtaposition of *The Obituary*'s multiple and simultaneous narrative perspectives opens possible "gestures of seeing."[60]

While "seeing" can suggest rendering something visible in an ocular sense, *The Obituary*'s relationship to "seeing" has much more in common with the haptic sense of seeing as grasping and understanding:

Reader, you may be forgiven for asking: what, here, is a ~~novel~~ life? If endlessly eclipsing into the emptiness of the middle? May we offer a clou in R case. A solid griffe or claw from 'the past.' Which time-worn device [analepsis]. Deployed in wider noir genre. By way of photo inset. Or scintilla. The past + its objects, saying the great Walter B. Solely graspable in present as fragment or flash of illumination. At moment of extreme contradiction. Implying any flickering planetary molecule [+ its shadow, memory]. Animate or inanimate. Capable of unexpectedly impacting any other. Such as when understood, fully. Will restore to rightful status discerning Indigenous peoples. Who knowing nothing happening in any one planetary domain or moment. Ever definitively lost to any other.[61]

Writing about features of Benjamin's dialectical image, philosopher Max Pensky observes that, for Benjamin,

> under conventional terms "past" is a narrative construction of the conditions for the possibility of a present which supercedes [sic] and therefore comprehends it; Benjamin's sense, on the contrary, was that "past" and "present" are constantly locked in a complex interplay in which what is past and what is present are negotiated through material struggles, only subsequent to which the victorious parties consign all that supports their vision of the world to a harmonious past, and all that speaks against it to oblivion.[62]

In light of reading the dialectical image as a form of poetic apprehension where seeing is akin to seizing, reading and writing become modes for producing flashes of recognition. "Be further advised," warns *The Obituary*'s narrator, "only epiphanic afternoons shall herein be remembered."[63]

Rather than have the narrative congeal into a single telling, Scott inscribes *The Obituary*'s narrative across several overlapping temporalities and jarring ontologies. In this sense, my reading of the narrative's various perspective framings recalls Lyn Hejinian's poetics of description as apprehension.[64] In her essay "Strangeness," invention and composition offer transformative and improvisational possibilities as a way of writing into a language of inquiry:

> Description should not be confused with definition; it is not definitive but transformative. Description, in the examples here, is a particular and complicated process of thinking, being highly intentional, while at the same time, because it is simultaneous with and equivalent to perception, remaining open to the arbitrariness, unpredictability, and inadvertence of what appears. Or one might say that it is at once improvisational and purposive. It is motivated thus by simultaneous but different logics.[65]

The significance of the blurred configuration between "simultaneous" and "different" is that it relates description to a metonymic process that, because metonymy implies a form of movement between or across relationships, also instigates other ways of thinking and knowing, even as it shifts the connections between things known to an unknown or unknowable.

The Obituary's narrative overlap and narrative diffusion are but two examples of experimental strategies that dilate the novel's narrative space so that it becomes a space of apprehension in the sense that Hejinian understands it. For instance, the boisterous noises produced by *The Obituary*'s (often seemingly bodiless) floating voices are projected – like the use of "scintilla" or "photo inset" in a film noir – against the gaps that interrupt and dis-locate their speech and the reader's ability to see them fully embodied. Scott's experimentally overlaid narrative builds upon the layers to produce visibility in accretion, which I examine in the following section.

NARRATIVE AND TEMPORAL OVERLAP: APPREHENDING THE SPACE OF TRANSLATION

I now return to consider various forms of overlap, and examine the disconjunctive play of surfaces in *The Obituary*'s experimentally composed narrative, in order to focus on the effects of narrative diffusion and its impact on opening a space of translation. This attention to what is overlaid leads me to consider the novel's palimpsest portrayal of time, where past and present coexist – a feature that is exhibited in the plural and indeterminate nature of the narrative's various perspective framings. In their merging together, the diffusion and redistribution of temporality as well as the incorporation of various speakers into a dis-conjoined palimpsest "space" acquires three-dimensional and thus architectural significance.

In terms of "space," the incorporation of various angles of vision as well as the superimposed time frames are mainly anchored in or around the figure of the triplex, the place and space from which most of the action emanates. To quote one of *The Obituary*'s narrators: "If material conditions shape the spirit, we may empirically declare the Triplex the place where what is happening is the place."[66] Indeed, the triplex is a ubiquitous part of Montreal's architectural landscape. It being an apartment building with "two sets of stairs. Outside. Plus inner, dropping directly down from upper flat door," each tenant has his or her own private entrance.[67] "We are proud of this architectural peculiarity," notes the Bottom Historian, "where each exit, no matter how high, permits unique access to exterior, so that every tenant may call her flat her house."[68] With its spiralling iron staircases, this "architectural peculiarity" also implies that its inhabitants live in close proximity to their neighbours. In this tri-stacked dwelling place, the three floors that typically constitute the triplex's layout, and its long, narrow middle corridor (thus the many references in the novel to the triplex as a "railway flat"), together mean that, both literally and figuratively, voices occasionally float through the cracks in the floorboards, wafting like ghosts into others' apartments.

While each floor cannot be said to represent a specific time period, the triplex's vertical structure does become a symbol for the sedimentation of time. The novel achieves such a depiction by representing the site of the triplex where Rosine lives as the burial place of the Crystal Palace, a nineteenth-century exhibition hall that existed prior to the triplex and that is now buried underneath it. Situated at 4999 Settler-Nun in Montreal's present-day neighbourhood known as the Mile-End, the novel also suggests that the Crystal Palace served as a smallpox hospice (ca. 1885) before was destroyed by fire.[69] Still, such a disastrous fate does not relinquish the Crystal Palace to the space of a historical factoid in the novel's footnotes. Instead, voices and portraits of the Crystal Palace erupt into the narrative, suggesting a living-dead figure. Such a layered construction is also reflected in the character of Rosine, who, herself a liminal figure between the living and the dead, is haunted by her uncertain ancestry, an aspect to which I shall return below.

To consider the flicker of presence and absence in the novel, what comes into focus only to fade out again, is to liken the play between what is absent and what is present to a series of entries and exits that are characteristically spectral. "What haunts are not the dead but the gaps left within us by the secrets of others," reads the epigraph to *The Obituary*.[70] As scholars Angela Carr and Kate Eichhorn point out, the collapsing of various time frames in the novel is a formal attempt to create a porous structure that will allow buried secrets to be unearthed, revealed rather than concealed.[71] "So our future novel is not about the ancestors but rather the persistent *pull* of the ancestors on the present."[72] Such a layering of temporalities is figured, at least symbolically, in the architectural remains of the Crystal Palace. Interestingly, not only does the adapted wooden-walled Crystal Palace stand as a translation of its original, glass colonial model, but such a translation also determines its fate: "Hélas, one hot June-wind night, alleged spark from cigarette catching hay in carriage house.

And spreading to Crystal Palace's wooden walls, which in departing from pure glass-+-iron mother-country model meaning Palace instantaneously burning. To ground."[73] A symbol of European wealth and power, the Crystal Palace is the allegorical sign of colonization, its pylons still rotting under the modern-day triplex. "What struck me especially, and this is how I see the novel now," says Scott in an interview, "is that a whole life happens at the level of the city, 'under' which are other unspoken presences ... *The Obituary* is a look behind where what has allegedly 'passed,' reconsidering it as an element of 'now-time.'"[74]

The creation of a "now-time" is further accentuated by Scott's ubiquitous use of the present participle, even when referencing an event in the past. This verb tense has the effect of blurring the borders between one time frame and another. In the following example, the verbs ending in the clipped "in'" instead of "ing" make the action feel continuous.[75] What begins in one time line, ca. 1885, seems to persist irrevocably.

> Having puffed a joint for dessert, all by himself, outside l'École nationale de théâtre, the assistant's nodding, halfway down inner 4999 Settler-Nun stairway, whose façade, red-orange painted brick, pressed peeling metal cornice, reading 1908 in middle, curiously resembling a dollhouse: one little brick floor piled atop another. Up up up. Yet, numbered downward, toward bottom, #4995 directly over buried pylons of former magnificent Crystal Palace, built for agricultural + commercial exposition purposes. Where ca. 1885, mid rows of faces on iron beds erupting like plastic bubbles into fetid putrid pus, lay Shale Pit Workers! of neighbouring Saint-John-Baptiste, dying in smallpox epidemy, raging in our filth-+-vice-ridden city. The 'night soil' not yet bein' plucked from alleys, overflowin' + floatin', thawin', joined by offal, floatin' downhill from overflowin' privies, down lanes where children playin' in first warm April suns. Further contaminatin' leakage from refuse barrels, vegetable leavin's, broken sewers, all rushin' in filthy ruisseaux. As if to welcome th' pestilence, just gettin' off th' train. Which Palace's wooden walls, quarantined for duration, catchin' spark from carriage house one hot June night +
> burnin'
> down.[76]

If the quote I've chosen seems excessively long, its length nevertheless serves a purpose. For example, it shows that the style of the writing makes it difficult to cut or trim passages without losing important pieces of context. While the action is clearly marked by date-specific temporal references that should divide the past from the present, the use of the present participle brings the action to the forefront of the story, making it feel as though it were happening in the present time frame. The "night soil," a playful euphemism for the city's garbage, contaminates more than the soil, alleys, and streams; indeed, the entire space of the story is temporarily subsumed by the poetic detail and sheer exuberance of the language. Words like "offal," to signify the putrid decomposition of animal flesh, and the use of "privies" instead of overflowing toilets, contribute a poetic density to the passage that further distances the reader's orientation. Where are we? When are we? As readers, it is not until we fall upon a reference to the Crystal Palace's walls several lines later that we are reminded that the action is technically taking place in the past.

Such an indeterminate use of temporality, the way the past seeps into the present in a continuous stream, defies the conventions of analepsis or flashback, which would typically work to cleave one novelistic moment from the other. In *The Obituary*, such a clear separation does not exist. Cleverly, the play of light in the sentence that follows the example provided above returns us to some semblance or version of the present moment: "Real light of day. Likewise falling through oeil-de-boeuf onto upper palier of stairway. Where old cop, Casse-Noisette to his friends, on knees, awaiting, en principe, as befitting diplômé de l'École Supérieure de Police de Paris: a search warrant."[77] Readers will remember, however, that the temporality in which the gendarme exists is contemporaneous with the early 1920s. "Indeed: In old gendarme's head, it's Paris. 1924."[78] He is enamoured with Rosine's grandfather, his "adored Jos. Dousse," his "beloved halfbreed danseur à claquettes"[79]: "Peacefully, they stroll. C-N in soft leather boots, fashionable à l'époque, laced to the ankle ... When ancient Casse-Noisette, geriatrically adrift in long bygone afternoon [...] about to tell a story, uttering: *NOW!*"[80] In another instance, after he hears or hallucinates a voice saying, "I wanted to fuck you all night,"[81] the gendarme imagines himself walking the streets of Montreal in search of Double Jos. Dousse. It is 1924. "[He is in] search of only man he ever really loving."[82] Hence, if the gendarme is "present" in the hallway of Rosine's apartment, he is nevertheless constantly eclipsing into fantasy, into other time periods, and presumably between the living and the dead. Like other characters in the novel, he too is haunted. He is haunted by his desire and obsession with his old wartime lover, Double Jos. Dousse, a fantasy that he has denied for so long that, "like all in R intrigue," his desire remains unspeakable – "his chain of words unable to emerge."[83] Of course, the gendarme may be haunted, but this does not preclude the fact that he too haunts the stairwell where he is ensconced. In fact, since he seems to more properly belong to a different epoch, he too, like the Crystal Palace and the nineteenth century Shale Pit Workers! who haunt it, may very well be a ghost.

The triplex, then, becomes the site of inquiry for the sedimentation of history in all its spectral layers. In such a layered form of writing, Scott's treatment of time has the effect of unhinging the present moment from its central and thus canonical position. It is here in particular that Scott's fractal narrative is reminiscent of Benjamin's historian: "A historian who takes this [the past as a precarious and living entity] as his point of departure stops telling the sequence of events like the beads of a rosary. Instead, he grasps the constellation which his own era has formed with a definite earlier one."[84] In place of a clear separation between various time frames, the reader finds a "landscape's history occasionally erupting into present"[85] a landscape where "phantoms = prime companions, o'er neighbourhood, o'er succeeding generations of recurring genetically torqued brats born on former Crystal Palace site, o'er former orchards + fields + men + this + that."[86]

As I have previously suggested, in palimpsest fashion, the Crystal Palace inhabits the triplex on rue Settler-Nun in quite the same way as the dead inhabit the space of the living: "Do not skyscrapers bear, deep within, straw huts? The person, her ancestors?"[87] For Carr and Eichhorn, the triplex furnishes the novel with an allegorical scaffold that mirrors its indeterminate references to genealogy, it is "a dwelling marked by its own disjunctive temporality."[88] While the triplex houses the imperial symbol of the city's colonial past, Rosine can also be said to "house" the secret lineage of her ancestors. Moreover, if the triplex is characteristically divided into three units, each with its own private entrance such that each occupant may call their suite their "home," so is Rosine divided into a tripartite structure of her own. She is at once the (possibly) dead woman lying on the bed, the fly doing a little erotic jig, and the basement historian also known as the lesbian modernist supplying the story with "facts" as she guards against "over-interpretation."[89]

The triplex is both lodging and tomb, a crypt for transgenerational secrets and trauma, and the fracturing of the character of Rosine too embodies this double ambivalence. More than a historical marker, however, the triplex also shapes the poetic space of the novel in the theoretical sense, thus linking the question of "what haunts" from the epigraph, by psychoanalysts Nicolas Abraham and Maria Török, to the wider question of Rosine, her ancestry, and the interrogative "who speaks when one speaks?" – a recurring question in Scott's work.[90]

Indeed, the question of "what haunts" directs our reading to the main protagonist, I/R/Rosine, whose Indigenous ancestry becomes entangled in a "murder mystery plot." I place the term in quotations so as not to belie the forced assimilation of Indigenous peoples and the communal repression of their genocide that is at the heart of the novel's "detective story": "on th' afternoon we are murdered, this set will turn malodorous ... Vrai, I mebbe back as a ghose."[91] Such a lapse of presence from the annals of history is evinced in the missing pages from the *Book of Genocides* (which was loaned to her by her landlord). Falling upon such an omission, Rosine, who is haunted by her Métis "inchoate origins,"[92] tears the yellowing pages from the book. In what will become a leitmotif for the violent treatment and subsequent effacement of Indigenous peoples from different texts (history [books], landscape, genealogy, etc.), the pages float through the streets of Montreal, blowing across the landscape as a bitter and ambivalent reminder of the historical violence and loss endured by many Indigenous families.[93]

Where *The Obituary* brings the past and the present into proximal space, blurring the clear distinctions between them, both Rosine, in relation to her family lineage, and the triplex, as it houses the city's colonial past expressed in the allegorical figure of the Crystal Palace, become crypts for the ineffable. Thus, in the novel's experiments with perspective and time, both Rosine and the triplex become carriers of transgenerational secrets that resist containment.

Instead of remaining buried within the subject, these repressed (his)stories take on rumourological airs as they float through novelistic space seemingly detached from a determining origin. They are fragments – voices detached from bodies, yellowing pages detached from books – that float through the novel without clear temporal markers or narratorial interventions. The (white) noise of the past provides a haunting soundtrack for the present, as snippets of conversations, stories and songs suture the narrative composition into a continuous present. This noise, as rumour, is the subject of the following section of this chapter.

ROSINE AND THE QUESTION OF WHAT HAUNTS

Almost everyone and everything bears some form of haunting in the novel. As Lianne Moyes points out, "Rosine, for example, is haunted by places that have been effaced, by languages written over those used around her, by people whose histories are not recognized – the entries missing from the book of genocides."[94] Indeed, if the novel is a queer intervention into the past and its transgenerational haunting, as Carr and Eichhorn aptly maintain, it is also about omissions, some deliberate, others tainted by more sinister undertones.[95] "Never say you're an Indian. If. You're. Not," Rosine's aunt tells her when pressed about her Indigenous heritage.[96] Perhaps the most violent form of omission, however, is the missing entry from the *Book of Genocides* that makes no mention of the forced assimilation of Indigenous peoples:

> Reaching for *Book of Genocides*, turning non-acid-treated leafs. Detaching as I touching. GER-many. Somalia. Armenia. Rwanda. Kosovo. Sudan. Eeeeeeast Teeeeeemor. Scrutinizing for la Gêne on which we standing, those going here before, stencilled in ice tunnel below bridge.[97]

Suddenly, the "bitter particles of those going there before," an ambiguous reference made in the novel's opening pages, takes on a new significance[98]:

> Turning pages of landlord's *Book of Genocides*. And finding no mention of the Gêne on which we ourselves standing – les cent-cinquantes-millions – vrai, I/R never thinking of that before: silent. Like falling snow on mountains. Letting th' yellowed leaves fly one by one. Out window. Then felt a wave of shame. And went to lie down.[99]

Like those bitter particles, the yellow leaves and snow that blow throughout the novel's pages acquire a new level of significance as they float across the city, further emphasizing that no part of the landscape is left untouched by the omission of the city's colonial past: "*walking down streets. Feet in autumn leaves. A shadow rustling behind. Possibly an ancestor.*"[100]

Such a past is not past, of course; its is very much alive in the present moment of the novel's depiction of a critical "now." Indeed, in the image that follows, the "leaves" from the trees become interchangeable with the "leaves" from the *Book of Genocides*. As their origin is no longer clear, they not only echo the indeterminate qualities of a rumour, but also recall Rosine's "inchoate origins": "Following pair of crumbled automn leaves. Wearing deep in their veins th' storm of generations. Blowing o'er parc … Blowing past triplex … O'er boul Saint."[101] Seated on the bus, I/R watches the yellowed pages of th' *Book of Genocides* as they land at the "foot of that old Con-fed Father, Georges Cartier's monument,"[102] a tribute to the city's colonial past. The pages are then swept up by the wind and are described as flying across the street "into parc Settler-Nun [formerly F's Field]," where they float like blossoms from an orchard, or like snow in a gentle breeze.[103] Finally, the pages land over the site of the former Crystal Palace, where there is no mention "of people camping there ere establishment of Gentleman's Raquette + Hunt, then glass-+-iron Crystal Palace's mille-et-une facettes."[104] The treatment of the blowing pages and the flagrant omission they represent bring the present into a critical state. It becomes the task of the historian/translator/writer/reader, then, to "cultivate a particular capacity for recognizing such moments."[105] This is precisely what I think *The Obituary* has set out to do – and with admirable success.

Scott suggests that the incorporation of the past into the present creates a flicker of presence, a form of existential translation of sorts, and no other figure in the novel embodies this flicker as overtly as the ghostly figure of *Face*, who haunts the triplex on rue Settler-Nun. Falling in and out of focus, the narrative describes the face that haunts the frame of the upper triplex window as attracting a crowd in the street below. Such a flicker of presence is analogous to the disjunctive temporalities linking the triplex, as crypt, to the burned-down Crystal Palace. Here, secrets act as phantoms haunting the subject (Rosine, the triplex, even novelistic space itself). In their ghostly appearances, such phantasmagorical sites/sight(ing)s operate in a manner that resembles Scott's use of the comma of translation in *My Paris*, where the dis-conjoined narrative surface allows the narrator's multiple affiliations to permeate one another. This is further elucidated in the way in which *Face* simultaneously attracts both a crowd and a barrage of stories at the foot of the building on rue Settler-Nun – hearsay – which turns the triplex into a widely contested space out of which disparate (hi)stories arise.

The triplex is the place, in other words, where rumours emanate:

> Here, Dear Reader, we begin our intrigue. Mid hangers-on [our natural element]. Gathered beneath 4999 Settler-Nun in the rain. Umbrellas raised smooth, or dehisce, like gangsters at a funeral. Heads shaved or impercipiently coiffed gazing up at contour behind venetians in darkening third-floor railway-flat window. Our wildest *élan*, ♥ [106] like Peter's, dutifully restrained. Eagerly awaiting, futurity oblige, dénouement of some devastating calumny or love tourniquet. – *Entoutkàs*, venturing the café-philosopher among us, goateed + pointedly down at the heel: – *Even if only about love. Are not love's overwrought requiems usually covering deeper pilferings or betrayals, lost lands, homes, or lost people in them?* Meaning our novel beginning drenched in the acerbic, therefore subject to countless deviations + only slowly, anteriorly, releasing its elixir.[107]

As the crowd waits for the mystery and reports regarding *Face* to be resolved, the scene depicts the uncertainty of the face's identity and origin with terms that are akin to those of a rumour:

> Gazing + unhurriedly opening, closing their odd-shaped umbrellas. Jostled, occasionally, by younger, more productive A-types rushing home to dinner. Who, themselves – if glancing up a sec at *Face* in Settler-Nun window – thinking [being somehow already negatively predisposed]: rumour having, a pervert [children looking away embarrassed]. While *Face* in situ behind sooty grey venetians denying, like everyone in this theatre, what *is*. And expounding what is not.[108]

While rumours accumulate at the foot of the triplex, they also accumulate across the landscape of the novel.

The accumulation of the rumour across space is both literal and figurative. In the literal sense, they take the form of gossip between the characters, who are, in one way or another, haunted by Rosine/*Face*. The triplex's landlord, for instance, who shares the same psychoanalyst as Rosine, has gathered several complaints/stories about her tenant and recounts them to her analyst, MacBeth. In a therapy session, the landlord confesses to MacBeth that Rosine was apparently seen "washing sex toys on the balcony [...] dildo like a stallion's. Who's she think she's kidding?"[109] Beyond her scandalous exhibition of her dildo, she is also apparently making such a racket "skipping non-stop up + down the stairs" that the other neighbour, Lena, "*saying crystal meth for sure ...*"[110] Meanwhile, due to complaints, *Face* is now under surveillance:

> Police officers from District 20 of le Service de police de la Ville de Montréal seeking individual living in Mile End borough.
> Object of various complaints from neighbours; of late, one or two reporting as possibly missing. Others claiming to see face in upper 4999 Settler-Nun window several times daily. No bank nor credit card transactions for a week.[111]

The traumatic uncertainty that *Face* represents for those living in the neighbourhood simultaneously points, in a figurative sense, to the threat of the indeterminacy of signification.

Meredith Quartermain addresses this anxiety in relation to *The Obituary*, albeit in an oblique manner, suggesting that such a form of disquiet is also embodied in the character of *I/th'fly*: "In *The Obituary*, the notion of words secreting some phantom significance is explicitly addressed (with a nice play on secret and secrete) ... At numerous junctures specific words trigger cracks, fissures and gaps signalling hungry ghosts of history, seemingly innocent colonial language which actually harbours murderous impulses (as casual as flyswatters)."[112] The inherent threat gestured to above lies in the image of words (signifiers) floating detached from meanings (signifieds). This is an image the reader is familiar with – at least in terms of the floating omission of Indigenous peoples from the novel's depiction of the *Book of Genocides*. It is the same kind of menace that threatens to engulf the "truth" regarding Rosine's family lineage, just as it is the same threat that has led to the shared repression and collective effacement of Canada's genocide of Indigenous peoples:

> ♥ No human lineage is certain. The family, like so many, faded on purpose into background. Replying when questioned: we know nothing beyond X generation. Not Grandma Prisc's proper family

name. Nor the language Grandpa speaking when talking to his mother. Everyone knew the words of the new concept anthem: *The Maple Leaf Forever*.[113]

To return to the stories that accumulate at the foot of the triplex, we could say that the entire novel serves such a purpose; these (hi)stories – as rumours – float across the novel's landscape seemingly unanchored in time and place, and therefore encrypt the narrative with undeniable anxiety.[114]

Indeed, one way to frame the rumour is to think of it as a story that runs against the grain, against the grain of the "truth of the story" in some sense. Rumours are carriers of an encrypted message that needs to be detected or interpreted. Embodying a life of their own, and alienated from any discernable sense of authorship, rumours are comparable to the contagious spread of disease, moving with the vampiric tenacity of the living-dead.[115] They are inhuman, careless. They roam completely detached from an apparent origin, and equally free from any sense of responsibility for their effects.

RUMOUR AS TRANSLATION

This inhuman quality recalls a few select passages in Paul de Man's "Conclusions: Walter Benjamin's 'The Task of the Translator,'" where, during the question-and-answer period of his talk, the question of the inhuman in Benjamin's "The Translator's Task" is broached.[116] Most interestingly, in relation to this section's focus on the rumour, de Man suggests that language is inhuman because it is impossible to fully comprehend. Cautioning against a reading of the inhuman as a secret, he argues that it should instead be viewed as the very (im)possibilities that are inherent in language. "The 'inhuman,' ... is not some kind of mystery, or some kind of secret; the inhuman is: linguistic structures, the play of linguistic tensions, linguistic events that occur, possibilities which are inherent in language – independently of any intent or any drive or any wish or any desire we might have."[117] Anchoring his claims in the example of the necessary but impossible task of translation, he suggests that translation is a way of reading the original. Of consequence here is the idea of translation as utopic. It is an impossible possibility. Necessary but impossible.[118] According to de Man, to understand this possible impossibility, we simply have to think of translation's irreversibility, "to the extent that you could not possibly get from the translation back to an original."[119] A translation will relate to the original in interesting ways, he suggests, raising some questions about aspects inherent in it, all the while destabilizing the text in the process.[120]

That is the great difficulty inherent in translation, that it necessarily changes certain aspects of the circulation of meaning within the text:

> And what happens to the original – I think can be said – the original is disarticulated, the original is reduced to the status of prose, is decanonized, all that by the process of translation, because the impossibility of translation is due to disruptions which *are* there in the original, but which the original managed to hide – in the same way that Benjamin manages to hide, from the reader, from the translator, from everybody who reads this text, manages to hide, for example, the inadequacy of any symbol in relation to what it means, by using symbols which are particularly convincing, which are particularly seductive, and which seem precisely to achieve what they want to achieve, what they mean to achieve.[121]

I am not suggesting here that translation is a rumour or vice versa. What I am suggesting, however, is a link between the detached meaning inherent in the passage from original to translation and the circulation of the rumour as a carrier of meaning – regardless of its truth factor.

In both instances, translation and rumour lead one to harbour a potential mistrust in the inhuman properties of language. The translation is stereotypically scrutinized and then criticized for straying from the original while the rumour becomes the (terrorizing) word on the street stripping one of one's good name. Here is de Man again: "That there is a nonhuman aspect of language is a perennial awareness from which we cannot escape, because language does things which are so radically out of our control that they cannot be assimilated to the human at all, against which one fights constantly."[122] Rather than approaching it with distrust, de Man contends that such insights bring about "a certain kind of critical examination"[123]:

> Things happen in the world which cannot be accounted for in terms of the human conception of language. And they always

happen in linguistic terms, or the relation [to] language is always involved when they have [happened]. And good or bad things, not only catastrophes, but felicities also. And they happen. In a sense, to account for them, to account for them historically, to account for them in any sense, a certain initial discrepancy in language has to be examined.[124]

Roland Barthes, for his part, addresses the inhuman element in language as "the terror of uncertain signs," which are traumatic in the sense that it is impossible in such circumstances for meaning to congeal: "In every society," he writes, "various techniques are developed intended to fix the floating chain of signifieds in such a way as to counter the terror of uncertain signs."[125] As Teresa de Lauretis remarks in an essay that begins with the same Roland Barthes quote I just used,[126] narrative, even as fiction, is one manner of stabilizing meaning:[127]

> That is the function of the linguistic message in the (advertising) image, whose polysemy would otherwise produce a traumatic suspension of meaning. Such an anchoring function is provided by narrative in literary function, where the rhetorical/figural dimension of language, in disrupting the stability of meaning, carries what Paul de Man calls "the persistent threat of misreading."[128] Or, as de Man puts it elsewhere,[129] reading a literary text "leaves a residue of indetermination that has to be, but cannot be, resolved by grammatical means."[130]

What is impressive about *The Obituary* is that it manages to make these floating, ghostly aporias visible precisely because its various overlaps prevent the narrative from congealing into a single (his)story. The encrypted and unanchored features of the narrative, therefore, open a space of translation that is akin to the undecidability of a rumour.

The rumourological version of the haunting, as one that carries the persistent threat of misreading, to echo Paul de Man, is not entirely surprising in a novel about how the secrets of the dead haunt the living. Nor is a passion for the rumourological surprising in a narrative that is only "slowly, anteriorly, releasing its elixir."[131] Meanwhile, as the narrative is subjected to "countless deviations," the better to outdo/outrun the suppression of a contagious secret, the time-sense of its pacing as well as its fantasmatic projections of the detached story, as rumour, keep the narrative in a constant state of anxiety, which I also read as a form of critical *vigil*ance.[132]

Moreover, with its barrage of voices and collaged temporalities, there is hardly any resting place for the reader, just as there is hardly a resting place for the dead whose voices float across *The Obituary* with the same living-dead tenacity of the rumour:

> Here, dear Reader, born of an instant's delight. Mere figment of the parents. Themselves pale projection of those going before. Here, we arriving in space where the sharp sensation something incontournable requiring our attention. For footprints exiting slushy court those in Grandpa's leaky teacup. Why, on this day of our lord, no shadow gliding back up stairs?[133]

In interviews, Scott refers to the scattered and slippery shards that constitute the narrative and its omissions as forms of ventriloquism. In her essay "The Sutured Subject," Scott writes: "For what it's worth, post-Freudian analysts like Abraham and Török also stressed that we are mostly haunted by the secrets of others, down through the generations, other voices that try to make us perform on the stage of society like ventriloquists."[134] The ventriloquizing quality of the narrative is referred to by the Basement Historian as stemming from the past's secret index:

> Children take words from the air, ventriloquizing omissions passed down generations. Hence Rosie's 'charrettes,' those famous Métis Red River carts with their wooden axles, capable of bearing giant loads, famously squeaking over rutted prairie. Which landscape's history occasionally erupting into present. As voiced by that Métis farmer on the radio decrying new floods banks raised to keep provincial capital Winnipeg burghers safe. Meaning the waters formerly rising on floodplain some genius planned the capital city on, flooding the outlying farmland instead.[135]

The words the children take from the air seem to float without a discernable origin or source. These rumourological utterances, in the figurative sense of their French meaning as *des bruits ou mots qui courent*, are best captured in the image of the disfigured *Book of Genocides* and the pages of said book, which continue to blow across the landscape of the novel, ultimately offering their own image of a haunted landscape.

CONCLUSION:
PASSAGES THROUGH LANGUAGE

The Obituary is a profoundly (and impressively!) genre-busting text that, akin to Avital Ronell's critical posture of "responsible responsiveness" discussed in chapter 1, does not attempt to foreclose the object and subject of its inquiry through analytical synthesis. Legibility is produced as narrative, and temporal overlaps create the possibilities for new significations to occur and erupt in the dialectical blur. With her overlapping and experimentally composed narrative, Scott proposes a radical way of opening a path to thinking through issues of legibility and inscription by pointing to those places in language (which includes history, representation – or at least a critique thereof – etc.) that lead to a void or negative – a gap – in the subject's place. This quality of negation makes visible that which has been blurred or effaced, rendered unamed, unameable, ineffable, unthought – hence the novel's articulation of transgenerational trauma and the subject of the future as a crypt that bears the inscriptions of an unspeakable past.

This unnamed and unnamable other (story, subject, etc.) is performatively dis-conjoined across various temporal strata that (irre)vocably interrupt the flow of narrative progression or progress itself. Where I have attempted to link the terror of uncertain signs with the groundlessness and contagion of the rumour, I have done so in an attempt to imagine what these unpredictable and unhinged narratives might reveal. What is it, in a rumour, that we cannot imagine seeing? What teratological threat threatens to topple understanding? Is that the (inter)zone of trauma? Is that the task of translation? – to quell the terror of aporias that are un-doing their source(s)? In her conclusion to the novel, Scott closes on the word "Engleeeeeeesh." Does this mark the illegible as a conclusion in and of itself?

Perhaps the most readily available avenue for thinking through the above-mentioned questions is to consider the manifestedly visual signs of overlap in the novel's use of brackets, symbols, crossed-out words, and warped spellings – all of which reroute signification in interesting ways. While I have not specifically lingered on these features,[136] I would like to close this chapter with an anecdote regarding Scott's evocation of crossed-out passages in at least one public reading of *The Obituary* I've seen. In choosing to end on this particular anecdotal note, I hope to underscore the noisy features of such a mercurial composition, and how – in its excess – the reader must wander through its layered passages[137] which are constantly shifting and undoing the ground(s) on which the text is built (even in the simultaneous moment in which they are read).

If one has ever had the delight of listening to Scott read from her novel, he or she might remember that she does not gloss over those passages in *The Obituary* that are bifurcated: "We are loath to go ~~Father~~ farther" (20), "There being no redemption in ~~origins~~ extinct matters" (117), "Is she lying there next ~~th' absent one beside her~~ stuck like that?" (139). When Scott encounters a word that has been crossed out she reads it – does not skip over it. In other words, she'll say the word that's crossed out, then say "that's crossed out" before moving on to its substitution.

The vocable presence and the dis-articulating tactics that Scott gives to these moments of erasure coalesce to form new significations that underscore (and underwrite) the very vocable-ness of the text's ineffable components. One utterance is simultaneously underwritten/overwritten by the other that overlaps it. Translatability is the "voice" of that dis-articulated overlap: the multiplication of (possible) utterances across an uneven, three-dimensional plane; a plane of language that is also a dwelling place – like a house – for the unsaid, or what is difficult or (nearly) impossible to ~~say or~~ represent, the buried speech that is at the heart of the soundless gap between languages and its (mis)apprehension.

4

The Snag of Translation and the Before Unapprehended Relation of Things

There continues to be a suggestion that we are somehow surrounded by other spaces in which exciting, ungraspable things occur.
Renee Gladman, "The Sentence as a Space for Living: Prose Architecture"

THE BEFORE UNAPPREHENDED RELATION OF THINGS

To enter this chapter, we must enter first with the sound of the English Romantic poet Percy Bysshe Shelley in our ears and consider translation, like poetry, as "the before unapprehended relation of things [that] perpetuates their apprehension."[1] And we might balance what might be presumed as wayward movement, or as a form of progress to some form of imminent seeing or foretold insight, with a form of close attention to the notion of apprehension and its multitudinous, even disharmonious meanings: in regards to the future, as anxiety or fear; in terms of what is imaginable, as understanding or grasp; in the sense of an arrest, as (lawful) snag or abiding snare.

I will not propose a defence of translation. Translation is already "a form of castigation,"[2] and as such it is already brimming with such defences, "at arm's length, touching, and pushing *away*,"[3] as Nathanaël writes so eloquently in *Hatred of Translation*. What I do want to consider, with a further quote from Nathanaël in mind, is that "if translation is belated (Benjamin), it is also apprehensive (Ortega y Gasset): it anticipates itself. It is foreknowledge which is so calamitous."[4] This careful consideration, this form of attention, to what will be necessary, even in (or given) the destructive impulse of language, which I imagine is part of the calamity referred to above, at the same time, entices me to enter this chapter, also, with the sound of the poet and translator Sawako Nakayasu's *Say Translation*, "say translation as open art practice as open as matter and anti-matter," which is said alongside a choir of voices voicing the multitudinous possibilities and challenges of translation: "Toni Morrison, Lara Glenum, Arielle Greenberg, Keith Waldrop, Douglas Robinson, María Irene Fornés, Anne Waldman, María Sabina, Jerome Rothenberg, Jacques Rancière, Ryoko Sekiguchi, Cole Swensen [...]"[5] The choir in Nakayasu's translation pamphlet offer supporting texts – texts that turn and tear, expose and interrupt our habits and expectations towards translation.

Of course, and as is made apparent throughout the previous chapters of this book, what is meant by "translation" signifies much more than the translated text or the act of translating. Translation is also the body of knowledge produced by the relation between texts, by the translated text as well as the act of translating, to say nothing of the act of reading. In *Say Translation*, Nakayasu asks us to think about translation in the multifarious sense of the term and to wonder if its future can be other than how we presently imagine translation functioning. Her book does not ask us to fathom the unimaginable. On the contrary, its supporting texts already suggest that translation can be thought of, even practised, otherwise. This is also what this book has sought to ask of translation: can translation be imagined and understood as something other than how it has come to be understood? And if so, how might we approach translation differently?

In his lectures gathered in *Comment vivre ensemble*, or *How to Live Together* in its English translation, Roland Barthes introduces the idea of *des textes d'appui* – "tutor texts" is Kate Briggs's translation. In *This Little Art*, her beautifully decanted book-length essay on translation, Briggs explains what Barthes has in mind: supporting texts are "the texts that brace us, the ones we lean on, testing them to see if they'll support our weight; the texts we always seem to be in conversation with, whether directly or indirectly; the texts that enable us to say or to write anything at all."[6] In regard to the present book, translation is *my* tutor text. It is the text I come back to again and again, trying to gain insight into its nature. I admire Briggs's choice of "tutor" as the translation for the French word "*appui*" because it grants the expression a quality of polysemy: the word tutor can account for both the edifying nature of a text and its supportive features, which are largely, I imagine, preparatory.

But the truth is, translation is not always a very sturdy tutor. Leaning against it, you come to realize, actually, that translation can leave you quite groundless. This is neither a negative appraisal nor a positive one, but an observation that relates to the complex fantasy that is induced in order to supposedly get to the other side of a thought or image structure in one language and then into another, as if there were only ever two. "Translation only ever gives the illusion of being transitive," points out Nathanaël in *Hatred of Translation*.[7] When we think beyond the idea of translation as passage, we might instead observe translation's disintegrative states: "the moment at which the texts come to pieces; the boundary, amplified, is extenuated, it ceases to exist."[8] The extenuated boundary is not one of accommodation or communion. It is rather, as I have come to understand it, a relational body, "the instabilities instigated by translational acts [that] are written into the text."[9] This volatility captures well the vital course of my questioning here, especially in relation to what a poetics of translation might make thinkable. It is precisely the knowledge produced out of the volatile and disintegrative character of translation that I want to think about.

For José Ortega y Gasset, for example, but this is true of many others who have written on translation or other artistic practices, language does not allow everything to be said. In all languages, the possibility of saying one thing entails the silencing of something else. Translation may be impossible, he writes, it may very well be a utopic enterprise, he continues, but the splendor of translation is that it augments our network of intellectual approaches considerably by carrying other languages within it, not just one's own: it carries over precisely what is not "said" in the language one is translating or reading in.[10]

The recurring image here, of translation as carrier, pairs well with the image, mentioned earlier, of translation as tutor or supporting text. Given that I had qualified this relationship as one susceptible to groundlessness, it might serve to better qualify this groundlessness as the unstable nature of translation, whether in terms of its "destruction of all identifiable coordinates," its inability to render something from one language into another, or the way such a rendering often leads to unexpected openings and encounters. "The knowledge that is required to translate a work produced by someone else is not given in advance for any translator," explains Kate Briggs in a live Q&A during the Windham Campbell Prizes Virtual Festival.[11] "I think translation is a knowledge producing, knowledge seeking process" she continues.[12] The instabilities and complex relations brought about through translation, which are also evoked in Ortega y Gasset's essay on translation, as a form of latent, seeping silence, tie translation to the original's underground, its alternative archive. It is there, in their distortions and differences, in their wearing down, that I imagine translation's similarities to Shelley's description of poetry as the "before unapprehended relation of things that perpetuates their apprehension." What I retain, then, whether I am yoking the words of a twentieth-century Spanish philosopher and Romantic poet together or reading Briggs, Nathanaël, or Nakayasu, among others, is the choice to forgo the idea of arriving at a theory and to instead "follow translation through its own thinking," and to consider, too, that the thinking it makes thinkable cannot be arrived at in advance, which also suggests that the nature of translation is rather uncertain, by which I mean not given in advance.[13] That much I can almost say for certain.

IN FLUX TRANSLATION

This book began as a foray into thinking about translation, and it became a book about translation *as* thinking. It was the work of others that instilled this particular nuance in my line of inquiry. Reading Erín Moure, Chus Pato, Fernando Pessoa, PME-ART, and Gail Scott – among so many others – was like simultaneously creating chance associations that scrambled, in their respective works as well as in their contact through my writing and thinking of them, not just notions of origin but the very notion and possibilities of translation. Relationships have thus been formed, and this book bears the imprint of those relations.

If you have moved through this book, reading linearly from chapter to chapter, then you will be aware of my fascination with the idea of an "originating" idea or thought that is not so much original in the sense of a beginning, but rather a vagabond figure whose arrival is both imminent and strangely also always on its way. Hence, it also calls "origination" into question. You will also know that along with this idea of scrambled or inchoate origins, I am also fascinated with time, and am most notably seduced by the idea of temporal ruptures.

The significance of time to translation, or rather the temporal dimensions of translation and its un-doings and un-readings, has thus far been a great source of interest to my study. In Erín Moure and Chus Pato's meeting-place in *Secession/Insecession*, time frames were paradoxically dis-continuous and co-existent. In regard to *The Book of Disquiet* and PME-ART's multiplicitous renderings of it, translation and art making blend and alter the sense of the duration of writing as translation: textual/diaristic artifacts orbit one another, form unpredictable meetings and relations where bookish worlds (almost) collide. In *The Obituary*, time plays a palimpsest role: past, present, and future speak through one another, like ventriloquists. It is a constantly-in-flux translation.[14] In this concluding chapter, I want to rehearse a question that gets carried over across the previous chapters: Do we have a concept of translation that accounts for thinking translation as duration – as a constantly-in-flux translation? And I want to add to that a few others: Is the definition of translation itself that which we might want to keep in flux? And how might we keep approaching translation differently? This is not to dilute the rigours of translational practices. On the contrary, what I am entertaining is the idea that the rigours of the practice are sometimes enfolded, dissimulated into other practices.

LIVING IN THE PRESENT TRANSLATION

I am interested in translation as an experiment in living in the present, and also in translation as uncertainty, hence its relationship to thinking and my interest in what it *simultanates*, a useful verb Renee Gladman has concocted to capture a kind of double consciousness, "a verb that would indicate one thing causing something else to run parallel to it."[15] By uncertainty, I mean that which is not definite, and I also mean something about the complex shape of our or a work's interiority, our and its aliveness at any given moment. Another way to frame it would be to copy here another useful question by Gladman: "When we move from our minds into language, from something that must be multilayered, full of fragments, full of complete feelings, like novels that exist in the shape of an instant, what are we doing?"[16]

As I write the question down, I am reminded of Anne, the protagonist-writer-translator in Nicole Brossard's novel *La Capture du Sombre* (*Fences in Breathing* in Susanne de Lotbinière-Harwood's English translation), which I will briefly return to at the end of this chapter. For the moment, I gather sentences from the opening pages of Brossard's novel, passages that might further our process of thinking about translation in these pages. I gather sentences from Lotbinière-Harwood's translation, such as:

> Like a foreigner, I want to dive into the landscape of a temporary world where meaning parts meaning as I move through it[17]; I am trying most of all to understand how, with a vertical body, it is possible to impale the real at the same speed as fiction. Then, without falling apart, I let immensity softly softly drop its Nordic melancholy blueness upon my shoulders[18]; I am constantly straining to keep urging life forward, that luminous and fascinating prey, and then I stay still for days at a time, surrounded by words and midnight graves. This time of urgency and vertigo forces me to heed what I call the *torment of grammar fast turning into abyss*. That's how it is[19]; In my language, I have exhausted the vocabulary that would have allowed me to name that intriguing, approaching black: raven, vulture, feline, the black of volcanic sand, of marble, of ink and soot, of leather, of cassocks, of niqab and chador, and of burnt corpse. I need other words for this darkness of nature and civilisation now encroaching[20]; Something silent goes through me when I think of the foreign language.[21]

Anne feels that she is at a breaking point, and that in order to process the daily calamities of everyday life (of nature and civilization), she must do so through another language, through translation, especially if she is to write. Which is interesting, because translation is its own form of opacity.

I don't mean this generally, and not specifically either, in relation to Anne. I am speaking to those parts in the process of translating where something or some part of the original cannot be rendered in another language, those parts, essentially, that require translation; Anne Carson refers to these moments as "metaphysical silences."[22] To better understand what I mean, it is useful for me to copy here a long passage by Nathanaël; it is one which has stayed with me throughout the years, even those preceding this project.

> Translation's disintegrative states have become something of a preoccupation; what I mean – and I'm still thinking this through – is that the instabilities instigated by translational acts are written into the text. Photographic processes have proven very instructive in relation to this. For example, Antonioni writes of the endless

inscription onto photographic film of visual, material information that escapes the eye's scrutiny. Prolonged development processes will reveal the ostensibly endless *latent* images contained in a single frame of film. In theory, one could expose an image ad infinitum, culling from the celluloid more and more infinite detail. But we know from a photographer such a Josef Koudelka, who practices a very sensitive relationship to time, that excessive development will produce a pitch black photograph – one could imagine this as the absolute, the most complete photograph, in which the intricate detail produces a solid, impenetrable mesh of opacity. In which everything is inscribed and nothing is legible. A corollary exists in translation, and it is the moment at which the texts – forgoing the bilateral language of source and target texts (with its tidy between, and problematic direction) – the texts, with their languages, enter into disintegrative states. It has something to do with proximities and loss of intelligibility. It has something also to do with vigilation. The moment at which one is most focused might be the moment one must close one's eyes out of sheer intensity. Something is, of necessity, eradicated, in one's apprehension of – disaster, say. Absolute vigil does not, cannot, exist. The senses cannot abide such demand.[23]

What continues to percolate for me is this idea of endless inscription as opacity veering toward obscurity, and of the obscurity of translation as being somehow tied to the notion of endless inscription and time, time that captures the dictates of different languages' grammars, their histories, the calamities of nature and civilization; I mean time and translation as a form of sapience; I mean translation as the widened aperture where every word and gesture has the potential to sink into "a blackness both opaque and nameless,"[24] "a feeling of both menace and tenderness"[25]; I mean translation and the way it unfinishes what was already finished,[26] like the prolonged development processes that Nathanaël writes about, the kind that reveals "the ostensibly endless *latent* images contained in a single frame of film."[27]

The wager of translation might very well be to harness or balance "the intricate detail" so as not to produce "a solid, impenetrable mesh of opacity" where "everything is inscribed and nothing is legible."[28] Yet that is exactly what the translator encounters, for before the translation is deemed "legible" in relation to its original, before the translation "supports" the original, props it up, gives it another life in a new language, the translator grapples with moments of opacity, grapples with the unapprehended relation of things: that "foreknowledge which is so calamitous," between the knowledge of the original and what enters or seeps into the words of its translation[29]; that moment when the word stops itself, to echo Carson again.[30] And to stop from toppling over into obscurity, the translated work thinks its way across *the snag* that discomforts the exercise, creates an alternative archive by way of the translator's reading of the text and the ability to write that reading in another language.

A THEORY OF SNAGS

For a theory of snags, we need to start with the poet, translator, and language activist Jen Hofer, who asserts:

> Translation stops me in my tracks. I might be going along (or in the case of how life feels lately, hurtling along) *como si nada* and then a word or phrase or image suddenly falters me, stumbling in my path, it's my body looming, an obstacle or blockage or snag or vortex that stops time and distends *como si nadara en un agua espesa y borrosa*. A bang. Something inserts itself where it does not belong. That's the poem, the snag. The snag is a call to attention, a reminder not to take language – or anything – for granted.[31]

That something that inserts itself where it does not belong, let's call it a stammer, a moment of hesitation.

At the same time, the theory of snags is about more than how to move from immobility to remobilization; it is also about what gets caught up in the run in the first place. Reading the prose writer Renee Gladman, the snag is something akin to a play between holding and beholding. In *Houses of Ravicka*, her third in a series of novels about the eponymous city (after *Event Factory* in 2010 and *The Ravickians* in 2011), the Comptroller, whose job it is to measure the subtle shifts and movements of buildings over time in order to create a geoscography, realizes that the location of one of the houses, no. 96, is a mystery. In the novel, each house has a counterpart existing in another part of the city. For example, house no. 32, which is situated in an area called cit Mohaly, is supposed to be house no. 96's counterpart, but where is no. 96? If no. 32 is situatable, shouldn't no. 96 be as well? The novel is largely about seeing beyond what the eyes can see: "No, perhaps I should begin by saying what it means to see or how measurements occur in time, because first you have to let go of the notion that sights enter the eyes, or merely the eyes."[32] The measurements occurring in time are, in large part, a way of accounting for the shifting buildings and their invisible structures, which are their temporal-spatial relations because, after all, they do more than occupy that space: they define it. But they are also the coordinates of the fleeting meeting place between the relations of one building to another, the beingness occurring in space and time, the movement and sedimentation of things and events across narrative, the relation of narrative across poetic time, and so on. Perhaps you are already hearing what I eventually hope we can hear together: that some of the most prevalent preoccupations embedded in the novel's drives and questions can be read quite unmetaphorically as preoccupations related to translation. And if you do not yet hear the music as clear, do not fret. The cadence shall insinuate itself through a slow method of accretion.

In her essay collection *Calamities*, Gladman often re-examines the aforementioned relationships, between the movement and sedimentation of a thought process to narrative and poetic time, and frames that uncertain relationship around a set of questions, such as this one: "Was it possible to say something was gathering outside of a thing with the intention of meeting something else when this something else was the larger space in which that first thing existed?"[33] While houses have subjectivity in *Houses of Ravicka* – the same as humans or similarly to humans – time, topographies, feelings, and events also convulse simultaneously through language.[34] But how do you account for this in a visual way? And in a simultaneous way? As Gladman herself notes in another essay, "there continues to be a suggestion that we are somehow surrounded by *other* spaces in which exciting, ungraspable things occur."[35] But how do you mark the relations between these other spaces?

I keep returning to Gladman because her thinking about her prose work helps me think about translation. I mean translation as that something, let's call it a practice or an artifact, that gathers outside of something else, something that is common to both, even though what they share is not properly theirs. I am thinking, too, of the way Erín Moure, in the afterword to her Galician-to-English translation of Lupe Gómez's poetry collection *Camouflage* (*Camuflaxe* in Galician), writes about the avant-garde as a recognition of a poverty – povera – that is an avant-garde for it is both social and ecological, takes only what it needs, accumulates not cash but community. It allows a deploying of language that both condenses like black holes – which show us that the universe is other than us and (im)possibly plural – and refracts like mirrors – which show us we are here.[36]

Moure's definition of the avant-garde is useful to this chapter's project in that she uses the work of Italian philosopher Giorgio Agamben to frame the poverty of the avant-garde, much like how I wish to frame translation in this essay as a "common use" that cannot be owned.[37] "This is not the poverty of humans deprived by the movement of Capital and its values of the very basics of food, education, housing, safety," she writes; instead of being measurable by wealth through accumulation, it is rather what we all own together.[38]

Of note, too, is the appearance of the notion of "obscurity" in the first sentence of her essay, where she writes that "camouflage is a hidden text that obscures nothing."[39] To my ears, Moure's "obscurity" here rhymes with Gladman's "*other* spaces in which exciting, ungraspable things occur" in the sense that if camouflage is the hidden text that obscures nothing, it also meets translation's wager to harness or balance the intricate details (of the original) without producing an obscure correlative (text) where, as we read through Nathanaël, "everything is inscribed and nothing is legible."

In Gladman's novel, the desire to amplify the camouflaged, the visible and invisible structures and customs, whether physical or conceptual, that we adopt and encounter in everyday life and that we, in many ways, naturalize or metabolize as habit, leads to a narrative that relies heavily on abstraction, on the black holes and mirrors that Moure writes about, and that must work their way out of that abstraction as a philosophical problem. The convulsion and simultaneity of time, topography, feelings, and events as they course through language are well captured in a sentence like the following, taken from the last section of *Houses of Ravicka*: "They were phantom structures built on top of and in between ... what would you call them? *Real* structures, *concrete* structures?"[40] You can see how the notion of structure here appeals to my study and the way I've attempted to frame translation as itself a thinking structure, or as "the arrangement and organization of mutually connected and dependent elements in a system or construct."[41]

Interestingly, but not surprisingly, Kate Briggs describes the translator in similar terms. In the style of a dictionary entry, she writes, "the translator: writer of new sentences on the close basis of others, producer of relations."[42] What I like about Gladman's treatment of buildings and structures in *Houses of Ravicka*, which closely resembles Briggs's treatment of the figure of the translator as a producer of relations, is the relationship her book magnifies between structures as built things and their mineral or geological parentage, which grants the whole picture an ecology or deep history. In that sense, *Houses of Ravicka* has much to teach us about structures, especially in terms of "the existing arrangement and mutual relation of the constituent parts of a material object, esp. as determining its distinctive nature or character,"[43] which we might think of in terms of the minerality of translation: the sedimentary quality of language that becomes in Ortega y Gasset's estimation, as we have seen, ever more exposed through translation poetics, but also through its qualities of disintegration, which understand the register of Gladman's structures' geoscography. Furthermore, *Houses of Ravicka* invites us to ask: how can we think about translation as relating to the structure or morphology of an organism, its shape and form? Better yet, how can we think of translation as an organism? To complicate things further, I might suggest that when we think about translation, we encounter it from the perspective of something already in movement, as something taking form, a new form perhaps, something that quite possibly has already occurred (commonly thought of as stepping over a line or a border, a context), or else as a possibility – the possibility of movement, of taking form or flight.

To return to *Houses of Ravicka*, the possibility of movement, between visible or invisible structures, aspires to a precarious form of apprehension: "we were all neighboring each other's crossings and each other's sightings of translucent, burgeoning structures, but each making a house out of that moment of seeing. I'm saying perhaps it was our moments of seeing that were the invisible structures in the first place."[44] Translation's resting face here is poetry, only not in the literary sense but in the sense of the poetic. Translation poetics also pertain to history: not translation in relation to history, but translation *as* history, as record keeper. Translation as storyteller, as the history of variation in form. That's what part of this book is about. About trying to understand, to open a portal into, what happens when things – time, feelings, events, and so on – pass through language, whether they are "real" structures or "concrete" structures, and what gets carried over and what gets left in the wake, what "suddenly falters us," stumbles in our path, to echo Hofer's version of the snag of translation. "It's a slippery movement, an open jaw, a stammer or wince whose sound is heard (mistakenly) as clear" to borrow too from Erín Moure in yet another striking essay.[45]

Although it would not seem at the outset that Gladman's novel involves translation, it is very much a novel in which one can extrapolate a lot *about* translation, especially translation as a call to attention. Like this book, the novel wonders what "acts upon itself in translation" (Nathanaël, *Je Nathanaël*). Here is Gladman again:

> I do not translate. I don't really know what it's like. But I also know of no other word which functions so brilliantly as a metaphor for everything I've said so far. At the core of my work is the question of the original – the event before it becomes memory, trying to locate oneself in the present, in language, which is always slightly behind the present. At the core of my reading, the majority of which is work in translation (from languages all over the world) is that same question of the original. I am captivated by the beauty of the problems of translation and find that these problems transfer easily to those of experience and language – how to construct a bridge between them, how the story of our experience changes once it enters language.[46]

Following Hofer's poignant image of the snag, as a force that stops us in our tracks and forces us to take note, this call to attention is like a sudden apparition or refraction that resists absorption, destruction, camouflage, invisibility. The snag does not course across the line or the sentence, it does not give it more fluidity, as we might assume translation might, yet it is not rigidity either. When Hofer or Gladman suggest that the snag stops them in their tracks, I think they mean something like, the snag reactivates something in language, in their process of thinking and reading and translating (whether on the page or in everyday life), such that the course of a line or a sentence refracts that call to attention and appeal to consciousness. Paradoxically, although the snag, as catch or obstacle, would seem foreign to the thing, it is actually integral, vital even; rather, it acts as a kind of maternal source. It decants, breathes new life and possibility into it, even as it carries within it a rather destructive impulse: "a foreknowledge which is so calamitous."[47]

THE RUN

It is interesting to think that, in translation, something temporarily gets immobilized (the snag) only to get remobilized. In terms of this remobilization, I want to add, to the jumbled thinking taking place here, the idea of the run. We could add to the mix here Roland Barthes and his image of the "stoppeuse." Briggs is useful here. In *This Little Art*, she recounts how, whether translating or writing, the difficulty of weighing different choices in the process of putting a text together will eventually have to be met with a decision, and with that decision and the sequence of decisions that will follow, comes the matter of "setting down language." Barthes, she writes,

> offers another image of feminized labour, but not the dressmaker this time, instead: the novel-writer as *stoppeuse*. In a lecture delivered on 2 February 1980, he says: when I was a child, I would see around me – it's a very familiar image from my childhood, especially since I had a childhood surrounded by women, my grandmother, my aunt, my mother – women obsessed with the risk of getting a hole in their stockings, stockings that were knitted (there was no nylon at that time), I don't know how stockings are made nowadays but at that time ... the hole would suddenly make a ladder down the stocking and I can still see the gesture, a bit familiar, a bit trivial, but necessary, whereby a woman would wet a finger in her mouth and apply it to the weave, cementing it with saliva, and in this way she would stop it.[48]

Even though I don't think we have to resort to Barthes in order to continue to access the idea of something being stopped in its tracks and the way we might work through it, I like the image of the snag here because the tear in the stocking runs amok rather than remaining immobile, lifeless.

But let's suppose something much more calamitous, like the idea that the run does not stop, not even with the benevolent wet finger or the ever-convenient practicality of a stitch. We might then also consider that the snag might outrun our efforts to tame or contain it, let alone understand it. And in that case, we need to also be able to think beyond it, and beyond death, even despite the challenge and impossibility this presents. There is a very interesting passage by Moure in an essay on translation, time, and Maurice Blanchot that illustrates well what I mean: "Translation, yes, always makes a present of a past, it is a present text in the presence of a text that has already ceased being written. It is the thinking beyond death that Blanchot says is impossible. Translation, perhaps, is its only possibility."[49] If translation is one possibility of running the course and outrunning what stops us in our tracks, of working perhaps beyond the logic of the snag, then in its outrunning, and in its thinking beyond death, translation is, perhaps, also a way of writing beyond the vanishing point and into the next composition or set of lines or divergent point of view, or, as Moure says, as a present text in the presence of a text that has already ceased being written.

Anne Carson makes a remark that is similar to Moure's reading of Blanchot, only she does so in relation to Homer's *Odyssey*. In the essay I alluded to earlier, "Nay Rather," Carson is interested in the untranslatable as a word that goes silent in transit, which I imagine as a kind of radical vanishing point.[50] The example she provides is from the fifth book of the *Odyssey*, but there are several instances in his poem where there are allusions to "a language apparently known only to gods."[51] Homer recounts how Hermes gave Odysseus a flower, "at the root it was black but like milk was the flower," a flower (*mōlu*) impossible to dig up unless you are a god.[52] Homer does not translate the word. They are four letters of the alphabet, Carson goes on to explain, "you cannot define, possess, or make use of them ... the plant is sacred, the knowledge belongs to gods, the word stops itself."[53] What distinguishes humans from gods is their immortality: they know how not to die.[54] What Carson presents is a way of thinking beyond the vanishing point, the point beyond which the eye can see, or the point beyond which the ears can hear, the one which we can assume is across the horizon, or at some distance from it. As Ortega y Gasset reminds us, translation bears precisely what cannot be said in the language in which one is translating or reading.

If it is helpful, we might consider another snippet from Moure's essay; one where she translates a passage by Blanchot on time:

> Time, time: the not-afterlife and its *step further yet* that can't be carried out inside time may lead outside time, without this outside being timeless. Rather, it is that place where time might tumble, stumble fragile, in keeping with the "outside-time in time" towards which writing would pull us, if we were allowed (vanished from "us") to write beneath the seal of ancient fear.[55]

This quote by Blanchot, and Moure's translation of it, together make me think of the way we might arrive at translation, or a poetics of translation, through Gladman's ruminations on narrative as that "something [that] was gathering outside of a thing with the intention of meeting something else when this something else was the larger space in which that first thing existed."[56] Translation, I believe, can offer that rich space of correspondence and misalignment in the intervals Gladman refers to. It is there that we "might tumble, stumble fragile" trying to put the complex shape of the interiority of one work into another. A note here before we proceed: Blanchot's (like Gladman's) "outside-time in time" is not timeless but preparatory, in the same way that thinking itself might be considered as preparatory, as incomplete, groundless, susceptible to freefall but also to intervals and rich spaces of correspondence, "dividing a singular moment into a series of discrete spaces."[57] Here, we are truly on the terrain of translation as thinking structure, a structure that houses possibilities for the uncertain, for a series of discrete spaces we might call the present of the book to come.

THE VIBRATING PRESENT AND *THE BOOK TO COME*

Thinking is a task. To paraphrase Rodolphe Gasché and his *The Honor of Thinking*, it is a task because it is preparatory – by which he means not of a founding character, and not an arrested form.[58] In those terms, the work or task or responsibility of thinking can be neither practical nor theoretical.[59] Thinking is something much wilder, riskier even. To me, this is also the task of translation, to find its way along the contours of the possibility of the uncertain. It is, to borrow a phrase from Benjamin from another context, the "caesura in the movement of thought," and I would add that, in those terms, it is the poetry of thought still to come.[60] And with this idea of translation as the caesura or breath line of thought, I want to proceed by invoking a text that is not overtly named in the previous chapters of this book, but that would serve as a magnificent interlocutor with the work, and that would frame or bookend its beginnings and endings in a way that is similar to the generative grammatical operations of the future anterior as it overruns the present without quite stopping at a future.

The fault of the future anterior is not in its overreach but in how it remains unfulfilled. Ever at the heels of its promise (or premise) to arrive when it has not yet properly departed, that fault, which I described in an unfulfilling way – not because it fails but because it does not end – is also a gesture that motions towards an opening: a gesture open to an encounter that radiates outward (translation's relationship to alternative relations to time would be one such example, but there are others).

From a readerly perspective, this radiant gesture is – at one time or another – a word or neologism plucked from the sinews of the sentence. Other times, it is a whole book decanted. Decanted by time (and its temporal coordinates), siphoned (cyphe(r)ned) by the process of reading, or poured through the lipped beaker of translation, from one mouth to another. Throughout this book, I have argued that this opening can be read through the poetics of translation, and more specifically that it can be read through the prism of translation as episteme. But if translation is to be considered a thinking structure, we must ask what it makes thinkable. Maurice Blanchot's *The Book to Come*, a book that opens with the sirens' song, is surprisingly useful in this regard:

> The Sirens: it seems they did indeed sing, but in an unfulfilling way, one that only gave a sign of where the real sources and real happiness of song opened. Still, by means of their imperfect songs that were only a song still to come, they did lead the sailor toward that space where singing might truly begin.[61]

The sirens' song reaches Ulysses and his sailors, whose ears have been sealed with wax. So, unlike the enchantment-leading-to-disappearance undergone by past sailors – and because Ulysses himself has been bound to the ship's mast – he survives the enchantment of the song, a song whose impossible afterlife circulates in the tales told in Homer's *The Odyssey*, where it can safely be heard. This is a heroic feat indeed, for – to echo Blanchot once more – the sirens' song is a song of the abyss that, once heard, opens an abyss in each word and beckons those who hear it to vanish into it.[62]

I am trying, over and over again, I am in the process of rehearsing, of getting the right steps to line up so as to understand something, glimpse something, about "an abyss in each word." In writing about Moure and Pato, I encountered the lure of falling, which had something to do with the love of poetry and Moure's felt relations with Pato's poetry in particular. Proximally, I also encountered Avital Ronell and her notion of an upward fall, which she describes as an ecstatic encounter not unlike Moure's account of finding Pato's poetry. In the case of Pessoa, he made himself into that abyss, multiple times over even, each time becoming his writing. But if we recall, *The Obituary* paints this abyss in quite different terms. The abyss in each word is death – not death *by* omission, but death *as* omission. In Nathanaël, the abyss in each word led to our thinking about friable boundaries, proximities, and loss of intelligibility. In Renee Gladman's *Houses of Ravicka* we encounter the problem of narrative as also a problem of translation, which to unravel requires a special kind of attention to the stutters and possibilities of poetic time.

This reading of narrative as an impossible song, as the afterlife of the song, could also be read in relation to translation. In other words, the previous chapters' emphasis on encounter, on temporal ruptures, on how narrative is an encounter with a present that opens onto "infinite movement" would all serve as prolific examples of how translation might also be understood under the guise of "an imperfect song still to come."[63] In this book, and in this chapter especially, I take "the imperfect song of translation," imperfect because of its deeply poetic nature, as both a theoretical and a philosophical undertaking (problem, task, duty, responsibility).

This encounter, between translation and poetry, is thematized as a shared relationship with both forms' ability to think and create within the interstices of various gaps and aporias. Indeed, in the opening pages of my introduction, my interest and investment in the poetic and epistemological possibilities of translation are clear. Translation becomes a way of giving a sign – of motioning towards the inexpressible, the inappropriable – of giving body to an idea or an image, a set of universal or particular claims – that (to borrow from Blanchot) when approached we can do nothing but come near to it.[64] I find it potent, even beautiful, to think that translation measures a trace or an absence, yet translation is more than a limit or a means of navigation. It is the possibility of travelling this distance, "of making the song into the movement toward the song, and of making this movement the expression of the greatest desire."[65] Yet little of this tells us what, exactly, translation narrates – if it does indeed narrate – although misalignments, poetic appointments, relations, and coincidences all seem part of it.

NICOLE BROSSARD:
NIGHT SINKING INTO NIGHT

Wondering about what translation might narrate or make possible, I want to bring Nakayasu's *Say Translation*, which opened this chapter, here again: "[...] say instead of book into translated book, say book into alternative structures of literature via translation, alternative structures of literature via translation."[66] There's a book on my desk that's helpful for thinking about "alternative structures of literature via translation," and about the *poesis* and *poetics* of translation as possibility and as limit. At least it helps me. The book is called *Fences in Breathing*, and it is by Nicole Brossard. As I mentioned in this chapter's introduction, it is a novel about a writer who suddenly needs to write in a language other than her own in order "to dive into the landscape of a temporary world where meaning parts meaning as [she, the protagonist,] move[s] through it."[67] It is a work largely interested in time: time in relation to the sentence, to translation, and to fiction. It is also a book about calamities, "the violence of the noise of civilisation."[68] In that sense, the novel is a brilliant companion piece to Renee Gladman's *Calamities*, a book of essays where she, like Brossard's *Fences in Breathing*, is fascinated by the attempt of putting one's thinking into language, into sentences, into the act of writing.

In the context of translation, the preoccupation is further complexified by the translator doing her best to put as much of the source material into the target text's thinking, there where the thinking in the source text might seep into the present of the translation:

> "Literature does not say that it knows something, but that it knows of something, that it knows about something" [...] The consequence of this *of*, of this *about* – what Barthes also calls literature's "precious indirection" – are that in addition to what is already known, literature can also tell us of what is not yet known, it can gesture toward further, *possible*, areas of knowledge, to what is unsuspected, unidentified, unknown.[69]

Translation is entangled in these alternate lines, these lines in movement, in many more ways than one: in the act of reading, in the act of translating, and in the translation that ensues. All these gestures, the pull of the sentences, these forms of "close action," allow for a kind of mutuality that has the potential to open onto something new.⁷⁰ To unpack this idea, here is Kate Briggs again:

> Here I am, writes Valéry, at my desk, with a famous book, set in its millennial fame. And here I am *arguing* with it.
>
> Arguing with it as freely as if it were a poem of my own on the table before me.
>
> In the process of translating it, the set book – once fixed in its fame, *these* necessary words in *this* necessary order – starts to unsettle. The immobile poem gets sort of remobilized [in translation]; each of its necessary lines looking now like a sequence of decisions, or indeed of accidents, made by a writing subject engaged in a similar kind of activity. Interestingly, this sensation of the poet at work, with its levelling effect – the labour of two writers at their desks, writing at very different times, in different ways (the one writing something on the close basis of what the other once produced) but both *writing* nevertheless – opens out onto a new boldness.⁷¹

This new boldness, this relationship of proximity you could say, constitutes small archives of translation as duration, as living in the present. Proximity, the narrator of Brossard's novel reminds us, remains difficult to comprehend. It's true that in *Fences in Breathing*, the narrator is not working on a translation in the strictest sense, at least not in the same way that Briggs invokes Valéry. But that does not preclude Brossard's protagonist from relating similar sensations and thought processes in relation to her own work in a foreign tongue: "Who am I becoming in the other tongue? Who translates what in the alternating patterns of words' shadow and desire's infinite renewal?"⁷² We could rest here a while to consider, too, the legions of self-translators who might also confirm that they too have felt the levelling effect Briggs describes or the interstices captured in the passage by Brossard. What interests me here, however, is the buoy and buoyancy of translation as two sentences that must reconcile expression and desire, silence and fullness, "making the song into the movement toward the song, and of making this movement the expression of the greatest desire," to return to that previously quoted passage from Blanchot's *The Book to Come*.⁷³

In Brossard's novel, translation's apprehensive quality resides in the calamitous potential of "two sentences touch[ing] in a single spot, resulting in a single syllable. Night ... it was a known fact: they were two sentences made to prevent the night from sinking into night. Two sentences sweeping the dark like emergency lights.[74] I see affinities here with Nathanaël's assertion of translation's foreknowledge, the way it anticipates itself. I also hear a bit of Ortega y Gasset's splendour of translation, not to mention Benjamin's dialectical image, in the illuminating quality Brossard grants to translation. But what is the night a metaphor for here? For calamities? Mundanity? Would the night simply be the night, without the vanguard of poetry? What kind of abyssal disparagement is safeguarded by the "emergency lights" resulting from the touch, collision, and meeting place of two sentences? And spoken by whom? Here are two sentences that cast a net where there is otherwise only freefall. Sentences that, in their meeting point, act as a snag. *There* where the sentence stops itself. Outrunning death even as it anticipates calamity. Is this freefall at all like the drive of translation? Its groundlessness? Its possibility of outrunning death?

In interestingly similar terms, Anne Carson recounts, in writing about the untranslatable in relation to Joan of Arc, how Joan never insisted that the voices that came to her had bodies or faces. When Joan's inquisitors asked her whether it was a single voice or many, she retorted, "The light comes in the name of the voice."[75] The sentence, Carson points out, stops itself.[76] "Its components are simple yet it stays foreign, we cannot own it."[77] In Brossard's calamitous image of night almost sinking into night, I wonder if there is not something too of Francis Bacon's "brutality of fact," which is yet another example Carson provides in her essay for those frayed moments of untranslatability. By "fact," Carson points out, Bacon implies "a sensible form that will translate directly to your nervous system."[78] According to Carson, the brutality of fact is the limit that leads to silence. "To grant sensation without the boredom of conveyance" is another terrific way Carson describes it.[79] One important differentiation, between Brossard and Bacon or Gladman and Bacon, is the painter's extinguishing of narrative whereas the writer, whether Brossard or Gladman, expounds or extols it. "Destroying clarity with clarity," to quote Bacon through Carson, "he wants to make us see something we don't yet have eyes for, to hear something that was never sounded. He goes inside clarity to a place of deeper refreshment, where clarity is the same and yet differs from itself, which may be analogous to the place inside a word where it falls silent in its own presence."[80] The idiom here is significant: either the word or clarity *falls*, or both. Also significant to note is the way we could use Carson's reading of Bacon's brutality of fact as a way of thinking of translation, as that which makes us see (or capable of reading/seeing) that which we cannot read, and as a form of clarity that does not have to be clarifying, in the same way that argument or explanation or description might be. Furthermore, it suggests that in its place of deeper refreshment, the groundlessness of translation doesn't function through reason. Once again, I hear Ortega y Gasset here and his insistence that translation carries what cannot be said in the language one is translating into. The original words and sentences may go silent in transit, but the new words continue to know of something in addition to what is already known. We might also think of Gladman, Brossard, Moure, and Blanchot in the way Carson describes how *clarity is the same yet differs from itself*, as that place inside a word where it *falls* silent in its own presence, which sounds a lot like Gladman's "something [that] was gathering outside of a thing with the intention of meeting something else when this something else was the larger space in which that first thing existed?"[81] and Moure's Blanchot's, "time may lead outside time, without this outside being timeless."[82] Listening again, we might also hear echoes of Shelley's "before unapprehended relation of things [that] perpetuates their apprehension."

I want to return to the simultaneity of Brossard's two sentences as safeguard against some abyssal plunge into obscurity, or in other words into the complete unknown, to be outside without the faith of the consistency of an inside where things, two sentences, move towards and in relation to each other. Elisabeth Grosz, in a book about architecture and space, writes about the relationship between such an inside and outside. "The outside is a peculiar place, both paradoxical and perverse. It is paradoxical insofar as it can only ever make sense, have a place, in reference to what it is not and can never be – an inside, a within, an interior."[83] While Grosz goes on to frame this outside and its comparability to two disciplines and enterprises – in her case architecture and philosophy– as fundamentally outside of each other and how they require a third space or position in which to interact, a space or position outside both, I think the same thought experiment can apply to translation. "To see what cannot be from the inside," she continues, "to see what cannot be seen is to be unable to experience this inside in its own terms. Something is lost – the immediate intimacy of an inside position; and something is gained – the ability to critically evaluate that position and to possibly compare it with others."[84] Submitting Brossard's two sentences that touched in a single spot to a third term, as Grosz suggests, rather than to one or the other's internal exigencies and constraints, and to a position that is outside of both, we find that they can be explored beside each other "as equivalent and interconnected discourses and practices."[85] This provides an enticing way of thinking about Gladman's ruminations on narrative, her neologism "simultenates," and Ortega y Gasset's account of translation as the ability to see what cannot be seen from the inside, to say nothing of how this challenges what we might think of as translation's harbouring of equivalences. We might also think about Nathanaël's poignant reading of translation's disintegrative states via an understanding of photographic overexposures.

CONCLUSION:
THE ECOLOGY OF THE SENTENCE

It is said that the German poet, philosopher, and translator Friedrich Hölderlin reworked his translation of Sophocles and his own writing with the ecstatic obsession that they were not, as Anne Carson puts it, "living or lively enough."[86] The liveliness and livingness of a poem preoccupied him immensely. Brossard's emergency lights and Gladman's beholding are, in that sense, Hölderlininan. There's a sense that the image, rather than the argument and rather than explanatory/expository prose, will touch (at) the thing, object or subject (beauty) in question like a ray of light. Working from a poetic register leaves the text open and just enigmatic enough that it sparks something in the reader who encounters it: joy, bafflement, awe. Brossard's protagonist, let us remember, is in the process of translating herself and her thoughts:

> The matters of the other language and of non-sense swirl through the air though I strive to put certain words in parallel I'm unable to make them touch in the right place sometimes a vagueness a slight gap sweeps the sentence away all at once and everything needs doing all over again I'm afraid to run out of words the same way one fears shortages of water gas or food I don't know how to make use of myself in the foreign language I struggle with this and the contour of mountains the pain is more mysterious than ever when I gaze at fields of sunflowers and reeds.[87]

The passage reminds me a great deal of a moment in Gladman's *Calamities*:

> I began the day wanting these essays to do more than they were currently doing and even had a book alongside that I thought would help me, but it turned out I wanted more from this book as well. It was hard to be a book about engineering in architecture when an essayist wanted you to be a book about structures in fiction.[88]

Gladman's collection of essays, *Calamities*, in fact, explores this principle in full. How can a sentence be about one thing while simultaneously being about something else? How can a book about fiction also be a book about architecture? How can writing also be drawing, and so on? In the Brossard and Gladman passages, there is the sense that the thing that is trying to be reached is elusive. The elusivity of it (if I may bend the term) creates in language a space for thinking. Both writing subjects exist in the sentence as a thinking process. There's something both literary and ecological about it. In yet another essay, Gladman writes: "I'm captivated by [...] how the story of our experience changes once it enters language."[89] There is tension between the "existing world" and the forthcoming world, which is the world of fiction, of literature, of translation.

Brossard's and Gladman's prose works explore the ecology of the sentence and how sentences bend time. In Brossard, the sentence is, for example, thought of as what plunges into the present and the unknown, suspending time.[90] These are "sentences that did things in grammar and in the wind."[91] There's a common experience, a kind of universality that recalls Moure's retention of the concept of the avant-garde through Agamben's *povera*, in the fact that language encapsulates but never fully owns anything. It continues to live, to simultenate (us, perhaps as we simultenate it). In the previous passage, Brossard points to an experience that is larger than the ineffable, which she so poignantly articulates as the point beyond words, "a moistness of life in its slightest splitting of sap and saliva, there where the mouth, caressing the dream's fine fabric, ventures all the way to the source."[92] It surprises and enthrals me a little to encounter, very explicitly, Barthes's *stoppeuse* and Hofer's snag in the previous passage by Brossard. The point beyond words, the recourse to the image of saliva, the fine fabric and the source where the sentence becomes a space for living: "How else might one divest oneself of one's I?" asks Nathanaël.[93]

There's a lot here, I know. And I am aware that I have presented an ensemble of possibilities in this chapter for thinking about and through translation poetics rather than a straight line through my subject and object of inquiry. The frays are as deliberate as they are rhythmic. Accretion has always been my preferred thought structure, after all. Hopefully, the moving parts presented here can continue to coalesce and morph in my reader's mind. As an experiment in living in the present, I admit that translation is both what brings me punctually into my thinking body and what brings me outward, reaching alongside many, many tentacular possibilities and constellations of text, to some version of the present. This chapter is written in praise and gratitude for the relationships forged through a thinking alongside, an alongside that, I suppose, I hope I never stop not translating.

Notes

INTRODUCTION

1. The relationship I define between translation and poetry parallels the one Avital Ronell thematizes between poetry and thought in the opening pages of her essay "On the Misery of Theory Without Poetry" (18).
2. Hejinian, *The Language of Inquiry*, 2.
3. Ibid.
4. Stephens [Nathanaël], *At Alberta*, 16.
5. Judith Balso's *Affirmation of Poetry*, a book that explores the nexus between poetry and thought or poetry as thinking, is a gem in this regard. The same can be said about Alain Badiou's *Handbook of Inaesthetics*, which I refer to in chapter 2.
6. Gladman, *Houses of Ravicka*, 123.
7. By "open" I have in mind Lyn Hejinian's account of the difference between an open and a closed text:

    We can say that a "closed text" is one in which all the elements of the work are directed toward a single reading of it. Each element confirms that reading and delivers the text from any lurking ambiguity. In the "open text," meanwhile, all the elements of the work are maximally excited; here it is because ideas and things exceed (without deserting) argument that they have taken into the dimension of the work. (*The Language of Inquiry* 43)

    In short, the open text invites the reader's active participation in the construction of meaning within the text; it simultaneously rejects the authority of hierarchies (those of the writer and those implicit in other structures as well – social, economic, cultural) and privileges the process of composition, either by the writer or future readers, over the product (43).

8 In German, *Die Aufgabe des Übersetzers*. All citations are taken from Steven Rendall's translation of Benjamin, "The Translator's Task." See also Harry Zohn's English translation of Benjamin, "The Task of the Translator," originally published in 1968 and revised in 1982.
9 Benjamin, "The Task of the Translator," 70.
10 Benjamin, "The Translator's Task," 152.
11 Other parallels, beyond the one proposed by Benjamin, are possible here as well, namely models of translation that fall in at least two categories: the instrumental and the hermeneutic. The instrumental model treats translation on the basis of communication and the transfer of meaning from one language to another. The hermeneutic model approaches translation as an interpretation that is mediated by social and cultural determinants (see Lawrence Venuti's "Introduction" to *Translation Studies Reader*). Different models will, of course, engender different translating strategies. Certain assumptions about language and textuality also give way to different understandings of the limits of translation. For some, translation is utopian in the sense that while it is necessary, it is also an impossible task. For others, translation is a question of utility: the diversity of languages logically requires it. (See Paul Ricoeur, "The Paradigm of Translation.")
12 Benjamin, "The Translator's Task," trans. Rendall, 152. In contrast, "The Translator's Task," trans. Zohn, includes the adjectives "unfathomable," "mysterious," and "poetic" (70).
13 Benjamin, "The Translator's Task," trans. Rendall, 152.
14 Ibid., 154.
15 Ibid., 152.
16 It is the musicality of the following passage by Erín Moure, from an essay on translation, poetics, and affect, that I choose to echo here when I write "something more or extra that lurches forward beyond words." In "Translation and Its Affective Challenges," Moure writes that "translation's affective challenge (and joy) then *is* this traversal, this seeding of a place *beyond* the text, where two texts shimmer and something *more* or *else* coalesces" (italics in original).
17 I have Benjamin's dialectical image in mind here, especially as it is articulated in a well-known passage from *The Arcades Project* (*Das Passagen-Werk* in German):
> To thinking belongs the movement as well as the arrest of thoughts. Where thinking comes to a standstill in a constellation saturated with tensions – there the dialectical image appears. It is the caesura in the movement of thought. Its position is naturally not an arbitrary one. It

is to be found, in a word, where the tension between dialectical opposites is greatest. Hence, the object constructed in the materialist presentation of history is itself the dialectical image. The latter is identical with the historical object; it justifies its violent expulsion from the continuum of historical process. (N10a, 3, 475)

18 de Man, *The Resistance to Theory*, 15.
19 I rehearsed this idea elsewhere, in an essay I wrote in 2016 on Daniel Canty's travel narrative *Les États-Unis du Vent*, titled "Stimulants, Influences, Narcotic Effects," which can be found at http://towncrier.puritan-magazine.com/reviews/etats-unis.
20 Elsewhere, in an entirely separate topography of circulation, Jeanette Winterson suggests that this kind of intoxicating quality of language is one where "you can slide into it … but you can't slide over it. The language is not about conveying information; it is about conveying meaning" (*Nightwood*, x).
21 For Antoine Berman, the mutual transformation of the original and its translation are framed within "the mediation of what is foreign." In *The Experience of the Foreign* he writes:
> The very aim of translation – to open up in writing a certain relation with the Other, to fertilize what is one's own through the mediation of what is foreign – is diametrically opposed to the ethnocentric structure of every culture, that species of narcissism by which every society wants to be a pure and unadulterated whole […] The essence of translation is to be an opening, a dialogue, a cross-breeding, a decentering. Translation is "a putting in touch with," or it is nothing. (4)

22 Avital Ronell, in "On the Misery of Theory without Poetry," refers to this space of enunciative overlap as "a trace of a relation to an ungraspable alterity" (18).
23 Benjamin, *The Arcades Project*, "Awakening" (N2a, 3, 462).
24 I am indebted to Erín Moure's English translation of Chus Pato's inaugural speech upon her investiture into the Royal Galician Academy on 23 September 2017. Her address, *Baixo o límite* (in English, titled *At the Limit*), treats several philosophical aspects of poetry – most notably its ability to speak beyond words and to make the unknown known in the tremor of the space of the caesura. After a brief section on the tension in Walter Benjamin's dialectical image, she writes:
> The poem provides a union of opposites, of counterposed materials not meant to be joined in synthesis, but which, in their detention, their caesura, allow a contemporaneity of language to be written that moves thinking into a space beyond argumentation, via the incalcula-

ble entity that is metaphor [...] As such, the poem does not advance from argument to argument, but exposes itself from threshold to threshold, from sill to sill. (34–5)

This little gem of a book arrived on my desk just as I was finishing the first draft of this book. While Pato's thinking – and Moure's translation of it – ghosts my own in the passage I bookmark with this note, and while it has helped me hone my thinking into a critical-poetical vocabulary that links poetry to translation and vice versa, I am equally grateful to both poets' work and thinking on the enunciative and epistemological possibilities of poetry, for they have allowed this work to perform leaps that would have taken me much longer to attempt on my own.

25 Except for the final chapter, the material presented in this book was mostly written before 2018, that is, before Avital Ronell's fall from grace (so to speak). I recognize that my engagement with the philosopher's work throughout these pages may be triggering for some readers.

26 Ronell, "Walking as a Philosophical Act."

27 For her part, Erín Moure calls this form of writing "intranslation" – a neologism she has coined to capture her "echolation-homage" of Chus Pato's work.

28 One might also think of Lyn Hejininan's distinction between a closed and an open text in her essay "The Rejection of Closure." *Inclined writing* relates to her conception of the open text in its embrace of that which exceeds conceptualization and has a quality of open-endedness, whereas a text written on the *decline* is a closed text that "delivers the text without any lurking ambiguity" (*The Language of Inquiry*, 43).

29 Ronell, "Street Talk," 126.

30 Benjamin, "The Translator's Task," trans. Rendall, 153.

31 Ibid., 153.

32 Ronell, "Street Talk," 108.

33 Umberto Eco asks a similar question in *Experiences in Translation*: "When is a translation no longer a translation but something else?" (61). Sherry Simon also quotes this passage from Eco in her chapter on "perverse translations," wondering when it is that a translation goes too far ("Paths of Perversity," 159). Simon's scholarship, particularly her notion of perverse translation, has been foundational for my own work and thinking about translation. While Benjamin and Ronell appear as recurring interlocutors throughout this book, Simon is perhaps the most underrepresented influence and interlocutor, and I would like to make her influence known here.

34 Waldrop, "Irreducible Strangeness," 110.
35 In "On Linguistic Aspects of Translation," Roman Jakobson distinguishes between three ways of interpreting verbal signs: *intralingual translation* uses other signs of the same language and is considered by Jakobson to be a form of "rewording"; *interlingual translation*, or what he calls "translation proper," is an interpretation using another language; and *intersemiotic translation*, which he also refers to as "transmutation," uses non-verbal signs such as a drawing or a painting (127). Jacques Derrida in "Des Tours de Babel" notes an important nuance in relation to Jakobson's models. According to him, Jakobson does not take into account the inherent plurality that accompanies every attempt at translation:
> He supposes that it is not necessary to translate; everyone understands what that means because everyone has experienced it, everyone is expected to know what is a language, the relation of one language to another and especially identity or difference in fact of language. If there is a transparency that Babel would have impaired, this is surely it, the experience of the multiplicity of tongues and the "proper" sense of the word "translation." (173–4)

36 Jakobson, "Linguistic Aspects of Translation," 429.
37 In the prefatory notes to *Insecession*, Moure describes intranslation in the following manner:
> I now recognize a third text alongside the readerly and the writerly: let's call it the intranslatable. The intranslatable is the unreaderly text which catches fire, burns in the mouth, an instance continuously outside any likelihood, whose function – ardently assumed by its scripter – is to contest the mercantile constraints on what is written. This text, guided, armed by a notion of *material*, prompts me to redact the following words: Dear Chus, I can neither read nor write what you produce, but I can *intranslate* it, like a conflagration, a drug, an insecession, an e(ri)nigmatic disorganization. (8, emphasis in original)

38 Moure, *Secession/Insecession*, 8.
39 For a detailed account of how *The Book of Disquiet* changes across time, see Richard Zenith's "Introduction" to his own translation (i.e., the Penguin Edition, 2002).
40 Twerdy, "Notes on the Art of Writing."
41 "Über den Begriff der Geschichte" in German.
42 Scott, *The Obituary*, 39.
43 Gladman, "The Sentence as a Space for Living," 93.
44 Canada Council for the Arts, "Book Publishing Support: Block Grants."
45 Badiou, *Handbook of Inaesthetics*, 36.

46 Ibid.
47 To understand these matters from another angle, it is helpful to remember that earlier in his essay, Benjamin posits that a work's translatability opens on to two questions: the first has to do with finding an adequate translator even though the work itself is not meant for the reader; in other words, a work of art is not aimed at an "ideal" receiver even though it may fall into the hands of a future reader who will claim responsibility for being addressed. The second question Benjamin poses has to do with a work's translatability and whether or not it allows itself to be translated ("The Translator's Task," trans. Rendall, 152). To this question he adds that "the translatability of linguistic constructions would accordingly have to be taken into consideration even if they were untranslatable by human beings" (152). The statement is a bit clearer in Harry Zohn's translation: "the translatability of linguistic creations ought to be considered even if men should prove unable to translate them" ("The Task of the Translator," 70). Thus, it might be that a work's translatability amounts to nothing except the remainder of an indifferent site. In other words, there is no guarantee that translatability will surge forth, for untranslatability is after all one of the effects of translation. In fact, there is the sense that translatability remains elusive and, in many ways, just beyond reach. The reason I am choosing to linger on this quote is that I think it encapsulates well translation's relationship and enmeshment between what a work illustrates and how it illustrates it. Thought another way, translatability springs forth in the undecidable gap between what a work "says" and what it "does."
48 Benjamin, "The Translator's Task," trans. Rendall, 152.
49 Chisholm, "Paris, *Mon Amour*, My Catastrophe," 181.
50 Code, *Ecological Thinking*, 117.
51 Briggs, "Q&A."

CHAPTER ONE

1 At the invitation of Dr Belén Martín-Lucas, an early version of this section, titled "In the altitudes of elation 'we look up and hold the folds of language inside us without any word for wind': at the start of the light we ask, what is *Secession/Insecession*?," appeared in *Canada and Beyond: A Journal of Canadian Literary and Cultural Studies* 6 (2017). Iterations of the research included in this chapter have also appeared in *Traduire / Translating: Intermédialités* 27, edited by Myriam Suchet (2016) under the title "Letters On The Move: Erín Moure and Chus Pato's *Secession/*

Insecession and Nathanaël (Nathalie Stephens)'s *Absence Where As (Claude Cahun and the Unopened Book)*."

2 Moure and Pato, *Secession/Insecession*, n.p.
3 Moure, in conversation with Christina Davis (Pato, Moure, and Davis, "Outside the Fold").
4 Daniel Aguirre-Oteiza makes a similar observation in his essay on the poetics and politics of difference.in *Secession/Insecession* titled "What Politics Where Breath Fractures?: (In)Translation and the Poetics of Difference" (2018).
5 Pato and Moure, *Secession/Insecession*, 158.
6 Ibid.
7 Ibid., 112.
8 Ibid., 123.
9 Ibid., 131.
10 Ibid.
11 Moure and Robichaud, "Geneviève Robichaud in Conversation with Erín Moure."
12 During interviews and public events, it is not uncommon for Moure to exclaim that she has gone to Chus Pato university – a claim also made by Hélène Cixous in relation to Clarice Lispector and her "learning experience 'at the school of Clarice'" (Cixous qtd. in Arrojo, "Interpretation as Possessive Love," 149).
13 Moure, in conversation with Christina Davis (Pato, Moure, and Davis, "Outside the Fold").
14 Pato and Moure, *Secession/Insecession*, 174.
15 Ibid., 175.
16 Ibid., 6.
17 From Aristotle's Eudemian Ethics (VII, 4, 1239 a 35–40), here referenced in Derrida's "Politics of Friendship," 353.
18 In an interview published in 2014, Moure states: "*Insecession* is my biopoetics nestled 'in *Secession*.' They appear 'with' each other because they are friend texts, reverberative" (Moure and Robichaud, "Geneviève Robichaud in Conversation with Erín Moure").
19 Spivak is one glaring exception, one that will be addressed later in this chapter.
20 I am indebted to the following scholarship on the subject of friendship: Jacques Derrida's *Politiques de l'Amitié* (1994) and its English translation by Gabriel Motzin and Michael Syrotinski, with Thomas Keenan, "Politics of Friendship" (1993); Avital Ronell's *Complaint: Grievance Among Friends* (2018); Maurice Blanchot's *L'Amitié* (1971) and its English translation by Elizabeth Rottenberg, *Friendship* (1997); Anne Dewey and Lib-

bie Rifkin's co-edited volume *Among Friends: Engendering the Social Site of Poetry* (2013); Andrew Epstein's *Beautiful Enemies: Friendship and Postwar American Poetry* (2006); and Ginette Michaud's *Juste le Poème, Peut-Être (Derrida, Celan) Suivi de SINGBARER REST: l'Amitié, l'Indeuillable* (2009). Whether explicitly quoted in this chapter or not, these works encouraged me to pursue my line of inquiry regarding translation's relationship to friendship.

21 Venuti, *The Translator's Invisibility*, 1–2.
22 Pato and Moure, *Secession/Insecession*, 162.
23 Ibid., 163.
24 Avital and Diane Davis, "Breaking Down 'Man,'" 377.
25 Ronell, "Walking as a Philosophical Act."
26 Ronell and Davis, "Breaking Down 'Man,'" 377.
27 Ronell with Davis, "Confessions," 243–4.
28 Davis, *ÜberReader*, xxiv.
29 Pato and Moure, *Secession/Insecession*, 160.
30 Ibid., 161–3.
31 Ibid., 159.
32 Ibid., 161.
33 Davis, *ÜberReader*, xxiv.
34 Ronell, "Walking as a Philosophical Act."
35 Ronell and Davis, "Confessions," 244.
36 My transcriptions.
37 I am reminded of Barbara Godard's text, "Women in Letters (Reprise)," in which she writes about dialogical form as a form of collaboration in the feminine, as "never completed and fixed in the words of a single text because it is situated in the (dialogic) space between texts. It is into this space that the reader must project herself, throw herself into the speculative activity of interpretation" (303).
38 Ronell and Davis, "Confessions," 245.
39 Pato and Moure, *Secession/Insecession*, 35.
40 Ibid., 34.
41 Ibid., 32–3.
42 Derrida, "Politics of Friendship," 382.
43 Pato and Moure, *Secession/Insecession*, 159.
44 Ibid., 169.
45 Ibid., 121.
46 Ibid., 158.
47 Aguirre-Oteiza, "What Politics Where Breath Fractures?," 239.
48 Ibid., 237–8.

49 Pato and Moure, *Secession/Insecession*, 174.
50 Ronell and Davis, "Breaking Down 'Man,'" 378.
51 Ronell, *Complaint*, 8.
52 Ibid., 9.
53 Blanchot, "Friendship," 291.
54 Ibid.
55 Ibid.
56 Ibid.
57 Michaud, *Juste le Poème, Peut-Être*, 141–2.
58 Ibid.
59 Venuti, *The Translator's Invisibility*; Spivak, "The Politics of Translation."
60 Ibid., 183.
61 Pato and Moure, *Secession/Insecession*, 148.
62 Although there are other models, Hélène Cixous's translations of Clarice Lispector and Sophie Seita's translations of Uljana Wolf offer two pertinent examples of the significance of friendship in regard to translation. See especially Cixous's *Vivre l'Orange* and Seita's translations of Uljana Wolf in *Subsisters: Selected Poems* (2017) and *i mean i dislike that fate that i was made to where* (2015). Erín Moure and Oana Avasilichioaei's *Expeditions of a Chimaera* (2009) would be another pertinent example, as would Moure's *O Resplandor* (2010). Other kinds of friendships, especially those forged between student and mentor, have been beneficial instigators for the translation of an oeuvre. The English translations of Jacques Derrida's work offer one such example:
> Derrida's translators have almost invariably been his American students. Under these conditions, the act of translation has contributed to the transmission of knowledge through a reciprocal empowerment whereby the philosopher's word is widely disseminated in a move that enhances the disciple's authority and establishes or sustains an interpretive community. (Godard, "Deleuze and Translation," 70)

63 Ronell, "Walking as a Philosophical Act," n.p.
64 Ibid.
65 Ibid.
66 Barthes, Roland. *Le Plaisir du Texte*; English translation *The Pleasure of the Text*.
67 Ronell, "Walking as a Philosophical Act," n.p.
68 Moure, *My Beloved Wager*, 271; emphasis in original.
69 Ibid.
70 Ibid.
71 Ibid., 272; emphasis in original.

72 Stephens [Nathanaël], *At Alberta*, 10.
73 Gladman, *Calamities*, 69.
74 Ibid., 70.
75 Stephens [Nathanaël], *At Alberta*, 10.
76 Moure, *My Beloved Wager*, 272.
77 Ibid.
78 Ibid.
79 Ibid., 249; emphasis in original.
80 Ibid., 250; emphasis in original.
81 Pato and Moure, *Secession/Insecession*, 34.
82 Ibid., 82.
83 Brossard, "And Suddenly I Find Myself Remaking the World," 284.
84 Ibid.
85 It may interest some readers to consult Rosemary Arrojo's critiques of experimental feminist translation strategies and theories. Useful readings include "Fidelity and The Gendered Translation" and "Feminist, 'Orgasmic' Theories of Translation and Their Contradictions." Her critical reading of Hélène Cixous's relationship to Clarice Lispector's work is also pertinent here: "Interpretation as Possessive Love: Hélène Cixous, Clarice Lispector and the Ambivalence of Fidelity."
86 Godard, "Theorizing Feminist Discourse/Translation," 43.
87 I am thinking here particularly of her involvement with the bilingual feminist journal *Tessera* (1984–2005). Although *Tessera* devoted the entirety of issue 6 (1989) to the exploration of translation, almost every issue in its lifespan included some element of translation (either in theory or in content). *Tessera* was also a notable language-oriented literary magazine in its dedication to showcasing experimental and theory-driven writing. As the note on the home page of its York-hosted archive explains,

> at the outset, the editors wished to present the innovative feminist theoretical writing being developed in Quebec to English Canadian critics and writers; by so doing, it fostered the development of "fiction/theory," the term coined in the third issue to name this body of experimental writing. *Tessera* created a dialogue between French and English speaking women writers and theorists by publishing in both official languages and providing a précis for each text in the opposite language. (http://tessera.journals.yorku.ca/index.php/tessera/index)

88 Elena Basile provides a thought-provoking reading of intimacy and translation in an article on Nathanaël's fuckable text, titled "A Scene of Intimate Entanglements, or, Reckoning with the 'fuck' of Translation."

89 For a more detailed reading of Godard and Brossard's author–translator relationship as well as a book-length study of gender and translation, see, among others, Simon's *Gender in Translation*.
90 Godard, "Theorizing Feminist Discourse/Translation," 46.
91 "Transformance" is also the term used to describe the re/writing project between Nicole Brossard and Daphne Marlatt. See Brossard and Marlatt's *Mauve* and *Character/Jeu de Lettres*.
92 Godard, "Theorizing Feminist Discourse/Translation," 46.
93 Pato and Moure, *Secession/Insecession*, 6-7.
94 Aguirre-Oteiza, "What Politics Where Breath Fractures?," 234.
95 Moure, "Writing *In Secession*," 81.
96 Barthes qtd. in Pato and Moure, *Secession/Insecession*, 9; emphasis in original.
97 Pato and Moure, *Secession/Insecession*, 8; emphasis in original.
98 Erín Moure has invented several neologisms to mark her various idiosyncratic approaches to translation. One of the most well-known is her use of the term trans*e*lation in regard to her approach to translating Fernando Pessoa's *O Guardador de Rebanhos*; the book is called *Sheep's Vigil by a Fervent Person*. As the prologue states, Moure's approach takes the form of "Trans-e-lations. Trans-eirin-lations. Transcreations" (ix). While I refer to Moure's idiosyncratic use of translation, I do not intend my use of the term to mean that she uncritically appropriates texts and uses them in the service of her own poetic practice. In fact, nothing could be further from the truth. Moure's translation and poetic practices are grounded in a poetics of hospitality – a preoccupation with making space for others than herself – something that arises everywhere in her writing, including in her co-authored book with Chus Pato.
99 The readerly text (lisible) is one that does not make demands on the reader as its meaning is presumed to be fixed – a meaning that is intact and waiting to be extracted, turning the reader into a passive consumer of that information (for example, the realism of nineteenth-century novels). These texts, according to Barthes, are concerned with the storyline and therefore demand a horizontal reading of the text; the writerly text (scriptible) is the text that is always in production, is open, self-conscious, and where the reader becomes an active participant in its meaning – which essentially blurs the line between the reader and the writer (for example, in works of modernist experimental literature). These texts require a vertical reading that imparts bliss or "jouissance" on the reader. See Roland Barthes' *S/Z: An Essay* (translated into and published in English in 1974) as well as his *The Pleasure of the Text* (translated into and published in English in 1975).

100 Pato and Moure, *Secession/Insecession*, 144.
101 Brossard, "And Suddenly I Find Myself Remaking the World," 286.
102 Aguirre-Oteiza, "What Politics Where Breath Fractures?," 235.
103 Ibid.
104 Pato and Moure, *Secession/Insecession*, 8.
105 Aguirre-Oteiza, "What Politics Where Breath Fractures?," 235.
106 Moure, in conversation with Christina Davis (Pato, Moure, and Davis, "Outside the Fold").
107 Pato and Moure, *Secession/Insecession*, 119.
108 Venuti, *The Translator's Invisibility*, 6.
109 Pato and Moure, *Secession/Insecession*, 122.
110 Brossard, "And Suddenly I Find Myself Remaking the World," 301.
111 Ibid., 284. Brossard's invocation of creative writing here serves as a further example of the blurred boundaries between writing and translation I previously gestured to, not just in terms of a creative approach to translation but in terms of moving away from hierarchizing the act of writing as supposedly distinct from or superior to that of translating – as if translating was not writing.
112 Ibid., 285.
113 Ibid., 286.
114 Ibid., 287.
115 Pato and Moure, *Secession/Insecession*, 6.
116 Canada Council for the Arts, "Book Publishing Support: Block Grants."
117 Ibid.
118 Moure addresses these issues in Pato, Moure, and Davis, "Outside the Fold"; Moure, "Translation and Its Affective Challenges"; and in a written conversation published by *Lemon Hound* (see Moure and Robichaud, "Geneviève Robichaud in Conversation with Erín Moure").
119 Pato and Moure, *Secession/Insecession*, 170.
120 The difficulty Moure has encountered publishing Pato's work in Canada is well documented. Although BuschekBooks in Ottawa is credited as the co-publisher of her translations of *Charenton*, *m-Talá*, and *Hordes of Writing*, in fact the house obtained Canadian copies from Shearsman, a publisher based in the UK. It is also worth noting that Canadian distribution of the work remained limited; it circulated without any promotional assistance.
121 Pato and Moure, *Secession/Insecession*, n.p.
122 In an interview, Chus Pato addresses Moure's influence on her work and thinking about poetry and translation:
> Lamentably, I know too little of Erín's poetry, but I am fortunate to know her, and we have spoken at length and deeply of poetry and translation over the years. I am very fortunate in that she decided to

translate what I write into English. I feel my debt to Erín can't be repaid, and I am not referring here to the expanded reception of my work; it is her gesture that I will not be able to repay, the gratuitousness and risk of that work, that intelligence, that emotion. The deep friendship we maintain has changed my work by making me reflect above all on questions that have to do with translation. To the point where I have come to see that every poem is in itself a translation, translation of the unsayable that is poetry into something writeable that is the poem. Above all, I'd say that Erín Moure's generosity sustains my writing and make[s] it possible, makes it possible for me to continue persisting in this foolhardiness, this grandeur of placing one word after another and then another. (Pato, Moure, and Davis, "Outside the Fold.")

123 Moure, in conversation with Christina Davis (Pato, Moure, and Davis, "Outside the Fold").
124 According to Jacques Derrida, the multiplicity of languages creates the conditions for translation's simultaneous necessity and impossibility. On Babelian confusion he writes that "tongues are scattered, confounded or multiplied [...] translation then becomes necessary and impossible" ("Des Tours de Babel," 170).
125 Ibid., 214.
126 Brossard, "And Suddenly I Find Myself Remaking the World," 286.
127 Godard, "Deleuze and Translation," 56; my emphasis.
128 Moure, *My Beloved Wager*, 168.
129 Ibid., 180.
130 Ibid., 261.
131 Aguirre-Oteiza, "What Politics Where Breath Fractures?," 239.
132 Pato and Moure, *Secession/Insecession*, n.p.
133 Moure, *My Beloved Wager*, 262.
134 Ibid.
135 Ibid., 252.
136 Pato and Moure, *Secession/Insecession*, 154; emphasis in original.
137 Ibid., 151.
138 Pato qtd. in Aguirre-Oteiza, "What Politics Where Breath Fractures?," 239. I am grateful to Aguirre-Oteiza for his observation.
139 Godard, "Deleuze and Translation," 60.
140 Pato and Moure, *Secession/Insecession*, 10–11.
141 It may be useful, too, to consider the way the reading subject becomes the writing subject. See, for instance, Simon's *Gender and Translation*, especially her reading of Barbara Godard's translation of Nicole Brossard's *Picture Theory* in the first chapter and particularly the section titled "Translating the Signifier: Nicole Brossard and Barbara Godard."

142 Nathanaël, *Asclepias: The Milkweeds*, 19. Emphasis in original.
143 Pato and Moure, *Secession/Insecession*, 11.
144 Ibid., 10.
145 Barthes, *The Pleasure of the Text*, 10. By "erotic intermittence" ("intermittence érotique" in French), Barthes has Sade in mind as he depicts the image of seductive edges that flicker in a complex choreography of collisions and ruptures: the pleasure of reading him clearly proceeds from certain breaks (or certain collisions)" (*The Pleasure of the Text*, 6). Furthermore, he continues,
> it is intermittence, as psychoanalysis has so rightly stated, which is erotic: the intermittence of skin flashing between two articles of clothing (trousers and sweater), between two edges (the open-necked shirt, the glove and the sleeve); it is this flash itself which seduces or rather: the staging of an appearance-as-disappearance. (10)
146 Simon, "Paths of Perversity," 119.
147 Elisabeth Tutschek's theorizing of a "dimension lapsisée" provides an interesting extension to Simon's perverse translation. In her PhD dissertation, *Dimension Lapsisée: Revised Subjectivity in Québécois Women's Narratives*, she elaborates a theory of translation based on the space of translation as an oscillating state that gives way to queer subjectivities. The term "dimension lapsisée," which is drawn from Nicole Brossard, names an interpretive device that Tutschek reconceptualizes with the aim of capturing the embodied language poetics of Montreal experimental writing since the 1970s. Such a threshold poetics teases out the various gender, linguistic, and cultural borderlands of the subject as she/he is re(con)figured in experimental writing. Here, reading Sedgwick's call to queerness in the form of gaps and lapses, alongside Tutschek's use of "dimension" and "lapse" to describe the queer translation practices of Montreal writers, is incredibly seductive.
148 Godard, "Deleuze and Translation," 60; my emphasis.
149 Moure, "Writing *In Secession*," 79; emphasis in the original.
150 Ibid., 80.
151 Pato and Moure, *Secession/Insecession*, 144.
152 Godard, "Deleuze and Translation," 62.
153 Ibid., 60.
154 Pato and Moure, *Secession/Insecession*, 82.
155 Ibid., 168.
156 Aguirre-Oteiza, "What Politics Where Breath Fractures?," 238–9.
157 Moure and Pato, *Secession/Insecession*, 120.
158 Ibid.
159 Ibid., 121; emphasis in original.

CHAPTER TWO

1 Earlier iterations of fragments from this text have appeared in *The Boston Review* (2017) *and* TRIC/RTAC (*Theatre Research in Canada / Recherches Théâtrales au Canada*) (2017).
2 Claudia Fancello, Marie Claire Forté, Nadège Grebmeier Forget, Adam Kinner, Ashlea Watkin, and Jacob Wren.
3 *The Book of Disquietude* translated by Richard Zenith and published by Carcanet Press, 1991; *The Book of Disquiet: A Selection* translated by Iain Watson and published by Quartet Books, 1991; *The Book of Disquiet* translated by Alfred Mac Adam and published by Pantheon Books, 1991; *The Book of Disquiet* translated by Margaret Jull Costa, edited by José de Lancastre, and published by Serpent's Tail, 1991. The aforementioned edition followed the Feltrinelli Italian edition published in 1986. Numerous re-editions followed the ones mentioned above – for example, *The Book of Disquiet* translated by Richard Zenith and published by Penguin Classics, 1998; *The Book of Disquiet* translated by Richard Zenith and published by Penguin Classics, 2002. The aforementioned text includes Zenith's revisions of his earlier editions and has since come to be considered a "standard"; *The Book of Disquiet: The Complete Edition* translated by Margaret Jull Costa and published by New Directions Press, 2017. The aforementioned edition is based on the Portuguese edition put together by the Pessoa scholar Jerónimo Pizarro – an edition that emphasizes the various phases of the book's composition from the Guedes phase to the one signed by Soares. Debates regarding the "best" translation in English are divided between Zenith's and Costa's.
4 Hospitality, in fact, is a theme that permeates much of PME's work – so much so, that it even becomes the umbrella term for a series of ongoing collaborations that explore the tensions between life and art by blurring the divide between performing and "playing" one's self, or between using language towards expository ends on the one hand and using it for artistic purposes on the other.
5 Benjamin, "The Translator's Task," trans. Rendall, 154.
6 Ibid., 152.
7 Ibid., 155.
8 I consider the work in relation to the notion of radical inscription in the sense that the book is unfinished and an anti-book of sorts, and that Pessoa published some of the fragments while leaving the vast majority unpublished. I also use the term radical in the sense of the fragments' afterlife as not one but many different books.

9. Pessoa in a letter to Adolfo Casais Monteiro, qtd. in Zenith, *The Selected Prose of Fernando Pessoa*, 259.
10. Pessoa, *The Selected Prose*, trans. Zenith, 265.
11. Zenith, Introduction to *The Book of Disquiet*, xi.
12. Ibid., xv.
13. Jackson, *Adverse Genres in Fernando Pessoa*, 162.
14. "In 1929 by *Solução Editora*; in 1930 in the prestigious Coimbra journal *Presença*; in 1931 in *Descobrimento*; and in 1932 again in *Presença*." Jackson, *Averse Genres in Fernando Pessoa*, 162.
15. Zenith, Introduction to *The Book of Disquiet*, xxviii.
16. The book was published by Lisbon's publishing house, Ática, with the collaboration of Jacinto do Prado Coelho, Teresa Sobral Cunha, and Maria Aliete Galhoz. Interestingly, nearly a decade elapsed before an English version, in four translations (!!), appeared at once in 1991: by Margaret Jull Costa, Alfred MacAdam, Iain Watson, and Richard Zenith.
17. Zenith, Introduction to *The Book of Disquiet*, xxviii.
18. Ibid.
19. Ibid., x.
20. Wren, *Authenticity Is a Feeling*, 235.
21. Twerdy, "Notes on the Art of Writing – and Rewriting."
22. Ibid.
23. Wren, *Authenticity Is a Feeling*, 237.
24. In an essay on translation and affect, Erín Moure writes: "Translation's affective challenge (and joy) then *is* this traversal, this seeding of a place *beyond* the text, where two texts shimmer and something *more* or *else* coalesces." Moure, "Translation and Its Affective Challenges"; emphasis in original.
25. de Medeiros, *Pessoa's Geometry of the Abyss*, 34.
26. Ronell, "The Test Drive" my transcriptions.
27. de Medeiros, *Pessoa's Geometry of the Abyss*, 2.
28. The Serpent's Tail edition was put together by Maria José Lancastre and subsequently translated into Italian by Antonio Tabucchi. Many texts that appear in the New Directions edition do not appear in Lancastre's selection for Serpent's Tail.
29. Margaret Costa, Introduction to *The Book of Disquiet*, vii–xv.
30. Ibid., xv.
31. Badiou, *Handbook of Inaesthetics*, 36; emphasis in original.
32. Ibid.
33. Ibid.

34 Derrida. "Des Tours de Babel," 165.
35 Ibid., 166.
36 By my use of "thing" I have in mind the kind of eccentric reading of an original text provided by Derrida in "Ear of the Other": "A text is original insofar as it is a thing, not to be confused with an organic or a physical body, but a thing, let us say, of the mind, meant to survive the death of the author or the signatory, and to be above or beyond the physical corpus of the text, and so on" (121).
37 A similar passage exists in Derrida's "Ulysses Gramophone": "According to a distinction I have hazarded elsewhere concerning history and the name of Babel, what remains untranslatable is at bottom the only thing to translate. What must be translated of that which is translatable can only be the untranslatable" (258).
38 Pessoa, qtd. in de Medeiros, *Pessoa's Geometry of the Abyss*, 15.
39 de Medeiros, *Pessoa's Geometry of the Abyss*, 3.
40 de Medeiros makes an identical observation in his chapter "Protocols of Reading" (21).
41 Wren, *Authenticity Is a Feeling*, 233–4.
42 See figure 5, which captures the permeable relationship between "the times" as news and the rewriting of the book.
43 Wren, *Authenticity Is a Feeling*, 234.
44 I am indebted to Avital Ronell's observation, in "Street Talk," that Benjamin's messenger in his essay "Karl Kraus" comes bearing more than news, as "news" can also be understood in the wider sense of a commentary on the times (111–12).
45 Benjamin, "Theses on the Philosophy of History," 258.
46 Ronell, "Street Talk," 112.
47 In French this is more obvious. A diary is a *journal intime*.
48 Ronell, "Street Talk," 108.
49 Ibid., 122.
50 Ibid., 124.
51 Ibid., 127.
52 Ibid., 128.
53 Ronell makes a similar observation in relation to Walter Benjamin in "Street Talk," 108.
54 Ramalho 2003a 2–3, qtd. in de Medeiros, *Pessoa's Geometry of the Abyss*, 13.
55 de Medeiros, *Pessoa's Geometry of the Abyss*, 95.
56 Pessoa, qtd. in Costa, *The Book of Disquiet: The Complete Edition*, x.
57 Costa, Introduction to *The Book of Disquiet: The Complete Edition*, xiii.

58 de Medeiros, *Pessoa's Geometry of the Abyss*, 96.
59 Wren, "Ways of Thinking."
60 Ronell, "Street Talk," 107.
61 Benjamin, "The Translator's Task," 153.
62 Derrida, "Des Tours de Babel," 179.
63 Benjamin, "The Translator's Task," trans. Rendall, 154.
64 Ibid., 152.
65 Ibid.
66 Ibid.
67 Zenith, Introduction to *The Book of Disquiet*, ix.
68 Ronell, "Street Talk," 126.
69 Ibid., 110.
70 Ibid., 113.
71 There are various ways to consider the proposition that Soares embodies the rumourological quality of Pessoa's oeuvre beginning with his containment – as Pessoa's semi-heteronym – of all the other heteronyms that shape and constitute Pessoa's oeuvre.
72 de Medeiros, *Pessoa's Geometry of the Abyss*, 53.
73 Ronell, "Street Talk," 121.
74 de Medeiros, *Pessoa's Geometry of the Abyss*, 61.
75 Ibid., 62–3.
76 Ibid., 63.

CHAPTER THREE

Earlier iterations of this research appear in a monograph on translation that has been edited by the IRTG (International Training Group) on Diversity in Montreal and Germany. The article in question bears the same title as this chapter.

1 Also referred to in English as "On the Concept of History."
2 "The Buried speech that creates a soundless gap between languages is at the heart of life in multilingual cities [which is most of them]. And of translation." So begins Scott's essay "Corpus Delicti" in *Permanent Revolution*, 45.
3 Simon, "The Paris Arcades," 75.
4 As a case in point, the first section of *The Obituary* is titled "Rose, Negative." Rose is a diminutive of Rosine – the name of the protagonist.
5 Lane-Mercier, "Gail Scott and Barbara Godard on 'The Main'" is an insightful read for anyone interested in the novel's depictions of nega-

tive forms of connectivity and how translation can be called upon to mediate overlapping cultural memories and narratives of personal loss – not through discrete languages but rather through constantly shifting spaces of difference (228).

6 *The Obituary*'s overlapping narrative structure is interesting to consider, not just in light of translation's dis-conjoined surfaces in the analogy of encounter between the arcades' metal and glass structure, but also alongside a reading of the arcades as "passages": passages that Benjamin collaged from a plethora of sources in his *Arcades Project*, but also Paris's (pedestrian) passages that linked various commercial attractions together.

7 Furlani, "La Flâneuse Montréalaise Translates," 373.

8 Ibid.

9 Scott, *My Paris*, 36.

10 Ibid., 121.

11 Ibid.

12 Ibid., 135.

13 Here is the specific passage from "How Writing is Written" by Gertrude Stein that Sherry Simon quotes in her article "The Paris Arcades":
> The comma was just a nuisance. If you got the thing as a whole, the comma kept irritating you all along the line. If you think of a thing as whole, and the comma keeps sticking out, it gets on your nerves; because, after all, it destroys the reality of the whole. So I got rid more and more of commas. Not because I had any prejudice against commas; but the comma was a stumbling block. When you were conceiving a sentence, the comma stopped you. That is the illustration of the question of grammar and part of speech, as part of the daily life as we live it. (78)

14 Simon, "The Paris Arcades," 74.

15 "I'm tempted to call it realism," Scott writes in her essay "My Montréal" (5):
> It's very possible the sound-effects that trouble my narratives and even my syntax, and that have always underscored my writing are, among other things, a formal response to the question of how to best represent my city. Its pulse, its tensions. Its ceaseless plethora of strong minority voices [...] constantly challenge any notion of authority. In such a context [...] thinking becomes, rather, a constellation, a pattern [...] Put another way, the French erupts into the English text, puncturing it, subverting the authority of both languages. It puts holes in memory as well. (5)

16 For further consideration of Benjamin's concept of the "dialectical

image" as well as his views on "historical materialism," please refer to Susan Buck-Morss's *The Dialectics of Seeing: Walter Benjamin and the Arcades Project* (1989); Michael Jennings *Dialectical Images: Walter Benjamin's Theory of Literary Criticism* (1987); Anthony Auerbach's "Imagine No Metaphors: The Dialectical Image of Walter Benjamin" (2007); and Rolf Tiedemann's "Dialectics at a Standstill: Approaches to the *Passagen-Werk*" (1988; 1999); as well as Max Pensky's "Method and Time: Benjamin's Dialectical Images" (2004).

17 Benjamin, *The Arcades Project* (N9, 7, 473).
18 Pensky, "Method and Time," 181.
19 See Benjamin's "Theses on the Philosophy of History" (1942, trans. Zohn in 1968), particularly sections 6, 9, 14, 16, and 18A.
20 Benjamin, "Theses on the Philosophy of History," 257.
21 Ibid., 258.
22 Scott, *The Obituary*, 126.
23 I borrow the specific phrasing of the above sentence from Andy Fitch's interview with Gail Scott in *Trip Wire: A Journal of Poetics* (issue 13), where he asks:
> Since your epigraph invokes a foundational component in the thinking of Nicolas Abraham and Mária Török, the concept of a transgenerational crypt, whereby the undisclosed, unprocessed trauma of one's parents (or, more broadly, one's preceding generation) produces inherited (though again unrecognized, misunderstood) symptomatic responses in the present, could you discuss how the tacit legacies of European colonization, the forced assimilation of Indigenous peoples in Canada, the agonistic multilingual/multicultural heterodoxies of Quebec, and/or the Benjaminian historical wreckage concretized amid Montréal's architectural textures manifest within *The Obituary*'s highly distinctive discursive form? (163)

24 Simon, "The Paris Arcades," 75.
25 Benjamin, "The Translator's Task," trans. Rendall, 162.
26 It may serve to be reminded here that Benjamin is not thinking of ordinary, everyday language. As Paul de Man notes in "'Conclusions'": "He's speaking of the very peculiar, unusual, and uncommon element in language called translation: something that language allows one to do, which is translation within language" (100).
27 Simon, "The Paris Arcades," 75.
28 Benjamin, *The Arcades Project*, "Awakening" (N2a, 3, 462).
29 Benjamin, "The Translator's Task," trans. Rendall, 155; my emphasis.
30 Benjamin, "Theses on the Philosophy of History," 254.

31 Ibid., 255.
32 Stein, "Composition as Explanation," 495.
33 Benjamin, "Theses on the Philosophy of History," 261.
34 Stein, "Composition as Explanation," 495.
35 Ibid.
36 Benjamin, "Theses on the Philosophy of History," 261.
37 Ibid., 263.
38 Stein, "Composition as Explanation," 495.
39 Benjamin, "Theses on the Philosophy of History," 256.
40 Ibid., 245.
41 It is useful to briefly consider here the political project of the Surrealists' technique of montage within the larger frame of the "institutionally structured history of painting," as its significance, I believe, can be applied to the literary (Surrealist) context in general and to Scott's use of a collage-inspired form in particular (Pensky, "Method and Time," 185):

> ... rejecting the model of the solitary creative genius, the method stuck together otherwise useless or discarded found objects – paper scraps, portions of painted canvas, newspaper, ticket stubs, cigarette butts, buttons – in a construction whose power to disorient and to shock lay to a large degree in the defamiliarization effect of seeing otherwise meaningless material objects suddenly removed from the context that determines their meaninglessness. (Ibid., 186)

What stands out in particular in the above passage is the idea of the method of montage working with the negative (the otherwise meaningless objects) against the grain of commodity culture and thus resisting its meaninglessness. Here is Pensky again:

> The materialist critic scavenges the detritus of history for those objects that resist incorporation into a triumphal story of capitalism as endless progress and that therefore express (in their very quality of trash) the frustrated utopian fantasies of a particular generation. (Ibid., 187)

42 Scott, *The Obituary*, 101.
43 Ibid., 103.
44 Ibid., 102.
45 In a review in *Jacket2*, Jane Malcolm aptly refers to these perspective framings as portals: "As readers, then, we peer through various portals – the doorways, the blinds, the "oeil de boeuf" windows, and an entire section entitled "VENETIANS THAT EVEN PRIVATE EYES HAVE TROUBLE SLEUTHING" – all of which happily conceal as much as they reveal." Malcolm, "We Peer Through Various Portals."

46 In an interview with Lianne Moyes, Scott herself suggests that what is left unsaid in the novel "is there as a kind of allegorical projection, opening the door not for less, but for more, meaning" (Moyes and Scott, "Architectures of the Unsaid," 131).
47 Hejinian, *The Language of Inquiry*, 2; emphasis in original.
48 Andre Furlani relinquishes this defiance of translatability, at least partly, to the temporal complexity of the gerund form, its capacity to maintain a perpetual present. Furlani, "La Flâneuse Montréalaise Translates," 373.
49 Scott, *The Obituary*, 117.
50 Ibid., 121.
51 Ibid., 160.
52 Ibid., 152.
53 Ibid., 12.
54 Carr and Eichhorn, "Temporality, Genealogy, Secrecy," 28.
55 Scott, *The Obituary*, 15–16.
56 Chisholm, "Paris, *Mon Amour*, My Catastrophe," 156–7.
57 Ibid., 159–60.
58 Ibid., 156.
59 Lianne Moyes, in her essay "Discontinuity, Intertextuality, and Literary History," found in *Wider Boundaries of Daring* notes the difficulty of doing justice to Scott's use of Benjamin's montage technique, describing it as "disjunctive images selected by the writing subject, images that affront readers with the disparate and conflictual histories hidden by the narratives of fine cuisine, haute couture, bohemian culture, cosmopolitanism, modernity, and so forth that constitute Paris" (15).
60 Chisholm, "Paris, *Mon Amour*, My Catastrophe," 181.
61 Scott, *The Obituary*, 118.
62 Pensky, "Method and Time," 180–1.
63 Scott, *The Obituary*, 12.
64 I am indebted to Bronwyn Haslam's linking of the poetics of indeterminacy with the poetics of description in her MA thesis "A Poetics of Apprehension: Indeterminacy in Gertrude Stein, Emily Dickinson and Caroline Bergvall" (2013).
65 Hejinian, *The Language of Inquiry*, 138–9.
66 Scott, *The Obituary*, 21.
67 Ibid., 21.
68 Ibid.
69 Ibid., 19.
70 The question "what haunts" also frames Scott's previous novel *My Paris* – except that in *My Paris*, rather than asking "what haunts," the question

is rather "whom does one haunt?" Such a question is lifted from the opening pages of André Breton's novel, *Nadja*: "Qui suis-je? Si par exception je m'en rapportais à un adage: en effet pourquoi tout ne reviendrait-il pas à savoir qui je 'hante'"? (9).
71 Carr and Eichhorn, "Temporality, Genealogy, Secrecy," 30.
72 Ibid., 28.
73 Scott, *The Obituary*, 59.
74 Scott and Moyes, "Architectures of the Unsaid," 135.
75 In "Architectures of the Unsaid," Scott admits to Moyes that the Gallic tonality of apostrophizing words such as "th'" or "in'" reveals a great deal about who is speaking: "[In this space,] we find people that don't speak well, and we find the shame of not speaking well or rather of not speaking like the well-educated. Thus, this apostrophe does something on two levels, both the sonic level and the informational level" (132).
76 Scott, *The Obituary*, 19.
77 Ibid., 20.
78 Ibid., 98.
79 Ibid., 148.
80 Ibid., 99.
81 Ibid., 140.
82 Ibid.
83 Ibid., 148.
84 Benjamin, "Theses on the Philosophy of History," 263.
85 Scott, *The Obituary*, 48.
86 Ibid., 20.
87 Ibid., 117.
88 Carr and Eichhorn, "Temporality, Genealogy, Secrecy," 27.
89 Scott, *The Obituary*, 16.
90 The question of "who speaks" is a recurring concern in Scott's work. In an interview with the poet, editor, and critic Sina Queyras, Scott professes that such a question is at the forefront of *The Obituary*'s concerns:
> Since starting to write prose "fiction," I have, like so many contemporaries, written with the awareness that both spoken and written, lines, phrases, theories, are borrowed. Kathy Acker was my first mentor in that respect. Formally, or even stylistically, speaking, I take what is punctually useful to me, often to cast it off or to give it diminished importance later. What is left accumulates into the writing subject "I" am becoming over time. I feel, with *The Obituary*, that I have achieved something I have been reaching toward as concerns novel time, as well as the question of who speaks when one speaks,

which is the real puzzle of the novel. (Scott and Queyras, "A Conversation with Gail Scott")

91 Scott, *The Obituary*, 16–17.
92 Ibid., 12.
93 As Scott herself remarks in an interview with Lianne Moyes, The Native presence is deeply embedded here [referring to the unsaid at the level of the city and its history] […] In other words, the unsaid in the family was also unsaid in the social context, the layer of silence ventriloquized back and forth. *The Obituary* is a look behind what has allegedly "passed," reconsidering it as an element of "now-time." ("Architectures of the Unsaid," 135)
94 Scott and Moyes, "Architectures of the Unsaid," 131.
95 Carr and Eichhorn, "Temporality, Genealogy, Secrecy," 28.
96 Scott, *The Obituary*, 22.
97 Ibid.
98 Ibid., 18.
99 Ibid., 22.
100 Ibid., 112; emphasis in original.
101 Ibid., 147.
102 Ibid., 23.
103 Ibid.
104 Ibid., 24.
105 Pensky, "Method and Time," 181.
106 The translation of the word "rumour" into the French language befittingly gives way to "des bruits qui courent" – an élan that says a great deal about the speed and temporality of the rumour as one that outruns the present moment, eclipses into fantasy.
107 Scott, *The Obituary*, 31; emphasis in original.
108 Ibid., 32.
109 Ibid., 92.
110 Ibid., 95.
111 Ibid., 102.
112 Quartermain, "How Fiction Works," 125–6.
113 Scott, *The Obituary*, 121.
114 This is not to say that this is the novel's only affective register. In fact, *The Obituary* is a rather funny novel as well, which says nothing about its decadent or expressionist features, and which would reward their own reading elsewhere.
115 Ronell, "Street Talk," 120.

116 In "The Translator's Task," Benjamin attributes the features of life to everything that has a history (153).
117 de Man, "Conclusions," 96–7.
118 Derrida makes a similar claim in his essay "Des Tours de Babel":
> "[…] tongues are scattered, confounded or multiplied according to a descendance that in its very dispersion remains sealed by the only name that will have been the strongest, by the only idiom that will have triumphed. Now this idiom bears within itself the mark of confusion, it improperly means the improper, to wit: Bavel, confusion. Translation then becomes necessary and impossible." (170)

119 de Man, "Conclusions," 97.
120 Ibid.
121 Ibid., 87–8.
122 Ibid., 100–1.
123 Ibid., 101.
124 Ibid.
125 Barthes, "Rhetoric of the Image," 39.
126 The article in question is on Djuna Barnes's *Nightwood*, another experimental novel that broaches questions of history and its "eccentric losers." I am indebted to Teresa de Lauretis, who in "*Nightwood* and the 'Terror of Uncertain Signs'" makes the link between the "inhuman" element in language and the embrace of a process of misreading that does not seek the congealment of (narrative or referential) meaning but that acquiesces to its indeterminacies – what de Lauretis refers to as "the otherness in it, the 'inhuman' element in language" (118).
127 Ibid., 117.
128 de Man, *Blindness and Insight*, 285.
129 de Man, *The Resistance to Theory*, 15.
130 de Lauretis, "*Nightwood* and the 'Terror of Uncertain Signs,'" 117.
131 Scott, *The Obituary*, 31.
132 I use the term in homage to a passage from Nathanaël's "Theatres of the Catastrophal":
> [In translation,] it is the moment at which the texts – foregoing [*sic*] the bilateral language of source and target texts (with its tidy between, and problematic direction) – the texts, with their languages, enter into disintegrative states. It has something to do with proximities and loss of intelligibility. It has something also to do with vigilation. The moment at which one is most focused might be the moment one must close one's eyes out of sheer intensity. Something is, of necessity,

eradicated, in one's apprehension of – disaster, say. Absolute vigil does not, cannot, exist. The senses cannot abide such demand.
133 Scott, *The Obituary*, 122.
134 Scott, "The Sutured Subject," 66.
135 Scott, *The Obituary*, 48.
136 Others have done so already and in ways that I'm not convinced I would have added to. See, for instance, Gillian Lane-Mercier's reading of *The Obituary* as sutured text ("Gail Scott and Barbara Godard on 'The Main'"), as well as Corey Frost's original insights into Scott's apostrophes ("Punc'd: Towards a Poetics of Punctuation in the Novels of Gail Scott").
137 Remember that for Walter Benjamin the arcades are passages in the most polysemic sense of the word.

CHAPTER FOUR

1 Shelley, "A Defence of Poetry."
2 Nathanaël, *Hatred of Translation*, 65.
3 Ibid., 53.
4 Ibid., 65.
5 Nakayasu, *Say Translation*, 2.
6 Briggs, *This Little Art*, 38.
7 Nathanaël, *Hatred of Translation*, n.p.
8 Nathanaël, "Theatres of the Catastrophal."
9 Ibid.
10 Ortega y Gasset, "The Misery and Splendor of Translation," 63.
11 Briggs, "Q&A," 23:00.
12 Ibid.
13 Nathanaël, "Theatres of the Catastrophal."
14 Nakayasu, *Say Translation*, 11.
15 Gladman, "The Sentence as a Space for Living," 93.
16 Ibid., 98.
17 Brossard, *Fences in Breathing*, 7.
18 Ibid., 7–8.
19 Ibid., 8.
20 Ibid., 9.
21 Ibid., 10.
22 Carson, *Nay Rather*, 6.
23 Nathanaël, "Theatres of the Catastrophal."
24 Brossard, *Fences in Breathing*, 10.

25 Ibid., 9.
26 Pato and Moure, *Secession/Insecession*, 158.
27 Nathanaël, "Theatres of the Catastrophal."
28 Ibid.
29 Ibid.
30 Carson, *Nay Rather*, 8.
31 Hofer, qtd. in Briggs, *This Little Art*, 137.
32 Gladman, *Houses of Ravicka*, 104.
33 Gladman, *Calamities*, 7.
34 Gladman, *Houses of Ravicka*, 146.
35 Gladman, "The Sentence as a Space for Living: Prose Architecture," 107.
36 Moure, "Of Camouflage," 107.
37 Ibid., 110.
38 Ibid.
39 Ibid., 107.
40 Gladman, *Houses of Ravicka*, 123.
41 OED, "structure," 3a.
42 Briggs, *This Little Art*, 45.
43 OED, "structure," 2b.
44 Gladman, *Houses of Ravicka*, 126.
45 Moure, "Retranslations are Writing."
46 Gladman, "The Sentence as a Space for Living," 96.
47 Nathanaël, "Theatres of the Catastrophal."
48 Briggs, *This Little Art*, 189.
49 Moure, "Translation as Step Outside Time."
50 Carson, *Nay Rather*, 8.
51 Ibid., 6.
52 Ibid.
53 Ibid.
54 Ibid.
55 Moure, "Translation as a 2-Step"; emphasis in the original.
56 Gladman, *Calamities*, 7.
57 Gladman, "The Sentence as a Space for Living," 92.
58 Gasché, *The Honor of Thinking*, 7.
59 Ibid.
60 Benjamin, *Arcades Project*, 475.
61 Blanchot, *The Book to Come*, 3.
62 Ibid., 4.
63 Ibid., 9–10.
64 Ibid., 4.

65 Ibid.
66 Nakayasu, *Say Translation*, 5.
67 Brossard, *Fences in Breathing*, 7.
68 Ibid., 86.
69 Briggs, *This Little Art*, 72.
70 Ibid., 140.
71 Ibid., 280.
72 Brossard, *Fences in Breathing*, 44.
73 Blanchot, *The Book to Come*, 4.
74 Brossard, *Fences in Breathing*, 90.
75 Carson, *Nay Rather*, 10.
76 Ibid., 10.
77 Ibid.
78 Ibid., 12.
79 Ibid.
80 Ibid., 14.
81 Gladman, *Calamities*, 7.
82 Moure, "Translation as a 2-Step."
83 Grosz, *Architecture from the Outside*, 16.
84 Ibid.
85 Ibid., 17.
86 Carson, *Nay Rather*, 16.
87 Brossard, *Fences in Breathing*, 68.
88 Gladman, *Calamities*, 73.
89 Gladman, "The Sentence as a Space for Living," 96.
90 Brossard, *Fences in Breathing*, 99.
91 Ibid.
92 Ibid.
93 Nathanaël, *Hatred of Translation*, 140.

Bibliography

Abraham, Nicolas, and Maria Török. *L'Écorce et le Noyau*. Paris: Flammarion, 1987.

Aguirre-Oteiza, Daniel. "What Politics Where Breath Fractures?: (In)Translation and the Poetics of Difference." *Journal of Spanish Cultural Studies* 19, no. 2 (2018): 233–45.

Arrojo, Rosemary. "Feminist, 'Orgasmic' Theories of Translation and Their Contradictions." *Tradterm* 2 (1995): 67–75.

– "Fidelity and the Gendered Translation." *TTR: Traduction, Terminologie, Rédaction* 7, no. 2 (1994): 147–63.

– "Interpretation as Possessive Love: Hélène Cixous, Clarice Lispector, and the Ambivalence of Fidelity." *Postcolonial Translation*, edited by Susan Bassnett and Harish Trivedi. London: Routledge, 2012.

Auerbach, Anthony. "Imagine No Metaphors: The Dialectical Image of Walter Benjamin." *Image and Narrative* 18 (2007): n.p.

Badiou, Alain. *Handbook of Inaesthetics*, translated by Alberto Toscano. Stanford: Stanford University Press, 2005.

Balso, Judith. *Affirmation of Poetry*, translated by Drew S. Burk. Minneapolis: Univocal, 2014.

Barnes, Djuna. *Nightwood*. New York: New Directions Press, 2006.

Barthes, Roland. *Le Plaisir du Texte*. Paris: Éditions du Seuils, 2002.

– *The Pleasure of the Text*. Translated by Richard Miller. New York: Farrar, Straus and Giroux, 1998.

– "Rhetoric of the Image." *Image–Music–Text*, translated by Stephen Heath, 32–51. New York: Hill and Wang, 1977.

– "Rhétorique de l'Image." *Communications* 4 (1964): 40–51.

– *S/Z: An Essay*, translated by Richard Miller. New York: Farrar, Straus and Giroux, 1974.

- *S/Z Essai Sur Sarrasine d'Honoré de Balzac*. Paris: Le Seuil, 1970.
Basile, Elena. "A Scene of Intimate Entanglements, or, Reckoning with the 'Fuck' of Translation." In *Queering Translation, Translating the Queer: Theory, Practice, Activism*, edited by Brian James Baer and Klaus Kaindl, 26–37. New York: Routledge, 2017.
Benjamin, Walter. *The Arcades Project*. Translated by Howard Eiland and Kevin McLaughlin. Boston: Belknap Press of Harvard University Press, 1999.
- "The Task of the Translator." In *Illuminations: Essays and Reflections*, edited by Hannah Arendt, translated by Harry Zohn, 69–82. New York: Schocken, 2007.
- "Theses on the Philosophy of History." In *Illuminations: Essays and Reflections*, edited by Hannah Arendt, translated by Harry Zohn, 253–64. New York: Schocken, 1985.
- "The Translator's Task." Translated by Steven Rendall. *TTR: Traduction, Terminologie, Rédaction* 10, no. 2 (1997): 151–65.
Berman, Antoine. *The Experience of the Foreign: Culture and Translation in Romantic Germany*. Translated by Stefan Heyvaert. Albany: SUNY Press, 1992.
Blanchot, Maurice. *L'Amitié*. Paris: Gallimard, 1971.
- *The Book to Come*. Translated by Charlotte Mandell. Stanford: Stanford University Press, 2003. 289–91.
- *Le Dernier à Parler*. Saint Clément de Rivière: Éditions Fata Morgana, 1984.
- "Friendship." *Friendship*. Translated by Elizabeth Rottenberg. Stanford: Stanford University Press, 1997.
- *Le Livre à Venir*. Paris: Gallimard, 1986.
Breton, André. *Nadja*. Paris: Gallimard, 1964.
Briggs, Kate. "Q&A." Windham–Campbell Prizes and Literary Festival. YouTube, 15 November 2021. https://www.youtube.com/watch?v=sCw8kp1_Kdc.
- *This Little Art*. London: Fitzcarraldo Editions, 2018.
Brossard, Nicole. "And Suddenly I Find Myself Remaking the World." In *Avant Desire: A Nicole Brossard Reader*, edited by Sina Queyras, Geneviève Robichaud, and Erin Wunker, translated by Oana Avasilichioaei and Rhonda Mullins, 284–304. Toronto: Coach House Books, 2020.
- *Fences in Breathing*, translated by Susanne de Lotbinière-Harwood. Toronto: Coach House Books, 2009.
Brossard, Nicole, and Daphne Marlatt. *Character/Jeu de Lettres*. Montreal: NBJ, 1986.

- *Mauve*. Montreal: NBJ, 1985.
Buck-Morss, Susan. *Dialectics of Seeing*. Cambridge, MA: MIT Press, 1989.
Canada Council for the Arts. "Book Publishing Support: Block Grants."
- "Book Publishing Support: Translation Grants."
Carr, Angela, and Kate Eichhorn. "Temporality, Genealogy, Secrecy: Gail Scott and the Obituary of Genre." In "Gail Scott: Sentences on the Wall," edited by Lianne Moyes in collaboration with Bronwyn Haslam. *Open Letter* 14, no. 9 (Summer 2012, special issue): 25–35.
Carson, Anne. *Nay Rather*. London: Sylph Editions, 2013.
Chisholm, Dianne. "Paris, *Mon Amour*, My Catastrophe, or *Flâneries* Through Benjaminian Space." In *Gail Scott: Essays on Her Work*, edited by Lianne Moyes, 153–206. Toronto: Guernica, 2002.
Cixous, Hélène. *Vivre l'Orange*. Paris: Editions des Femmes-Antoinette Fouque, 1979.
Code, Lorraine. *Ecological Thinking: The Politics of Epistemic Location*. Oxford: Oxford University Press, 2006.
Costa, Margaret. "Introduction." In *The Book of Disquiet: The Complete Edition*, translated by Margaret Jull Costa, vii–xv. New York: New Directions Press, 2017.
Davis, Diane, ed. *ÜberReader: Selected Works of Avital Ronell*. Champaign: University of Illinois Press, 2007.
de Lauretis, Teresa. "*Nightwood* and the 'Terror of Uncertain Signs.'" Special supplemental issue for W.J.T. Mitchell. *Critical Inquiry* 34, no. 5 (2008): 117–29.
de Man, Paul. *Blindness and Insight: Essays in the Rhetoric of Contemporary Criticism*. Minneapolis: University of Minnesota Press, 1983.
- "'Conclusions': Walter Benjamin's 'The Task of the Translator.'" Messenger lecture, Cornell University, 4 March 1983. *Yale French Studies* 69 (1985): 25–46.
- *The Resistance to Theory*. Minneapolis: University of Minnesota Press, 1986: 1–20.
de Medeiros, Paulo. *Pessoa's Geometry of the Abyss: Modernity and the Book of Disquiet*. Oxford: Legenda, 2013.
Derrida, Jacques. "Des Tours de Babel." In *Difference in Translation*, edited and translated by Joseph M. Graham, 165–248. Ithaca: Cornell University Press, 1985.
- *The Ear of the Other*. Translated by Peggy Kamuf. Lincoln: University of Nebraska Press, 1988.
- "Politics of Friendship." Translated by Gabriel Motzin and Michael Syrotinski, with Thomas Keenan. *American Imago* 50, no. 3 (Fall 1993): 353–91.

– "Ulysses Gramophone: Hear Say Yes in Joyce." In *Acts of Literature*, edited by Derek Attridge, translated by François Raffoul, 253–309. New York and London: Routledge, 1992.
Dewey, Anne, and Libbie Rifkin, eds. *Among Friends: Engendering the Social Site of Poetry*. Iowa City: University of Iowa Press, 2013.
Eco, Umberto. *Experiences in Translation*. Toronto: University of Toronto Press, 2001.
Epstein, Andrew. *Beautiful Enemies: Friendship and Postwar American Poetry*. Oxford: Oxford University Press, 2006.
Frost, Corey. "Punc'd: Towards a Poetics of Punctuation in the Novels of Gail Scott." In "Gail Scott: Sentences on the Wall," edited by Lianne Moyes in collaboration with Bronwyn Haslam. *Open Letter* 14, no. 9 (Summer 2012, special issue): 40–56.
Furlani, Andre. "La Flâneuse Montréalaise Translates." In *The Routledge Handbook of Translation and the City*, edited by Tong King Lee, 364–80. New York: Routledge, 2021.
Gasché, Rodolphe. *The Honor of Thinking: Critique, Theory, Philosophy*. Stanford: Stanford University Press, 2006.
Gladman, Renee. *Calamities*. Seattle: Wave Books, 2016.
– *Houses of Ravicka*. New York: Dorothy Project, 2017.
– "The Sentence as a Space for Living: Prose Architecture." *Tripwire Journal* 15, Narrative/Prose, 2019.
Godard, Barbara. "Becoming My Hero, Becoming Myself: Notes Toward a Feminist Theory of Reading." *Tessera* 3 (Spring 1986): 142–50.
– "Deleuze and Translation." *Parallax* 6, no. 1 (2000): 56–81.
– "Performance/Transformance: Editorial." *Tessera* 11 (Winter 1986): 11–18.
– "Theorizing Feminist Discourse/Translation." *Tessera* 6 (Spring 1989): 42–53.
– "Women in Letters (Reprise)." In *Collaboration in the Feminine: Writings on Women and Culture from Tessera*, edited by Barbara Godard, 258–306. Toronto: Second Story Press, 1994.
Grosz, Elisabeth. *Architecture from the Outside: Essays on Virtual and Real Space*. Cambridge, MA: MIT Press, 2001.
Haslam, Bronwyn. "A Poetics of Apprehension: Indeterminacy in Gertrude Stein, Emily Dickinson, and Caroline Bergvall." MA thesis, Université de Montréal, 2013. Papyrus: Institutional Repository. https://doi.org/1866/10627.
Hejinian, Lyn. *The Language of Inquiry*. Berkeley: University of California Press, 2000.
Jackson, K. David. *Adverse Genres in Pessoa*. Oxford: Oxford University Press, 2010.

Jakobson, Roman. "On Linguistic Aspects of Translation." In *Translation Studies Reader*, edited by Lawrence Venuti, 126–31. New York: Routledge, 2010.

Jennings, Michael. *Dialectical Images: Walter Benjamin's Theory of Literary Criticism*. Ithaca: Cornell University Press, 1987.

Lane-Mercier, Gillian. "Gail Scott and Barbara Godard on 'The Main': Borders, Sutures, Micro-Cosmopolitan Interconnectivity, and Translation Studies." In *Trans/Acting Culture, Writing and Memory: Essays in Honour of Barbara Godard*, edited by Eva C. Karpinski, Jennifer Henderson, Ian Sowton, and Ray Ellenwood, 225–43. Waterloo: Wilfrid Laurier University Press, 2013.

Malcolm, Jane. "We Peer Through Various Portals: A Review of Gail Scott's 'The Obituary.'" *Jacket2*, 2013. https://jacket2.org/reviews/we-peer-through-various-portals.

Michaud, Ginette. *Juste le Poème, Peut-Être (Derrida, Celan) Suivi de SINGBARER REST: L'Amitié, l'Indeuillable*. Montreal: Le Temps Volé Éditeurs, 2009.

Moten, Fred. *Black and Blur*. Durham: Duke University Press, 2017.

Moure, Erín. *My Beloved Wager: Essays from a Writing Practice*. Edmonton: NeWest Press, 2009.

– *O Resplandor*. Toronto: House of Anansi, 2010.

– "Of Camouflage." Afterword to Lupe Gómez's *Camouflage*, translated by Erín Moure. New York: Circumference Books, 2019.

– "Retranslations Are Writing." *Jacket2*, 25 October 2012. https://jacket2.org/commentary/retranslations-are-writing.

– [Eirin Moure] *Sheep's Vigil by a Fervent Person: A Translation of Alberto Caeiro/Fernando Pessoa's O Guardador de Rebanhos*. Toronto: House of Anansi, 2001.

– "Translation and Its Affective Challenges: Bodies, Spacings, and Locales from the Okanagan to the Deza, from Canada to Galicia." *Evening Will Come: A Monthly Journal of Poetics* 55, Affect feature (July 2015).

– "Translation as a 2-Step: Doing Nothing." *Jacket2*, 6 December 2012. https://jacket2.org/commentary/translation-2-step-doing-nothing.

– "Translation as Step Outside Time." *Jacket2*, 30 November 2012. https://jacket2.org/commentary/translation-step-outside-time.

– "Writing *In Secession*: Biopoetics and the Galician Imaginaire of Chus Pato in Canada." *Canada and Beyond* 5 (2015): 72–87.

Moure, Erín, and Oana Avasilichioaei. *Expeditions of a Chimaera*. Toronto: Book*hug, 2009.

Moure, Erín, and Geneviève Robichaud. "Geneviève Robichaud in Conversation with Erín Moure." *Lemon Hound*, July 2014.

Moyes, Lianne. "Discontinuity, Intertextuality, and Literary History." In *Wider Boundaries of Daring*, edited by Di Brandt and Barbara Godard, 163–89. Waterloo: Wilfrid Laurier University Press, 2009.

Moyes, Lianne, and Gail Scott. "Architectures of the Unsaid." In "Gail Scott: Sentences on the Wall," edited by Lianne Moyes in collaboration with Bronwyn Haslam. *Open Letter* 14, no. 9 (Summer 2012, special issue): 128–38.

Moyes, Lianne, Gail Scott, and Corey Frost. "In Conversation: Gail Scott, Lianne Moyes, and Corey Frost." In *Gail Scott: Essays on Her Work*, 208–29. Toronto: Guernica Editions, 2002.

Nakayasu, Sawako. *Say Translation*. New York: Ugly Duckling Press, 2020.

Naoufal, Nayla. "La Fabrique de Littérature." *Le Devoir*, 27 October 2014. https://www.ledevoir.com/culture/arts-visuels/422160/la-fabrique-de-litterature.

Nathanaël. *Asclepias: The Milkweeds*. New York: Nightboat Books, 2015.

– *Hatred of Translation*. New York: Nightboat Books, 2019.

– *Je Nathanaël*. Toronto: Book*hug, co-published with Nightboat Books (New York), 2019.

– "Theatres of the Catastrophal: A Conversation with Nathanaël." *Lemon Hound*, 14 February 2013.

Ortega y Gasset, José. "The Misery and Splendor of Translation," translated by Carl R. Shirley. *Translation Review* 13, no.1 (1983): 18–30.

Oxford English Dictionary. "Structure," 3a and 2b.

Pato, Chus. *At the Limit*. Translated by Erín Moure. Montreal: Zat-so, 2018.

Pato, Chus, and Erín Moure. *Secession/Insecession*. *Secession* translated by Erín Moure. Toronto: Book*hug, 2014.

Pato, Chus, Erín Moure, and Christina Davis. "Outside the Fold: A Conversation with/without Erín Moure and Chus Pato." *Stylus. the [woodberry] poetry room blog*. https://woodberrypoetryroom.com/?p=1904.

Pato, Chus, and Geneviève Robichaud. "Geneviève Robichaud in Conversation with Chus Pato (Translated by Erín Moure)." *Lemon Hound*, 6 February 2017.

Pensky, Max. "Method and Time: Benjamin's Dialectical Images." In *The Cambridge Companion to Walter Benjamin*, edited by David S. Ferris, 177–98. Cambridge: Cambridge University Press, 2004.

Pessoa, Fernando. *The Book of Disquiet*. Translated by Margaret Jull Costa. London: Serpent's Tale, 2010.

– *The Book of Disquiet*. Translated by Alfred Mac Adam. New York: Pantheon Books, 1991.

- *The Book of Disquiet*. Translated by Richard Zenith. Manchester: Carcanet Press, 1991.
- *The Book of Disquiet*. Translated by Richard Zenith. New York: Penguin, 2002.
- *The Book of Disquiet: A Selection*. Translated by Iain Watson. London: Quartet Books, 1991.
- *The Book of Disquiet: The Complete Edition*. Translated by Margaret Jull Costa. New York: New Directions Press, 2017.
- *The Selected Prose of Fernando Pessoa*. Translated and edited by Richard Zenith. New York: Grove Press, 2001.

PME-ART. *Adventures can be found anywhere, même dans la mélancolie*. Galerie Leonard and Bina Ellen Art Gallery, 23 October–1 November 2014, Montreal.

Quartermain, Meredith. "How Fiction Works: Gail Scott's *Heroine* and *The Obituary*." In "Gail Scott: Sentences on the Wall," edited by Lianne Moyes in collaboration with Bronwyn Haslam. *Open Letter* 14, no. 9 (Summer 2012, special issue): 112–27.

Ramalho Santos, Irene. *Atlantic Poets: Fernando Pessoa's Turn in Anglo-American Modernism*. Hanover: University Press of New England, 2003.

Ricoeur, Paul. "The Paradigm of Translation." In *Translation Studies* 1, edited by Mona Baker, translated by David Pellauer. 215–26. New York: Routledge, 2009.

Robichaud, Geneviève. "In the Altitudes of Elation 'We Look Up and Hold the Folds of Language Inside Us without Any Word for Wind': At the Start of the Light We Ask, What Is *Secession/Insecession*?" *Canada and Beyond: A Journal of Canadian and Literary and Cultural Studies* 6 (2017): 77–83.

- "Letters on the Move: Erín Moure and Chus Pato's *Secession/Insecession* and Nathanaël (Nathalie Stephens)'s *Absence Where As (Claude Cahun and the Unopened Book)*." *Traduire/Translating: Intermédialités* 27, edited by Myriam Suchet, 1–21.
- "Stimulants, Influences, Narcotic Effects." *The Town Crier*. March 2016.

Ronell, Avital. *Complaint: Grievance among Friends*. Champaign: University of Illinois Press, 2018.

- "On the Misery of Theory without Poetry: Heidegger's Reading of Hölderlin's 'Andenken.'" *PMLA* 120, no. 1 (2005): 16–32.
- "Street Talk." *Studies in 20th Century Literature* 11, no. 1 (1986): 105–31.
- "The Test Drive." YouTube, 12 March 2008. https://youtu.be/xVwoN2aLvLo?si=WjJ3wCcjR8KUpT83
- "Walking as a Philosophical Act." European Graduate School Video Lec-

tures. YouTube, 26 December 2014. https://youtu.be/6lJQNeoc2rI?si=F8SEWKRsXpOd1KfY.

Ronell, Avital, and Diane Davis. "Breaking Down 'Man': A Conversation with Avital Ronell." *Philosophy and Rhetoric* 47, no. 4 (2014): 354–85.

– "Confessions of an Anacoluthon: Avital Ronell on Writing, Technology, Pedagogy, Politics." *JAC: Journal of Composition Theory* 20, no. 2 (2000): 243–81.

Scott, Gail. "Corpus Delicti." In *Permanent Revolution*. 45–57. Toronto: Book*hug, 2021.

– "My Montréal: Notes from an Anglo-Québécois Writer." *Brick* 59 (Spring 1998): 4–9.

– *My Paris*. Toronto: Mercury Press, 1999.

– *The Obituary*. Toronto: Coach House, 2010.

– "The Sutured Subject." *Review of Contemporary Fiction* 28, no. 3 (2008): 62–72.

– Translator's Note on France Théoret's *Laurence*. *How2* 1, no. 4 (September 2000).

Scott, Gail, and Andy Fitch. "Gail Scott Interviewed by Andy Fitch." *Trip Wire: A Journal of Poetics* 13 (2017): n.p.

Scott, Gail, and Corey Frost. "Some Other Kind of Subject, Less Bounded." *How2* 1, no. 4 (2000): n.p.

Scott, Gail, and Sina Queyras. "A Conversation with Gail Scott." *Lemon Hound*, 8 December 2010.

Shelley, Percy Bysshe. "A Defence of Poetry." Poetry Foundation. https://www.poetryfoundation.org/articles/69388/a-defence-of-poetry.

Simon, Sherry. *Gender and Translation*. London and New York: Routledge, 1996.

– "The Paris Arcades, the Ponte Vecchio, and the Comma of Translation." *Meta* 45, no. 1 (April 2000): 73–9.

– "Paths of Perversity: Creative Interference." In *Translating Montreal: Episodes in the Life of a Divided City*, 119–61. Montreal and Kingston: McGill-Queen's University Press, 2006.

Spivak, Gayatri Chakravorty. "The Politics of Translation." In *Outside the Teaching Machine*, 179–200. London and New York: Routledge, 1993.

Stein, Gertrude. "Composition as Explanation." In *A Stein Reader*, edited by Ulla E. Dydo. Evanston: Northwestern University Press, 1993.

Stephens, Nathalie [Nathanaël]. *At Alberta*. Toronto: Book*hug, 2008.

Tiedemann, Rolf. "Dialectics at a Standstill: Approaches to the *Passagen-Werk*." Translated by Gary Smith and André Levefere. In Benjamin, *The*

Arcades Project, 929–45. Cambridge, MA: Belknap Press of Harvard University Press, 1999.

Tutschek, Elisabeth. *Dimension Lapsisée: Revised Subjectivity in Québécois Women's Narratives*. PhD diss., Saarland University, 2015.

Twerdy, Saelan. "Notes on the Art of Writing – and Rewriting." *Canadian Art*, 14 November 2014. https://canadianart.ca/features/jacob-wren-interview.

Venuti, Lawrence. Introduction to *Translation Studies Reader*, edited by Lawrence Venuti, 1–9. New York: Routledge, 2010.

– *The Translator's Invisibility: A History of Translation*. New York: Routledge, 1995.

Waldrop, Rosmarie. "Irreducible Strangeness." In *towards a foreign likeness bent*. Duration Poetics 1: 106–10.

Winterson, Janet. Preface to *Nightwood*, xi–xvi. New York: New Directions Press, 2006.

Wolf, Uljana. *i mean i dislike that fate that i was made to where*. Translated by Sophie Seita. New York City and Oakland: Wonder, 2015.

– *Subsisters: Selected Poems*. Translated by Sophie Seita. New York: Belladonna*, 2017.

Wren, Jacob. *Authenticity Is a Feeling*. Toronto: Book*hug, 2018.

– "Ways of Thinking." *Adventures can be found anywhere, même dans la mélancolie*. Leonard and Bina Ellen Art Gallery, 23 October–1 November 2014, Concordia University, Montreal.

Zenith, Richard. Introduction to *The Book of Disquiet*, translated and edited by Richard Zenith, 3–21. New York: Penguin, 2002.

Index

Abraham, Nicolas, and Maria Török, 96, 114, 168n23
Adventures can be found anywhere, même dans la mélancolie, 6, 18, 61–2, 68
affect, 40, 150n16, 164n24; affective, 7, 9, 17, 39, 57, 77, 150n16, 160n118, 164n24, 172n114
afterlife, 9, 11, 13–14, 19–20, 63–5, 77, 80, 83–5, 138–41, 163n8
aporia(s), 4–6, 9–11, 22, 60, 121, 123, 141
apprehension, 4, 6, 11, 17, 20–1, 89, 99, 108–9, 124–5, 128, 131, 135, 145, 170n64, 173–4n132
Arcades Project, The, 20, 89, 94–5, 99, 103, 106–7, 150n17, 167n6
art, 16, 52, 72, 75, 78, 103, 163n4; making, 17, 129; object, 71–2, 87; performance art, 62; practice, 126; work(s) of, 8–10, 13–14, 22, 63, 65, 68, 154n47

Badiou, Alain, 22, 74–80, 84–5, 149n5
Benjamin, Walter, 7–14, 20–2, 63–5, 73–108, 113, 119–20, 125, 139, 144, 150n11, 150–1n17, 151–152n24, 152n33, 154n47, 165n44, 167n6, 167–8n16, 168n26, 170n59, 173n116, 174n137

betweenness, 3–5, 36
biopoetic, 6, 17–18, 25–8, 45, 54, 56, 59, 155n18
Blanchot, Maurice, 37–8, 137–45, 155n20
Book of Disquiet, The, 6, 13, 19–20, 59, 61–77, 79–87, 129, 153n39, 163n3
boundary, 17, 41, 84, 127; boundaries, 3, 10, 16, 20, 21, 44, 53, 106, 141
Briggs, Kate, 126–8, 135, 137, 143
Brossard, Nicole, 5–6, 21, 23–4, 43–52, 129, 142–7, 159n89, 159n91, 160n111, 161n141, 162n147

Canada Council for the Arts, 22, 49, 51
Carson, Anne, 130, 132, 138, 144–6
certitude, 12, 32–4
cipher, 9, 15
continuing life, 14, 20, 83, 99
correspondence, 18, 51–2, 56, 60, 139; corresponding, 18, 31, 50
Costa, Margaret Jull, 19, 61, 74, 82, 163n3, 164n16
crypt, 86–7, 96, 114, 116, 123, 168n23

de Man, Paul, 9, 119–21, 168n28
de Medeiros, 72–6, 82, 86–7
Derrida, Jacques, 36–7, 51, 54, 64, 75–6, 83, 87, 153n35, 155n20,

157n62, 161n124, 165nn36–7, 173n118
dialectical image(s), 11–12, 20–1, 23, 89–103, 108, 144, 150–1n17, 151–2n24, 167–8n16

echolation, 25–6, 55
echolation-homage, 18, 28, 60, 152n27
ecology, 24, 135, 146–7; ecological, 24, 36, 134, 147
epistemological, 4, 16, 33, 65, 141, 151–2n24
equivalent, 14, 18, 94, 108, 146; equivalence(s), 5, 10, 26, 56, 146
errant, 20, 52, 84, 88; errant futurity, 13, 84–5, 88
ethics, 30, 32, 35, 38–9, 104
experimental, 6–7, 15–17, 41–4, 51, 65, 90, 93, 97, 107, 109, 158n85, 158n87, 159n99, 162n147, 173n126
experimentally: composed, 104, 109, 123; engaged, 13

feminist, 17, 43–8, 51, 158n85, 158n87
Fences in Breathing, 129, 142–3
fidelity, 10, 17, 78, 158n85
foreign, 6, 30, 46, 51, 53, 130, 136, 143, 144, 146, 151n21
foreknowledge, 125, 132, 136
friend, 28–30, 35–41, 51–2, 60, 66, 76, 155n18

Galicia, 18, 42, 51, 54
Galician, 17–18, 25–6, 40–2, 48–55, 133, 151–2n24
gap(s), 3–6, 11–12, 90, 97–110, 118, 123–4, 141, 146, 154n47, 162n147, 166n2
Gladman, Renee, 5–6, 21, 23, 41, 125–36, 139–48
Godard, Barbara, 44, 46, 52, 55–8, 156n37, 157n62, 159n89, 161n141, 166–7n5, 174n136

Hejinian, Lyn, 3, 4, 103, 104, 108, 109, 149n7
heteronym(s), 19, 62, 65–8, 78, 81, 86, 166n71. *See also* semi-heteronym; Soares, Bernardo
hospitable, 59, 62
hospitality, 32, 35, 38, 53, 159n98, 163n4
Houses of Ravicka, 23, 132–5, 141

illegible, 67, 102, 123
impasse(s), 5, 7, 9, 11, 13
in-between, 3–5, 7, 22–3, 57, 59, 63, 85
inclination, 12, 31, 33, 35, 52, 56, 59–60
inclined writing, 12–13, 20, 25–8, 31, 34, 36, 51–2, 57, 59, 152n28
indeterminacy, 4, 23, 90, 103–4, 107, 118
Indigenous, 91, 107, 114–15, 118, 168n23
innovative, 10, 14–15, 158n87
inquiry, 4, 7, 10, 12, 16, 31–2, 40, 108, 113, 123
interval(s), 5, 9, 25, 38, 90, 139
intimacy, 30, 48–9, 69–70, 79, 145, 158n88; intimacies, 56
intimate, 38, 42–5, 57, 63, 69, 72, 78–9, 158n88
intranslation, 18, 22, 46–8, 152n27, 153n37
invisible, 15, 23, 30, 41, 43, 46–7, 71–2, 104, 133–5; invisibility, 23, 30, 38, 100, 104, 136

Jakobson, Roman, 17, 19–20, 153n35
jetztzeit, 95, 101

knowledge, 12, 20, 24, 33–4, 63, 72, 97, 104, 126–8, 132, 138, 142, 157n62

Language of Inquiry, The, 3–4, 103, 149n7, 152n28

legible, 5, 102, 131, 134; legibility, 6, 10–13, 100–1, 105, 107, 123

MacAdam, Alfred, 19, 164n16
mastery, 12, 32–3
montage, 94–5, 97, 102–7, 111, 169n41, 170n59
Moure, Erín, 5–6, 12, 17–32, 35, 39, 41, 45–60, 104, 128–9, 133–41, 145, 147, 150n16, 151–2n24, 152n27, 153n37, 155n12, 155n18, 157n62, 159n98, 160n118, 160n120, 160–1n122, 164n24

Nathanaël, 5, 41, 56, 125–31, 134, 136, 141, 144–8, 158n88, 173n132
now-time, 95–6, 101, 102, 111, 172n93

Obituary, The, 11, 14, 20–3, 89–93, 95–7, 100–29, 141, 166–7nn5–6, 168n23, 171n90, 172n93, 172n114, 174n136
"On the Concept of History," 166n1
ontic, 4, 7, 10, 16–17
ontology, 78, 88; ontologies, 108
opacity, 130, 131–2
origin(s), 13, 64, 80, 85, 114–17, 119, 122, 128
Ortega y Gasset, José, 125–8, 135, 138, 144–6
overlap, 10–16, 20–3, 48, 53, 79, 87, 90–109, 123–4, 151n22; overlapping, 6, 11, 15, 23, 89–93, 97, 100, 108, 123, 166–7nn5–6

Pato, Chus, 5–6, 12, 17–60, 104, 128–9, 140–1, 151–2n24, 152n27, 155n12, 159n98, 160n120, 160–1n122
performance, 13–20, 44, 53, 61–3, 68–72, 77–9, 84, 88
Pessoa, Fernando, 5–6, 13, 19, 20, 22, 59–69, 71–86, 128, 141, 159n98, 163n3, 163n8, 166n71
philosophy, 20, 22, 34, 52, 55, 58, 74–5, 84, 145
PME-ART, 5, 6, 13, 18–20, 61–88, 128–9, 163n4
poetic: components, 6, 8, 15, 24; enterprise, 75, 78; expression, 10, 17; juxtaposition, 9–12, 16, 20–3, 41, 89, 97; practice, 16, 18, 26, 159n98; properties, 7–9; structure(s), 5, 23, 103; thinking, 15, 22
poetics of: apprehension, 170n64; description, 108, 170n64; difference, 155n4; friendship, 18, 26, 30; hospitality, 159n98; indeterminacy, 170n64; love, 36; punctuation, 174n136; translation, 4–8, 10–13, 16, 20, 23, 28, 76, 92–3, 127, 139–40, 142

queer, 17, 51, 93, 105, 115, 162n147

reader, 8, 20–31, 37–40, 45–9, 55–63, 73–4, 88, 91–6, 100–24, 146, 150n47, 156n37, 159n99; readerly, 45–6, 140, 153n37, 159n99
relations, 4–5, 16, 35, 58, 96–7, 128–35, 140–1
Rendall, Steven, 8, 150n8
rewriting, 6, 13, 19–20, 43, 61–70, 76, 88
Ronell, Avital, 12–14, 31–41, 53, 65, 73–87, 123, 141, 149n1, 151n22, 152n25, 152n33, 155n20, 165n44, 165n53
rumour, 13, 79–87, 96, 115–23, 172n106
rumourological, 13–14, 19, 79–87, 114, 121–2, 166n71
rumour-text, 13–14, 79, 83–4, 87

Scott, Gail, 3–6, 11, 14, 20–3, 89–116,

123, 128, 166n2, 166–7n5, 167n15, 168n23, 169n41, 170n46, 170n59, 170–1n70, 171n75, 171–2n90, 172n93, 174n136
Secession/Insecession, 6, 17, 25–30, 34, 36–7, 42, 44, 47–60, 104, 129, 153n37, 154–5n1; seeing, 24, 39, 61, 71–2, 105–8, 123, 125, 132, 135, 145
semi-heteronym, 19, 62, 66–67, 81–86, 166n71. *See also* Soares, Bernardo
sight, 23–4, 100, 106–7, 116
sighting(s), 20, 89, 135
Simon, Sherry, 56, 89–99, 152n33, 162n147, 167n13
snag, 3, 12, 21, 125–6, 132, 136–8, 144, 147
Soares, Bernardo, 19, 61–7, 72–88, 163n3, 166n71. *See also* semi-heteronym
source (text/language), 10, 13, 19, 25, 29, 38, 52, 56, 68, 71, 83–5, 122, 131, 142, 147, 173–4n132
structure(s), 4–10, 13–17, 20, 23, 28, 30, 34, 60, 91–119, 127–48, 149n7, 151n21, 167n6
stutter, 21, 40; stuttering, 55, 57–8
survival, 14, 83

target (text/language), 14, 19, 25, 52, 56, 84, 131, 142, 173–4n132
"Task of Translation, The," 63, 123, 139
temporal, 11, 15, 21, 23, 77–80, 93, 104–14, 123, 128, 133, 140–1, 170n48
temporality, 11, 21, 36, 73, 80, 83, 92, 99, 109, 112, 170n48

"Theses on the Philosophy of History," 20, 78, 89, 95, 101–3
This Little Art, 126, 137
touch, 5, 8, 15, 21, 49, 53, 56, 143–6, 151n21
touching, 56, 115, 125, 143
transelation, 159n98
translanguaging, 11, 17, 90, 92, 104
translatability, 5, 9, 11, 13, 20, 22, 76, 84–9, 96, 104, 124, 154n47, 170n48
translational, 64–5, 127, 129–30
translation poetics, 24, 135, 148, 151n21
"Translator's Task, The," 7–9, 13, 20, 63, 75, 90, 99, 119, 150n8, 154n47, 173n116

uncertain, 12–14, 21, 68, 110, 121–3, 128, 133, 139
uncertainty, 21, 23, 77, 117–18, 129; uncertainties, 3, 90, 105
undecidability, 13, 33, 65, 73
untranslatable, 75, 138, 144, 154n47, 165n37
untranslatability, 75–6, 144, 154n47

Venuti, Lawrence, 30, 38, 48, 50
visibility, 30–1, 43–4, 100, 109
visible, 4–9, 15, 22–3, 30–1, 40, 44–2, 79, 82, 87, 90–1, 100–7, 121–3, 134–5

Watson, Iain, 19, 163n3, 164n16

Zenith, Richard, 19, 66–8, 85–6, 153n39, 163n3, 164n16
Zohn, Harry, 8, 150n8, 154n47